People of the Pharaohs

.

People of the Pharaohs

From Peasant to Courtier

·

HILARY WILSON

Michael O'Mara Books Limited

First published in Great Britain in 1997 by
Michael O'Mara Books Limited
9 Lion Yard
Tremadoc Road
London SW4 7NQ

A CIP catalogue for this book is available from the British Library

ISBN 1-85479-218-0

Designed and typeset by Florencetype Ltd, Stoodleigh, Devon

Printed and bound in Great Britain by Clay Ltd, St Ives plc

Contents

•

Time Chart of Egyptian History

Dynasties	Dates BC (approx)	Period	Royal names associated with period (Hellenised version in brackets follows original name)
	5200–4600	Early Predynastic	
	4600–3150	Late Predynastic	Serk (Scorpion), Narmer (Menes?)
1 & 2	3150–2686	Archaic	Aha (Menes?), Uadji, Den, Djer, Peribsen, Khasekhemwy
3–6	2686–2181	Old Kingdom	Djoser, Seneferu, Khufu (Cheops), Khafre (Chephren), Menkaure (Mycerinos), Unas, Teti, Pepi
7–10	2181–2040	First Intermediate	Akhtoy, Neferkare, Intef
11&12	2040–1782	Middle Kingdom	Intef, Montuhotep, Senusert (Sesostris), Amenemhet (Ammenemes)
13–17	1782–1570	Second Intermediate	Sebekhotep, Neferhotep, Khendjer, Seqenenre, Khyan, Apopi, Kamose

Dynasties	Dates BC (approx)	Period	Royal names associated with period (Hellenised version in brackets follows original name)
18–20	1570–1070	New Kingdom	Ahmose, Amenhotep (Amenophis), Tuthmose (Tuthmosis), Hatshepsut, Akhenaten, Tutankhamen, Horemheb, Seti (Sethos), Ramesses, Merenptah
21–26	1070–525	Third Intermediate	Nesbanebded (Smendes), Pasbakhaniwt (Psusennes), Shoshenq, Osorkon, Taharqa, Psamtik (Psammetichus), Wahibre (Apries)
27–31	525–332	Late	Persian Kings (Cambyses, Darius, Xerxes), Nectanebo
32 (Ptolemaic)	332–30	Graeco-Roman	Ptolemy, Cleopatra, Caesarion
Roman Emperors	30 BC–323 AD		Augustus, Tiberius, Nero, Domitian etc. to Diocletian

During the Intermediate Periods there were many kings within a very short space of time. Often they were no more than local princes whose authority was strictly limited, and on occasion several of these kings ruled concurrently from different capitals. During the Third Intermediate Period the Egyptian throne passed into the hands of a succession of foreigners. Dynasty 22 was descended from Libyan prisoners of war brought back to Egypt by Ramesses III. Thebes broke away from their rule to establish an independent kingship as Dynasty 25, the rulers being Nubian princes allied by marriage to the Theban religious aristocracy. At the same time, the native ruling house in the Delta city of Sais resisted the Assyrians, but this Dynasty was brought to an end by Cambyses' invasion in 525 BC. Persian rule was never popular because the Emperors conducted it by means of satraps or deputies, rather than in person. When Alexander freed the country from the Persians in 332 BC, he was made King of Egypt and, on his death in 323 BC, his regent Ptolemy took the crown, establishing the last dynasty of Pharaohs. Egypt became a province of Rome after Octavian's defeat of Cleopatra at Actium. The Byzantine forces capitulated to the Arab invasion in AD 642.

MAP OF EGYPT

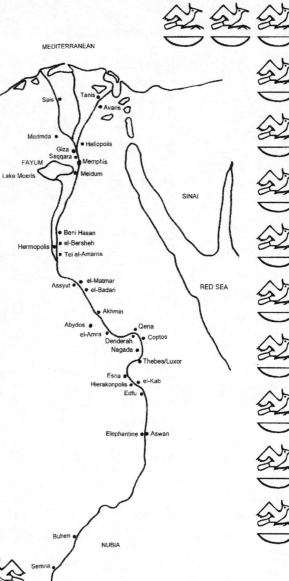

MEDITERRANEAN

Sais •   Tanis •
       • Avaris

Merimda •
     • Heliopolis
Giza •
Saqqara •
FAYUM   • Memphis
Lake Moeris   • Meidum

SINAI

• Beni Hasan
• el-Bersheh
Hermopolis   • Tel el-Amarna

• el-Matmar
Assyut •   • el-Badari

RED SEA

• Akhmin

Abydos •   • Qena
el-Amra •   • Coptos
   Denderah
   Nagada •
     • Thebes/Luxor

Esna •   • el-Kab
Hierakonpolis •
Edfu •

Elephantine • • Aswan

Buhen •
   NUBIA

Semna •

The border is made up of the lapwing hieroglyph, used as the determinative
for 'people' or 'commoners' and the basket sign, meaning 'all' or 'every'.

Resources

•

BETWEEN THE MEDITERRANEAN SEA coast in the north
and the First Cataract at Aswan in the south there arose one of the
most remarkable of all civilizations, ancient Egypt. This 1,000 kilo-
metre-long oasis, formed by the Nile in the north-eastern corner of
Africa, was known to its people as *Ta Mery*, the Beloved Land. The
inhabitants of the region called themselves Blacklanders in reference
to the dark, rich soil to whose fertility they owed the success of
their economy. This acknowledgment of their dependence on the
Nile and their link with the land itself are emphasized in the nature
ascribed to the ram-headed god Khnum who was thought to control
the flow of the river from his home in the caverns beneath
Elephantine Island. He was also a creator god who moulded
Egyptians out of the black alluvium deposited on the land in the
annual miracle of the Inundation and is often portrayed as a potter
seated at his wheel, fashioning two mud figures for each person – the
physical body and the spiritual *ka*. Once Khnum had breathed life
into the clay, the resultant human being, a product of the very soil
of the land, became a real Blacklander, a true Egyptian.

The Nile was called simply the River, and was personified by a
portly man with pendulous breasts, wearing the broad-belted loincloth of a boatman and a coronet of water plants. This was Hapy,
the god of the Nile's flood. It was to Hapy that the Egyptians
prayed every year at the beginning of the Inundation season, begging
the god to send a 'good Nile'. If the flood level was too low, the
vitalizing silt would not be spread over a large enough area and
the harvest would be poor. If the waters rose too rapidly or too
far, permanent plantings such as palm groves and orchards might
be damaged and the sowing would be delayed by the waterlogging

of the land. There was the potential for famine at both ends of the scale. On Seheil Island, where the main cult temple of Khnum stood, a rock-cut stela records a disastrous famine caused by seven successive years of low floods. The inscription was carved in the Ptolemaic period, but purports to be a historical record from the reign of King Djoser, first king of the Third Dynasty and builder of the Step Pyramid at Saqqara. The scene is set with Djoser bemoaning the famine-stricken state of his realm: 'I was in mourning on my throne, those of the palace were in grief. My heart suffered great affliction because Hapy had failed to come in time for a period of seven years.'

The King sought out the source of the river, asking: 'In which place is Hapy born? Which god dwells there?'

The reply came: 'There is a town in the midst of the deep, surrounded by Hapy. It is called Yebu [Elephantine]. It is the first of the southern towns . . . the water is named "Twin Caverns" . . . It is the sleeping place of Hapy. There he is rejuvenated in his time. It is the place whence he brings the flood.'

The text goes on to explain how Khnum appeared to Djoser in a dream and promised to end the famine: 'I shall make Hapy gush for you. There will be no year of lack and want anywhere. Plants will grow weighed down by their fruit. . . . Gone will be the hungry years. Shores will shine in the excellent flood. Hearts will be happier than ever before.'

In gratitude Djoser ordered his Governor of the Southlands, based at Elephantine, to turn over an area of land in that region, together with all its revenues, to the temple of Khnum. Whether or not this is a true story or a complete fiction, it is clear evidence of the long-standing association between the river, the King and the health of the land and its people.

Although Hapy is often shown presenting the bounty of the river to the other gods and had no major temples dedicated to him alone, he was revered throughout the length of Egypt and was recognized in many local guises. Districts or estates were represented by Nile gods, each wearing the local standard or emblem as a crown, so that each stretch of the river had its own Hapy. Two Nile gods representing the northern Delta region, Lower Egypt, and the southern valley, Upper Egypt, differentiated by the papyrus stems or flowering reeds of their diadems, were often shown tying a knot with their heraldic plants around the hieroglyph for 'unite' (fig. 1). This scene, symbolic of the unification of the two parts of the country under one king, is often found as an element in the decoration of the King's throne. The Unification was a momentous event in Egyptian history which is thought to have happened around 3100 BC, though, for ever after, the original dual nature of the state was recognized in the most common designation for the country, the Two Lands. The dualism inherent in this appellation is apparent in the Biblical name for Egypt, *Misraim*, which is a word in the dual form. The King called himself Lord of the Two Lands and claimed the protection of the Two Ladies, the patron goddesses of Upper and Lower Egypt. These were Nekhebt, the vulture, wearer of the White Crown, and Wadjet, the cobra, wearer of the Red Crown, two of the most ancient national deities.

The King also claimed to be Guardian of Maat, a word usually translated as truth and justice, but really meaning much more than this. Maat was personified by a goddess wearing in her headband the feather against which a dead man's heart would be weighed in the scales of justice, in order to judge his worthiness to enter the next world. Maat was order, equilibrium and rightness, a code of behaviour for all creation. The King was the upholder of the rule of Maat, maintaining in fine balance all aspects of life in

Figure 1 *Unification*: Two Nile gods representing Upper and Lower Egypt tie a knot with their heraldic plants, the flag iris and the papyrus, about the hieroglyph for 'unite'.

Egypt. He was the gods' representative on earth and the people's representative before the gods. The King was also thought to have influence over the natural world. By performing the appropriate rituals in due season, he ensured a good Inundation, a rich harvest or a successful vintage. Disasters such as flood, fire or famine were upsets in the rule of Maat which might be seen as manifestations of the gods' displeasure.

Many of Egypt's poorest citizens, living on a knife-edge between survival and starvation, understood only too well the importance of keeping the balance of Maat. The stability of their position depended, for a large part, on the predictability of the Nile's rise and fall. Even in the earliest periods, records were kept of the height reached by the flood waters. On the Palermo Stone, a year-by-year record of the kings of Egypt from before the Unification to the Fifth Dynasty, the reigns are recorded in rows of boxes, each box being flanked by the palm-rib hieroglyph for 'year'. Inside every box are inscribed very curt details of what were considered to be the important events of the year it represents. The crucial event of each and every year was the Inundation which is recorded in a separate space at the foot of each year division. There were several places along the river where the height of the rising waters was measured. One such Nilometer is on Elephantine Island. It is a stone staircase on the riverbank, descending into the river itself. As the waters flooded up the stairway, the level of the Inundation was marked on its wall and annual records were kept conscientiously by the priests of the temple there. The author of the Palermo Stone must have had access to such archives when compiling his historical survey.

Some time before the Unification, the Egyptians had adopted a calendar based on the river's cycle. It had been noticed that the Nile started to rise at the same time that Sirius, the brightest star in the heavens, became visible at dawn. This occurs on or about 19 July in the modern calendar. The Greek historian Herodotus noted how unusual it was for a river to flood in the hottest part of the year:

> As to why the Nile behaves as it does I could get no information from the priests, nor from anyone else . . . why the water begins to rise at the summer solstice, continues to do so for one hundred days, and then falls again so that it remains low throughout the

winter . . . Nobody in Egypt could give me an explanation of this, in spite of my persistent attempts to discover why the Nile should behave in the opposite way to all other rivers.

The Egyptians associated Sirius with Isis, the wife of Osiris. They called the star Sopdet and the Greeks knew it as Sothis. The year was divided into three seasons of four months, each month having thirty days, with five extra days added to make up the civil year of 365 days. Since this takes no account of leap years, the civil calendar slipped apart from the agricultural Sothic calendar by one day every four years and only once in approximately 1,460 years did the two calendars coincide. The dawn-rising of Sirius, the day known as the Opening of the Year, marked the first day of the Inundation season when the river began to rise as rains in the Ethiopian highlands swelled the waters of the White and Blue Niles and the River Atbara. The hymns sung to the Nile god at this time were so popular and well known, rather like seasonal carols, that they were copied by student scribes practising their handwriting:

> Hail to you Hapy, sprung from the earth, come to nourish the
> land of Egypt!
> Secret in his ways, of darkness by day, to whom his followers
> sing!
> Who floods the fields that Re has made, to nourish all who
> thirst.
> He lets the waterless desert drink his dew falling from the sky. . . .
> . . . When he is sluggish, noses clog and everyone is poor.
> . . . When he floods, the earth rejoices, and everyone laughs and
> smiles.
> . . . Songs to the harp are made for you, one sings to you with
> clapping hands . . .

The first community organization was directed at making the best use of Hapy's bounty. A system of irrigation canals, dykes and catch basins ensured that every part of the country would have its share of the mineral-rich flood waters. The resultant chequer-board pattern of irrigated land gave rise to the hieroglyph which represents an estate or agricultural area, and in country districts of modern Egypt the fields retain the same gridlike appearance. Ancient Egyptian society was very conservative. Once the Egyptians had found a system which worked, its success was apparently

Figure 2 *One Man and his Dog:* A gardener raises water by means of a *shaduf.* Waterlilies bloom in the pond which is surrounded by clumps of papyrus and cornflowers, a pollard willow and a pomegranate tree.

attributed to its being sanctioned by the gods and once established, methods and techniques for exploiting the Inundation remained in use almost unchanged for more than 3,000 years. Even the *shaduf,* a primitive but effective means of lifting water from one level to another (fig. 2), introduced during the Middle Kingdom, is still in use in rural areas.

While water was the primary resource of the country there were many other natural benefits of living in the Nile Valley. For the greater part of its length from Cairo to Edfu, the cliffs which border the river plain on both banks are of limestone, the stone which was used for the bulk of major building works. At Tura in the Mokkatam hills to the south-east of Cairo, the purest white limestone was quarried to be used for the outer casing on pyramids. Limestone is still being extracted from those same quarries. South of Edfu, sandstone predominates and at Aswan the Egyptians quarried the pink, red and black granites which were favoured for obelisks, shrines and the lining of tombs. In the desert regions beyond the valley there were deposits of other stones valued either for their hardness, their colour or the ease with which they could be worked. From before the Unification slate, breccia, diorite and schist were being used for high-quality storage jars, vases and bowls which were deposited in graves. Alabaster or calcite was extensively used for similar ritual and decorative wares throughout the Dynastic Period. Basalt and quartzite were in demand for statuary and sarcophagi in all periods and the Romans exploited the quarries at Gebel Dokhan where they extracted both imperial purple and black porphyry.

Of far more practical use to the majority of the peasant population was the abundance of flint which occurs naturally in the limestone areas. Flint was worked into blades, axes, spear heads and arrow points and continued to be used for agricultural and butchery tools long after the Egyptians had discovered copper. Copper itself was extracted from ores like malachite and azurite found in the Eastern Desert, to be used in the manufacture of tools and both household and ritual implements. The earliest copper objects to be found in Egypt date from the Badarian Period, c. 4500 BC. For decorative purposes and as a highly regarded medium of exchange for foreign trade the Egyptians relied on gold. The gold deposits in the quartz rocks of the southern desert regions between the Nile and the Red Sea, and down into what is traditionally called Nubia, were so extensive that to other nations the Egyptians' use of gold seemed extravagant. King Assur-uballit of Assyria wrote to the King of Egypt requesting gold as a gift between friends: 'Gold in your country is as common as dirt; one simply gathers it up. Why then do you keep it all for yourself? I am building myself a new palace so send me as much gold as I will need for its adornment. . . . If your purpose is one of true friendship you will send me much gold.'

With water to irrigate the fields and home-produced tools to work them, the Egyptians were almost self-sufficient. The one resource in short supply was wood. Tree roots found in regions which are now high desert show that the area of natural vegetation was more extensive in ancient times and that the climate was not always as harsh as it has become, but the tree species of ancient Egypt were much the same as those found in the country today. The native acacias, tamarisks and sycamore figs produce bent, knotty planks and only short lengths of trunk suitable for beams. A country which relied heavily, if not entirely, on boats for all its transport needs clearly had to have a good and dependable source of serviceable timber. This was found in the areas of the Lebanon and Northern Syria where cedar and pine trees grew to great size. At some very early time in Egypt's history, the people of the Nile Valley became aware of the availability, not far from their borders, of this most precious resource. The Palermo Stone records the arrival in Egypt of boatloads of timber, some of which was used in monuments built by the kings from the First Dynasty onwards. Control over the ports through which the wood was exported, if not over the forests themselves, was a pressing concern for kings of all eras, since a supply of timber was essential to so many aspects of Egyptian life.

Among the trees native to Egypt, the date palm was the most important, providing food, building material and fibres for all types of basketry and cordage. Dates probably accounted for a large part of the carbohydrate content of the peasant diet and were the most common flavouring agent for the national drink, beer. Each date palm produces between 40 and 80 kilograms of fruit annually and these may be dried so that dates are available throughout the year. Another tree, the dom palm, was also widespread in the southern part of the country, though now it is much rarer and only found upstream of Qena. This tree is differentiated from the date palm in the tomb of Sennedjem at Deir el-Medina by its forked trunk. Dom palm nuts, each the size and shape of a small capsicum, have the appearance of varnished wood and grow in bunches. The outer fibrous layer was soaked and pulped to be baked in bread. Dom palm kernels were burned to make the charcoal nuggets used for incense burning. In the tomb of Pashed, also at Deir el-Medina, a palm tree is shown as the Tree of Life beneath which the tomb-owner stoops to drink water.

Also in Sennedjem's tomb may be seen the other most typical and most beloved tree of the ancient Egyptians, the sycamore fig. This tree with its oval leaves and small clusters of yellowish fruit is usually drawn in the 'lollipop' shape of the hieroglyph for 'tree' showing that the sycamore was *the* tree of Egypt. The goddess Hathor, one of the most popular deities revered by Egyptians of all levels of society, was known as the Lady of the Sycamore. She was thought to wait at the edge of the desert on the path between this world and the next, offering rest in the shade of her sacred tree and sustenance in the form of fruit and water to the dead souls on their journey to eternity. The sycamore or wild fig produces two or three crops a year of fig-shaped fruits which are less sweet than those of the true fig, but sycamore trees grew wild throughout Egypt while fig trees were usually confined to the orchards and gardens of the wealthy.

Since honey was a luxury commodity, available only to those who could afford to employ beekeepers, dates and sycamore figs provided most of the sweetness in the diet. The date palm hieroglyph was one of the signs used to represent 'sweet' or 'sweetness'. Another, used in the name of Sennedjem which means 'sweet brother', was a pod which could be the fruit of the carob tree. The earliest evidence for the carob tree in Egypt comes from Middle Kingdom Thebes where carob wood was found in the roofing of a tomb. The carob tree may have been introduced from Arabia or the Eastern Mediterranean area, perhaps at the same time as another fruit tree, the pomegranate.

The scarlet flowers and distinctively-shaped fruits of the pomegranate became popular elements in jewellery, wall friezes and the inlaid decoration of temples and palaces. Pomegranate wine was a middle-class substitute for real grape wine. It even featured in the love poetry of the New Kingdom as in an extract from a papyrus in the British Museum: 'Hearing your voice has the same effect on me as pomegranate wine, I live by hearing it. Each glance you make in my direction sustains me more than food and drink.'

All these fruit-bearing trees were utilized as sources of timber, the sycamore especially in boat-building. Other trees like the ben tree and the balanites tree were prized for their fruits or seeds which were pressed for their oil, as were those of the castor oil plant which still grows wild in Egypt. The olive was another introduction, probably during the early New Kingdom. It may have been brought to Egypt by the Hyksos, people of Canaanite origin who occupied the northern part of the country during the latter half of the Second Intermediate Period. Olive leaves and twigs have been found in Eighteenth Dynasty funerary wreaths, but most olive oil which, like castor oil, was used by the Egyptians for lighting as well as in cooking, was imported from Canaan, implying that the native Egyptian crop was not sufficient to supply local demands.

After the cultivated grains and other food crops, the most useful types of plants were the reeds, rushes and sedges which formed extensive reed beds on both banks of the Nile and for almost the whole of its length. Reeds were used for building both dwellings and boats. Matting, baskets, sacks and even sails and sandals were woven from the leaves and stripped rind of these useful plants. Some provided food, like the sedge *Cyperus esculentus* which produces wrinkled brown tuberous nuts now known as tigernuts. The crop is thought to have been one of the earliest sources of food exploited and perhaps deliberately cultivated in ancient Egypt. The plant emblem of Upper Egypt was a flowering rush, traditionally shown as a flag or iris with a red standard and a blue fall, but, since this plant cannot be identified in Egypt today, it is impossible to say to what extent ancient artists might have exaggerated the colours of the petals. The plant has long since become extinct in the country of which it was once considered to be so typical.

By far the most important of all the water plants of the Nile was, without doubt, the papyrus plant which had so many uses that it is easy to see why it was chosen as the national emblem of Lower Egypt, the area of the most extensive papyrus marshes. A single papyrus stem was the hieroglyph for 'green', 'sturdy' and 'fresh'. The name of the serpent goddess Wadjet of the Delta city of Buto translates simply as 'the Green One'. Of all its practical uses the most well known is the writing material from which derives the modern word 'paper'. The development of writing was at the heart of the success of Egyptian society. The Egyptians believed in the magical power of the written word to contain the essence of everything it described. Writing was a powerful tool in the hands of Egyptian scribes, a tool which they used to establish Egypt's reputation as an educated and sophisticated society with an efficient and dedicated bureaucracy.

Every aspect of life in ancient Egypt was governed by the intimate relationships between the people and their gods. Religion was not a way of life for the Egyptians, life was their religion. Their deities were very different from the distant, abstract beings of other civilizations. They lived amongst their followers in temples which were conceived not as places of communal worship but rather as palatial homes for the most affluent and influential members of Egyptian society. The gods were the first citizens of Egypt. The sound economic base provided by the Inundation, the availability of a wealth of natural resources, and a thriving tradition of literacy enabled the ancient Egyptians to enjoy life to the full and to celebrate their joy in the honour paid to their gods. This fully-rounded civilization survived for about 4,000 years, displaying a degree of success and stability envied by other societies which lasted for less than half that time.

Hieroglyphs associated with the land

| irrigated land, estate, district | flowering sedge of Upper Egypt | papyrus clump of Lower Egypt | hill country, desert, foreign land |

Names used by the ancient Egyptians for their own country

| Tawy 'The Two Lands' | Ta Mery 'The Beloved Land' |

Kemet
'The Black Land'

CHAPTER 1

The Farmer

•

THE FERTILE NILE VALLEY, refreshed and revitalized every year by the Inundation, was a great enticement for settlers driven towards the river by the gradual desiccation of the lands bordering the Sahara Desert. The first farmers combined the exploitation of pockets of wild grains with the hunting and domestication of native species of sheep, goats and cattle. The wadis provided grazing as well as cover for game such as antelope, gazelle, ostrich and hare. The river itself was home to hippopotami and many species of fish. Wildfowl thronged the reedbeds and marshes. The land was ideally suited for people who followed a farming lifestyle, though it was not completely free from hazards. There were crocodiles in the river and lions, hyaenas and jackals prowled the desert fringes. Several types of venomous snakes and scorpions were common throughout the country.

However equable the climate or productive the soil, however rich in natural resources the land, the success of the civilization was largely due to the constant exercise of man's ingenuity and determination in overcoming and taming the forces of nature. These forces were often revered, sometimes in animal form, as tribal or regional fetishes, worshipped as local deities in primitive shrines and placated with offerings. Two of the oldest deities who gained national status were Hathor, the benign cow-goddess who nurtured the King, and her consort Horus, the falcon-god of the sky, whose right eye was the sun and whose left eye was the moon. Hathor, a mother-goddess, the patroness of women and promoter of sexual love, and a funerary deity, appealed to people of every social status, both the living and the dead. The earliest kings claimed not only to be protected by Horus but also to be incarnations of the god himself. Many cities or provinces recognized their own

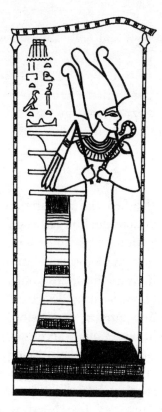

Figure 3 *Osiris*: The shrouded figure of the King of the Dead stands before his emblem, the *djed* pillar, beneath a simple canopy. As King and a god of agriculture he bears the crook and flail sceptres.

versions of Horus and used the falcon as a standard. One of the most significant centres of Horus-worship was Edfu where, in the Ptolemaic temple dedicated to the hawk-god, carved scenes depicted the god's continuous battle against his enemy Seth, the god of chaos, storm and violence. If Horus represented the productive land and peace, Seth personified the desert and conflict. These two aspects of existence in the Nile Valley, neither of which could exist without the other, dramatically display the Egyptian concept of Maat, the world in equilibrium.

Some of the earliest versions of Egyptian myths are found inscribed in the tomb chambers of late Old Kingdom pyramids. These *Pyramid Texts* are the oldest sources of information about the beliefs of the ancient Egyptians and are, in many cases, contradictory, inconsistent and almost incomprehensible in modern terms. The principal deity with whom the King was associated and who, in later periods, came to be recognized as the Ruler of the Underworld, was the agriculture-god Osiris (fig. 3). The myths explain how this son of the earth-god Geb had been appointed by his father as Egypt's first King. He instructed the Egyptians in farming techniques, the manufacture and use of tools, the domestication of animals, the growing of crops and the propagation of vines. His sister-wife Isis taught the women how to make bread and beer from grain, how to spin and weave linen from flax and how to care for children and the sick. Together Osiris and Isis defined the proper worship of the gods and promised a life after death for those who lived a blameless mortal existence according to the rules they had established. Osiris, the god closest to the hearts of all Egyptians from the King down to the humblest peasant, was the first farmer and the role-model for all his followers. The most acceptable offerings to such a god, and by association all other deities, were the products of the land itself, returning the god's gifts in kind.

Bread and beer were the chief components of the diet for all Egyptians, rich and poor, young and old alike, and both were made from grain. There were several words in the ancient Egyptian language for grain, but one term in particular graphically expresses the significance of grain in the life of the people. This was *ankhet*, a noun derived from the verb 'to live' and so describing corn as 'that which gives life'. This fact alone would make the farmer the most important contributor towards the health and prosperity of the people, but the producers of grain had a doubly influential role. The ancient Egyptians never used money as it is understood by modern society. There were no coins in general circulation until the Ptolemaic Period. For some 4,000 years, the civilization functioned and flourished with a barter economy in which 'prices' of basic commodities were expressed in terms of measures of grain. In a very real sense the farmers of Egypt grew the country's wealth and upon their success, or failure, depended the whole structure of their society.

The earliest evidence for the cultivation of grain crops in the Nile Valley comes from the Predynastic Period around 4500 BC, notably from the Fayum. This oasis to the south-west of Cairo is fed by the Bahr Yusuf which branches off the Nile just north of Assyut and runs almost parallel with the river at the western edge of the cultivable plain. The Fayum was intensively exploited for agricultural purposes throughout Dynastic history. The lake was known to the ancient Egyptians as *Mer Wer*, the Great Lake, hence its Greek name, Moeris. Land was reclaimed from the lake at several periods, especially during the Twelfth Dynasty when kings built their pyramids and summer palaces in the region. The greatest increases in both the available agricultural land and the population of the Fayum occurred during the Ptolemaic era when about 1,200 square kilometres of land was under cultivation, though much of that has since reverted to desert. This compares with an estimate for the whole country at the same time, as calculated from inscriptions in the temple of Horus at Edfu, of a little under 25,000 square kilometres. The Romans also settled in the Fayum which became one of the principal grain producing areas of the Roman Empire.

In prehistoric times wheat, barley and flax were cultivated on the shores of Lake Moeris and continued to be the most important crops of Egypt in all periods. The type of barley grown was much the same as the modern crop, whereas the ancient wheat species was emmer, a primitive form of wheat with fewer, smaller grains per ear than modern types. Emmer is lower in nutritional value than barley which, until the late New Kingdom, was the more important cultivar. Both cereals were used for bread and beer.

The Inundation reached its height in mid-August. As the flood waters overflowed the banks, they covered the lower-lying land beyond to such a depth that in many areas boats were needed to cross the fields. Catch basins were created by dyking and, from the late Old Kingdom onwards, canals channeled the flood waters in a less haphazard way. Lesser channels directed the water far away from the river itself enabling the maximum area possible to be irrigated. The fields which were naturally flooded received the best of the mineral-rich silt carried by the Inundation. Fields which were artificially irrigated by opening dykes to allow water to run over them, were also fertilized, but to a lesser extent since some of the alluvium would have been deposited en route in the canals. The most labour-intensive higher-lying land, irrigated with water raised by means of the *shaduf* and sheer muscle power, was likely to be the least productive. Ridges of earth like miniature dykes divided the fields into small plots so that water could be contained in a limited area and allowed to soak into the soil.

The provision of water for the fields and the maintenance of irrigation works were communal responsibilities, but local land-owners, especially the provincial noblemen, were more immediately involved with such work than the national government. In his tomb in the cliffs above modern Assyut, Kheti, the Governor of the Upper Sycamore and Viper Province wrote his autobiography around 2100 BC describing his efforts to improve the irrigation works of his province:

> [By way of monument I replaced an old channel with] a canal of ten cubits width. I excavated it for the arable land . . . I supplied water in the highland district. I made a water supply for this city . . . in the upper lands which had not seen water. I made the elevated land a swamp. I caused the water of the Nile to flood over the ancient landmarks. I made the arable land [plentiful with] water. Every neighbour was supplied with water and every citizen had Nile water to his heart's content. I gave water to every citizen alike and everyone was content with his lot.

The best fields could produce two harvests a year if suitably irri-gated for the second crop. The introduction of the *shaduf* in the early New Kingdom made this a less arduous task and increased both the quantity of the grain harvest and the area of land avail-able for crop-growing. The *shaduf* is a simple mechanism which seems to have originated in Mesopotamia. A long pole which is either balanced on an upright, such as a brick pillar or a forked wooden post, or suspended from a timber framework, is pivoted so that it may be swung from side to side as well as up and down. At one end of the pole is hung a bucket, anciently of leather or basketwork, and at the other end is a counterweight, usually a mass of mud and stones. The operator pulls down the pole to fill the bucket with water, then allows the counterweight to raise it up to a level where it may be emptied into a channel, gulley or cistern at the edge of the field. The *shaduf* was also used for watering ornamental gardens as shown in the Theban tomb of Ipuy, but a gardener caring for vegetable plots had a less easy life. He had to carry water in jars suspended from a yoke over his shoulders (fig. 4). Much of his day would have been spent going back and forth between the garden and the water supply. Student scribes were warned about the hard life of the gardener, amongst

Figure 4 *A Hard Life*: Gardeners tend a vegetable patch, shown as a grid of small plots divided by ridges of soil. One brings water in jars suspended from a yoke.

other trades, in a work composed by teachers who wished to emphasize the worth of education:

> The gardener carries a yoke, his shoulders are bent as with age. The yoke causes a swelling on his neck which festers. In the morning he waters the vegetables and in the evening he tends the herbs, while throughout the middle part of the day he toils in the orchard. He works himself to death in a job which is harder than all other professions.

The hard work involved in growing cereals was not much less. The Inundation season was followed by the season of Emergence during which the waters subsided. This was the winter-spring season of tillage and planting. Once the land had dried out enough to be worked, the first task was to turn the earth. On the so-called Scorpion Macehead, a Predynastic king is shown wielding a hoe or mattock of a type which continued in use for thousands of years. A similar implement is still used by Egyptian peasant farmers to till their fields. Larger areas were worked with a plough of very primitive design being no more than a sharpened, fire-hardened stick which was pressed into the earth by the ploughman and dragged through the ground by a pair of oxen (fig. 5). This action did little more than carve a series of grooves in the soil. There was no knife arrangement to cut a furrow and no angled board to turn the soil. The ploughman steered his machine by means of

Figure 5 *Ploughing and Sowing*: Sennedjem drives his piebald plough team across the field. His wife follows behind sowing seed corn.

handlebar-like uprights and the oxen were harnessed to a yoke or the reins were simply attached to a board wedged between the animals' horns. Such scratch ploughs were first used in the Archaic Period and, despite their inefficiency, continued in use unchanged in design for about 2,000 years. Men with hoes followed the plough to break up the clods of earth and produce a good tilth, so that the soil was rendered suitable for sowing.

Seed corn was provided from the harvest of the previous year. Since grain was so valuable, the use of seed corn was strictly controlled and all withdrawals from the granaries were carefully recorded by scribes. The amount allowed to any farmer would depend on the area of land he wished to plant and some complicated calculations were needed to assess what was required. Many things had to be taken into account, such as the quality of the soil which was in turn dependent on the height of the Inundation that year. Last year's harvest might have been poor, which would mean there was less seed available than the farmers were demanding, so a rationing system would be applied to ensure that the grain was distributed fairly. This was particularly important in periods when a succession of low Inundations had led to the depletion of stocks of corn. The First Intermediate Period was such a time when the failure of the harvest several years running caused considerable instability throughout the country. Farmers looked to local rulers rather than the Crown for help in sustaining the agricultural base of their economy. In Kheti's autobiography he

Figure 6 *Grain for Min*: Ramesses III performs the rite of cutting the first sheaf of grain as part of the Harvest Festival of Min.

describes how he shared his wealth with his less fortunate people: 'I was rich in grain so when the land was in need I maintained the city with grain by the sackful and by the basketful. I allocated each citizen grain for himself; and the same for his wife, and for the widow and her son. I remitted all taxes which had been levied by my forefathers.'

The seed was broadcast, scattered by hand from a basket slung on the sower's shoulder. Following behind him, a flock of sheep or goats, or sometimes a herd of pigs, was driven on to the field to tread in the seed. This gave the corn the best chance of germinating and prevented too much of it being eaten by birds or being burnt by the hot sun. Except when a second crop was grown, there was rarely any need to irrigate the fields further after their thorough soaking during the months of Inundation, but a certain amount of tending was required during the growing season. Fields were probably enclosed with stake or picket fences, or with simple barriers of thorny brushwood, to deter animals from trampling or eating the crop. A Middle Kingdom story known as the *Tale of the Eloquent Peasant* described how a path ran along the edge of a barley field between the standing crop and a waterway. A peasant taking his produce to market was forced by an unscrupulous landowner to lead his donkeys so close to the field that one of the animals snatched a mouthful of grain. The peasant's donkeys and their loads were immediately confiscated and the peasant himself was beaten for theft. Doubtless this is an exaggerated story, but it shows that there were recognized boundaries and rights of way around the fields and both landowners and those who used the public paths had recourse to the law to uphold their rights.

Farmers would employ children to scare away the pigeons and sparrows which could wreak havoc in a field of sprouting corn. Some weeding would have been necessary, as indicated by the weeds shown in the wall painting of a cornfield from the tomb of Menna dating from the middle of the Eighteenth Dynasty. The remains of funeral garlands and decorative elements in furniture and jewellery show that cornflowers, poppies and mayweeds were all common.

The growing and ripening corn, in particular barley, was thought to be the responsibility of an ancient agriculture-god called Neper who was absorbed into the nature of the god Osiris at a very early era. In the Coffin Texts, a collection of magical and religious literature inscribed on coffins during the Middle Kingdom to help the deceased on their perilous journey to the next world, Neper is described as 'this grain-god who lives after death', a reference to the 'dead' seed corn sprouting to be 'reborn' and live again as the crop ripens. In one 'spell' the deceased is identified even more closely with the life and death of Neper: 'I live and grow as Neper whom the honoured ones cherish, one whom Geb [god of the earth] hides. I live and I die, for I am barley, and I will not perish. . . . I have gone forth in truth and my shape is raised up.'

The myths of Osiris, the son of Geb, tell of his successful rule as the first King of Egypt, his murder and dismemberment at the hands of his jealous brother Seth, his burial and his resurrection to become King of the Dead. This is a perfect analogy of the crop cycle. His death was seen as the reaping of the harvest, his dismembered body represented the threshed grain, his burial was analogous with the planting of the seed and his resurrection was promised by the growth of the new crop. At the great Festival of Osiris held at Abydos, saucers holding a mixture of barley and silt were buried by pilgrims who saw in the germination of the grain a promise of a good harvest to come. Similar 'Osiris beds', made of wood and shaped like the mummiform figure of the god himself, were included in tombs as symbols of the hoped-for resurrection. Osiris himself was often portrayed with skin coloured black, imitating the Nile mud, or green, the colour of sprouting barley. Osiris-Neper may be identified with agriculture-gods in many other civilizations. For instance, a pagan corn-god survives in the English folk tradition of Old John Barleycorn who was cut down, beaten and buried and yet 'still got up again'.

The female counterpart of Neper was Renenutet, a goddess intimately associated with the King in the form of the uraeus serpent. This cobra deity protected the King from enemies by spitting fire or venom into their eyes from her perch on the King's brow. Occasionally she was shown as a cobra-headed woman suckling the infant King and was also thought to nurture the crops, so influencing the prosperity of the land and its people. Not surprisingly, Renenutet was most popular in the Fayum where village chapels were dedicated to her by the field workers who sought her blessing on their labours. The feast days of Renenutet were celebrated at the end of the season of Emergence and the beginning of the third season, the summer season of Drought.

One very important event in the crop cycle in Egypt was not part of the Osiris myth. This was the visit of the tax assessors. Since grain was the most common negotiable currency, the harvest gathered from a field was effectively the income of the field's owner and as such was subject to income tax. Teams of surveyors were sent to inspect the ripening corn. They measured the fields to calculate the area under cultivation which would be compared with records from previous years. Samples of grain would be tested and the receipts for the issue of that season's seed would be consulted in order to judge the quality of the crop. On the basis of all this information, an estimate would be made of the expected yield. The tax demand issued by the Inspector of Fields was for about 20 per cent of what he estimated the harvest would be. Much could happen in the time between the taxman's visit and the harvest. Pests such as mice, rats, birds and insects could decimate a crop. Fire was not uncommon in a hot, dry climate and there was always the possibility of theft or vandalism by human agents. By the time the harvest was completed the actual yield could be well short of what had been predicted.

At the time of the harvest the goddess Renenutet, Lady of the Threshing Floor, was again remembered and her symbol, like a crescent moon woven from straw, is shown hovering above the harvest workers. Similar fetishes, like European corn-dollies, may have been hung in barns and granaries and even in homes as charms to bring luck to the harvest. The major religious festival of the season was that of the procreative god Min who is shown as a shrouded human figure with permanently erect phallus. His crown is a low cylindrical cap surmounted by two tall plumes, the same as that worn by Amen at Luxor with whom Min is closely associated. His sceptre is the flail, a threshing implement which was also carried by the king as a symbol of royal authority. Min, as a god of agriculture and fertility like Osiris, is often portrayed with black or green skin. His festival, known as the Coming Forth of Min, was held at the very start of the harvest season. Since the harvest was a central feature in the lives of the majority of the population, this was a very important event for the people. It was celebrated in style at the major cult centres of Coptos, Akhmin and Luxor, and in a more modest way in agricultural communities throughout the Two Lands. Its celebration at Thebes is shown in some detail in reliefs in the mortuary temple of Ramesses III at Medinet Habu.

The highlight of the festival of Min was the parade of the god's cult statue, which rested on a float draped with a red sequined cloth and was carried on the shoulders of twenty priests. Unlike most religious processions, in which the god's statue was hidden from human gaze in a shrine shrouded with a linen curtain, Min was displayed for all to see. The statue of this god, with his face, hands and huge erection coloured with shiny black bituminous paint to represent the soil of Egypt, was a powerful image of the fertility of the land. The god's sacred animal, a pure white bull symbolizing virility and procreation, was led at the head of the parade which included the royal family, attendant priests, musicians and a military escort. The rituals which accompanied the general carnival atmosphere included a series of hymns with actions which were not quite as dramatic as medieval mystery plays, but which were less formal than the daily temple rites and involved an audience. The hymns celebrated Min's potency, his powers of regeneration and rebirth and his influence over all growing things. In one of the hymns, called the *Mime of Min who Resides in the Garden*, he is closely associated with Osiris. At one point in the festival four birds representing the Sons of Horus were released to take the news of Min's blessing on the King to the four corners of the world. As a harvest festival, the most significant act was the symbolic cutting of the first sheaf of grain, performed by the King himself (fig 6). The ceremonies illustrated at Medinet Habu are accompanied by inscriptions which explain what is happening, though the language used is rather archaic and difficult to interpret. The cutting of the corn is described thus:

> Now comes the attendant priest, bringing the sickle of black copper decorated with gold, and a sheaf of wheat to be presented to the King. . . . Now the King cuts the grain with the sickle by his own hand. The wheat is put to his nose then placed before Min. . . . An ear of wheat is given to the King.

Possibly, the placing of the wheat 'before Min' took the form of offering the newly cut grain to the White Bull and his acceptance of it was seen as a good omen for the harvest. The Bull of Min himself was probably thereafter butchered and formed the main dish at the festival banquet. A trough planted with lettuces shown as tall pointed plants of the cos variety, is also a prominent element in the scenes of the festival. Lettuces were considered to have aphrodisiac properties and the white sap which exudes from their cut stems was identified with semen. Even the shape and exaggerated size of the plants, as shown in these reliefs, were symbolic of the god's permanently priapic state, hence the choice of lettuces as a suitable offering to the primeval god of fertility.

Figure 7 *The Threshing Floor*: Cattle are driven round the threshing floor as men rake the ears of corn under their hooves to crush and separate the grains from the husks.

At harvest time the corn was cut with wooden sickles set with flint blades. The corn was cut just below the ears leaving the straw standing for separate collection. In a painting from the tomb of Ti at Saqqara, pipers are shown playing a tune to help the reapers keep the rhythm of their strokes. Gleaning was a task set the children. In the Theban tomb of Menna, two young girls are shown fighting over the grain dropped by the reapers. Obviously, if a child had found a good patch of dropped grain she would guard it fiercely.

The cut grain was collected in large baskets and transported to the threshing floor where it was deposited in heaps. Threshing, the process of freeing grain from the husks, was carried out on a circular flat area of beaten earth which may have been paved with limestone slabs or with a sort of concrete made from gypsum. The corn was raked from the edges into the middle and under the hooves of cattle or donkeys which were driven around the floor, trampling the ears to squeeze the seeds out of their tough, inedible cases (fig. 7). The next process was winnowing. Winnowers, their heads bound with cloths which were almost certainly drawn across their mouths and noses to prevent the inhalation of too much dust, tossed the threshed grain into the air from wooden or basketwork scoops so that the lightweight chaff was blown away by the breeze while the heavier grain fell to earth. The separated grain was measured into baskets or sacks which were meticulously counted and their number recorded by scribes before being carried to the granaries for storage.

In earliest times, grain was stored in brick-lined pits, perhaps with a replaceable lining of reed matting and a thatched, or animal hide roof. The type of grain silo found in the farmyards of the larger estates was a beehive-shaped structure of mudbrick, plastered and possibly lime-washed. The silo was filled from the top and grain was taken out through a wooden shutter door low down in the wall. The largest estates, the temples and the government buildings had free-standing granaries with grain bunkers protected within substantial walls. The entrance to such a granary would have been guarded by a doorkeeper and the deliveries and extractions of grain were recorded, like deposits and withdrawals from a bank, by a battery of ledger clerks. An accountant, whose title was Counter of Grain, was responsible for keeping the books and an Overseer of the Granary was in charge of the overall running of the grain stores, just like a modern bank manager. The Overseer of the Double Granary of Egypt was one of the most important finance officers of the country, rather like the Governor of the Bank of England. Locally, granary officials were responsible for releasing grain, which was the main element in the wages paid to state employees, and for receiving the proportion of the grain harvest demanded by the state as taxes. The Rhind Mathematical Papyrus is a collection of tables and worked examples, some of which are the sort of practical calculations which would have been used by tax assessors and granary officials, including methods for calculating the capacity of a cylindrical granary and hence the value of the grain stored in it, and others for calculating the comparative values of bread and beer based on the cost of their basic ingredients. Tax officials visited farms at harvest time to collect the grain according to the tax demands issued earlier. There was summary punishment for any farmer who was late in paying his dues or who could not produce the amount demanded.

Landowners could lease out their land to tenants who paid an agreed portion of their harvest as rent. A bundle of papyri found in the Eleventh Dynasty tomb of Meseh at Thebes included letters and accounts from the files of Heqanakht, who kept a careful watch over the management of his agricultural estates, even while he was away from home on business. He instructed his steward as to what crops to plant and what extra land to rent: 'Now, as for all the affairs and all the business of the plot where I sowed flax previously – do not allow anyone else to use this land before you. You shall sow the plot with northern barley – do not sow emmer there unless it turns out to be a high Inundation, then you may sow it with emmer.'

Heqanakht went into detail about the rent he considered reasonable for cereal fields: 'You assessed for me the rent of 13 arouras of land in terms of northern barley . . . as being 65 sacks from those 13 arouras of land (that is producing only 9 sacks per aroura) which is rather tight. For 20 arouras this would mean a rent of 100 sacks of northern barley. . . . Make sure that Heti's son Nakht is sent down to farm 30 arouras of land for us on rent at Per-Haa. They shall take the rent for it from the *men*-cloth woven there but, if they have already sold the emmer which was in Per-Haa they shall pay the rent with [the proceeds from] this instead.'

Vegetable growing was largely the responsibility of individual householders. Plots may have been allocated to workers on the larger estates as part of their wages, so that they could supplement the family income by bartering surplus produce in the market-place. Pulses would have formed a significant part of the vegetable crop. Peas, beans and lentils were valuable sources of protein in a largely low-protein diet. Garden produce like onions, lettuces and cucumbers is often depicted in heaps of offerings. Some of the leafy bundles shown with them may represent the hemp-like plant meloukhia which is considered a traditional Egyptian vegetable of great antiquity and is still cultivated in kitchen gardens throughout the country.

The third major crop grown by Egyptian farmers was flax. Early evidence for the spinning and weaving of linen from the fibres of flax stems comes from the Fayum in the form of a scrap of woven fabric dating from *c.* 5000 BC. The fineness of the thread depends

Figure 8 *The Flax Harvest*: Flax stems are pulled up by the roots, tied in bundles and the seed heads removed by dragging the stems through a wooden comb set in the ground.

on the age of the plants when they are harvested. Younger, green stems produce the finest, whitest cloth, while the fully matured stems provide the raw material for matting and cordage. Some of the flax crop had to be allowed to ripen properly to produce seed for the next season. Linseed is a source of oil which could have been used for lighting as well as in the polishing and preserving of wood. To harvest flax, as shown in the papyrus of Mutemwiya in the British Museum, plants were pulled up by the roots since the stems were the most important part of the plant. The seed heads were removed by dragging bundles of stems through a wooden rake or comb set into the ground (fig. 8). Until the introduction of cotton during the Roman period, linen was the principal fabric employed in the manufacture of clothing. During the Ptolemaic Period, a fine linen fabric known as byssus was produced in temple workshops. The King held the monopoly on the export of this cloth which was highly valued throughout the Classical world.

Most farmers derived their income from a mixture of crop-growing and animal husbandry. The richest were the owners of the largest number of cattle. Herds were the subject of a biennial census which was vividly portrayed in the painting in the tomb of Nebamun at Thebes and in the model from the tomb of Meketre. Scribes were on hand, to count the cattle and to record their age, condition and, probably, their breeding record. Two types of cattle are identifiable in such scenes. The older breed, shown in the reliefs from the causeway of Khufu at Giza, had long, lyre-shaped horns. The shorthorn breed is the type shown in the model of a fattening shed from the Eleventh Dynasty tomb of Meketre

Figure 9 *The Cattle Shed*: Varicoloured cattle are shown in pens with mangers and water troughs. Two men prepare fodder for the herd, while another hand-feeds a piebald ox.

at Deir el-Bahri. The cattle were of many different colours, red, black, white, dappled, piebald and spotted (fig. 9).

There were three major religious cults surrounding bulls. The most important was that of the Apis Bull, supposedly the earthly receptacle for the spirit of the creator-god Ptah of Memphis. When the Apis died the priests of his cult searched for his replacement in the same way that Tibetan monks search for a new Dalai Lama. The bull had to be black with a white crescent moon on his forehead, the shape of a vulture with outspread wings across his back, the sign of the scarab under his tongue and the hairs of his tail should be double. The life of the Apis was one of great luxury with all the food and female company he could desire. It is likely that farmers would send their prize cows to stud at the Apis sanctuary to improve their herds with divine blood. Similar bull cults were recognized at Heliopolis where the black Mnevis Bull was worshipped as an incarnation of the sun-god Re, and at Hermonthis where Montju the warrior god was represented by Buchis, a white bull with a black face. Animals were pastured in water meadows all along the Nile, but the best grazing lands were in the Delta

Figure 10 *The Lonely Goatherd*: A goatherd beats an acacia tree to shake down foliage and pods for his flock to eat. A couple of impatient animals brave the tree's thorns to help themselves.

marshes. The beasts were marked with bronze brands. The temples employed scribes and accountants to keep records of the considerable herds they owned to provide meat offerings for the gods. The size of the temple herds was often increased after a military campaign when the king donated captured livestock to religious foundations.

Cattle-breeding was the height of animal husbandry in Egypt and beef was the most prestigious meat though it was restricted by its value to the upper classes. For the majority of the population, beef was the meat of daydreams. Even the upper middle classes would have tasted beef only rarely, if at all, although they would provide a quantity of the best joints for their afterlife by way of pictures, models and written lists. In most moderately affluent households 'small cattle', meaning sheep and goats, were more accessible sources of meat, with goats being more common. Goats were more adaptable to the available scrub grazing and were easier to milk than cows whose level of domestication made them unpredictable and liable to kick. Flocks were grazed in the wadis on the edges of the desert (fig. 10). The hooked shepherd's staff was used as a sceptre of royal authority and the short crook was the hieroglyph for 'ruler'. The Canaanite kings of the Fifteenth Dynasty, were known as 'Rulers of Foreign Lands', *Hekau Khasut*, which is now rendered as Hyksos. *Hekau* is written with the crook sign which may be why Josephus calls the Hyksos the 'Shepherd Kings'.

Workers employed in non-agricultural jobs, found pig-breeding to be a lucrative cottage industry. Workmen at Amarna bartered hogs in the city to bring in a little extra income for the village families and pig bones form a large proportion of the animal remains from such settlements. Pigs were also an important part of village ecology, being fed on human refuse. Meat other than beef is never shown on tomb or temple offering tables. Despite widespread consumption by the population as a whole it is possible that there was some sort of taboo on the depiction if not the eating of 'small cattle' or pigs in a religious context. Herodotus wrote about an apparent religious restriction on the eating of pork: 'Pigs are considered unclean. If anyone touches a pig accidentally in passing, he will at once plunge into the river, clothes and all, to wash himself. . . . Swineherds, though of pure Egyptian blood, are the only people in the country who never enter a temple.' Since it is clear that ordinary Egyptians ate pork in quite large quantities when they could afford it, and since no Egyptian, unless he was serving as a priest, had the right to enter a temple which was the residence of a god and therefore the ultimate in private property, both Herodotus's statements appear to fall down. He may have recorded the situation as he observed it in c. 400 BC but his description cannot be taken as typical of earlier periods.

Cattle and goats were kept also for their hides, and sheep, from the Middle Kingdom onwards, for their wool. Cow-skin was used to make the seats of chairs, as shown by the painted cowhide pattern on the seat of Tutankhamen's 'ecclesiastical' throne. Oxen were also very important as draught animals, and a small tenant farmer who could not afford to keep plough oxen of his own would have to negotiate the loan of a pair from a wealthier neighbour, as shown by surviving contracts of hire.

Wild game was acceptable both as offerings to the gods and on the rich man's table. Scenes of hunting are quite common, though this pastime was an upper class privilege and certain quarry was the exclusive preserve of royalty. The hunt of the wild cattle from which, ultimately, the farm animals were domesticated, was recorded by several kings including Amenhotep III who issued a series of inscribed scarabs to advertise his hunting skills.

A messenger came to tell His Majesty that there were wild cattle in the desert of the district of Shetau. . . . the people of the district were ordered to keep watch on these cattle. His Majesty, commanding that they should surround them with a net and a dyke, . . . ordered that the total of these cattle should be counted and the number of them came to 190. The number of cattle which His Majesty brought in by his own prowess on this day was 56. His Majesty rested for four days. . . . then His Majesty mounted again in his chariot and the number of these cattle brought in by him was 40 making a total of wild cattle [captured] 96.

From this description it can be seen that Amenhotep, by coralling and probably lassoing, was capturing the animals alive. It would be considered wasteful to slaughter so many beasts all at once, just for the sake of sport.

Wild game was often captured for the fattening sheds. A painting from the Twelfth Dynasty tomb of Khnumhotep at Beni Hasan shows stockmen feeding oryx. Farmyards also contained fattening pens for poultry, principally ducks and geese, many of which were captured from the wild. Poultry were also subject to the biennial livestock census as painted in the tomb of Nebamun. Birds were kept for their eggs too, but ducks and geese lay less frequently and less regularly than hens which were unknown in Egypt, except for specimens kept as curiosities, until the Late Period. The force-feeding of geese with a sweetened barley mash was part of the poultryman's job, presumably to increase the weight of the birds and also, possibly, to promote the growth of the liver on the same principle as the traditional production of *foie gras*. The Rhind Mathematical Papyrus includes calculations of the quantities of feed necessary for fattening poultry. Similar calculations were available for working out the rations for cattle.

Arable farming, animal husbandry and market gardening formed a broad-based agriculture in which the majority of the population of ancient Egypt was directly involved. The success of this system is shown by its ability to support non-productive members of society – priests, bureaucrats, artists and soldiers – and so to create a varied and viable culture. The Egyptian farmer was the pillar on which this culture was founded.

Hieroglyphs associated with the Farmer

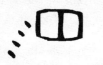

corn measure, 'grain'	three ripples, 'water'	hoe, mattock 'beloved'	sickle

bull, 'cattle'	ram, 'sheep'	peasant's crook	shepherd's crook, 'sceptre', 'ruler'

CHAPTER 2

The Builder

•

ONCE A RELIABLE and sustainable food source had been established, the next priority for any pastoral or farming community was to provide shelter from the elements for themselves, their families and possessions. Nomadic herdsmen and hunter-gatherers leave little evidence of the sort of shelters they built. Some of the oldest house-like structures in the world, found close to Wadi Halfa, just beyond the southern border of modern Egypt, seem to have been tent rings, irregular circles of large sandstone blocks which had been used to hold down the edges of tents made from matting or animal skins stretched over a light wooden framework. These structures, built over shallow pits lined with sandstone slabs were at least semi-permanent. This site dates from the late Palaeolithic and similar tent rings, with carefully laid tufa slabs forming vertical enclosure walls, found at Dunqul, the southernmost of the Egyptian oases in the Western Desert, have been dated to c. 50000–40000 BC.

Rock paintings found in the south-western region of Gebel Uweinat show domed huts similar to those built by cattle-herding tribes of East Africa today. The Uweinat site is thought to represent a change from hunting to a settled cattle farming lifestyle around 6000–5500 BC and also demonstrates that the fringes of the Sahara Desert were much more amenable to human habitation and exploitation in the Neolithic era. Even at that early period, however, people were migrating towards the more promising pastoral lands of the Nile Valley and settlements were being established.

In the south, the site considered typical of the Egyptian Pre-dynastic culture before 5000 BC is el-Badari, 30 kilometres upriver from the modern city of Assyut. Badarian remains include several settlements which might be called villages. At Matmar and el-Badari itself little remained apart from storage pits – probably primitive granaries, lined originally with mud or basketwork – and the ashes from fires showing that the sites were settlements. The houses themselves were almost certainly round and constructed of woven reeds daubed with mud. The buildings at Hemamiya are more recognizable as dwellings. They too were generally round with low walls formed from limestone chips and blocks held together with mud. The roofs were probably conical or domed and made of reeds or straw thatch over a wooden or bent-reed frame. Other buildings were clearly storage huts for grain, tools or animal fodder and some may have been used as barns for the animals themselves.

Around 3600 BC the first rectangular houses so far identified appeared at el-Mahasna north of Abydos. These wattle-and-daub structures were made with woven plant materials supported on wooden posts and plastered over with mud. Primitive shrines shown on Predynastic artifacts, such as the Hunters Palette, indicate an arched shape with the corner posts extending above the level of the eaves. A structure of this type became the hieroglyph for 'shrine' and 'sarcophagus' or 'burial'. The rectangular floor plan of a one-roomed hut with an entrance in the middle of one long wall was the hieroglyph for 'house' or 'building'. Oval buildings were typical of the earliest known farming village, Merimda-Beni-Salame, some 60 kilometres north-west of Cairo dating from c. 4900 BC. The occupants of Merimda combined herding with growing crops. The settlement displays a measure of prosperity with houses large enough to be partitioned into eating and sleeping areas, and arranged in streets. The partitions, like the fences surrounding the houses providing courtyards and animal pens, were made of reeds woven with grasses and supported by wooden posts. Similar panels or hurdles are still produced in peasant areas of modern Egypt, though maize stems and sugar cane leaves have largely replaced reeds as the principal materials. The top edges of these panels are neatened by tying off the loose ends in a series of knots giving a fringe effect. The ancient origin of this technique is shown by the use of the *beker* frieze in the painted or carved decoration of walls. Each element of the frieze is a stylized representation of one of the knots along the top of a reedwork panel.

The commonest sources of building materials were the reeds and grasses so abundant along the Nile, especially in the Delta region.

Where trees were either scarce or too valuable as food sources to be felled for timber, reed bundles took the place of wooden roof supports and posts. Although the woven panels were often smothered with a layer of mud to make them stronger and more permanent, very substantial buildings could be made using reeds alone. This technique is still employed by the Marsh Arabs of Iraq whose reed buildings bear a striking resemblance to the traditional Egyptian shrine shape, with decorative sections of wall which are similar in pattern to the latticed façade of Egyptian dwellings as represented in tomb stelae. The plant species used were principally the common reed and the giant reed, both perennials with flat tapering leaf blades and bamboo-like stems which grow to three metres in height. These reed stems are individually quite rigid but when bound in bundles they can become as sturdy as timbers. Both species are still common in marshy areas of Egypt, forming extensive reed beds. The giant reed also tolerates drier conditions to colonize the banks of irrigation channels. The flowering heads are plume-like and when blown by the wind they take the shape of the reed hieroglyph which was a common alphabetic sign. A bed of flowering reeds was the hieroglyph for 'countryside' and 'peasant'. The bent reed stem with two leaflets on each side of its base was the sign most often used for 'king', symbolizing the epithet 'He of the Reed'. The identification of the monarch with this humble plant shows how important the link was between the King and his land.

Another plant used extensively for building purposes was the sedge *Cyperus papyrus* which grows as tall as five metres. The huge papyrus swamps which existed in pharaonic times have completely vanished as drainage of the marshes and changes in irrigation methods, notably the building of the Aswan High Dam, have destroyed the plant's natural habitat. In recent years, papyrus plants have been reintroduced into Egypt as a cultivated crop to provide the tourist industry with the raw material for that most typical of all Egyptian souvenirs, decorated papyrus sheets. The colour of papyrus gave rise to the use of a stylized stem as the hieroglyph for 'green' or 'fresh'. It also meant 'lucky' or 'fortunate' and amulets in the shape of the papyrus stalk with its bell-shaped flower head were carved from a green stone to be worn as a lucky charm. The uses which the Egyptians had for papyrus, as mentioned by Herodotus did not include building. By his time, *c.* 400 BC, the tradition of building with reeds may have died out, or perhaps he never visited the areas where it persisted, for buildings were still being made of reeds in the First Century AD when another Classical author, Diodorus, wrote about Egypt: 'It is said that the ancient Egyptians built their houses of reeds, a tradition still to be seen amongst the shepherds today. They care for buildings of no other materials saying that reeds have always served them well.'

The product which remains the most important of all building materials is mudbrick. The oldest bricks found in Egypt come from Predynastic sites in Upper Egypt, and by the Archaic Period bricks were being used extensively in buildings of all sorts. Some Predynastic ceremonial palettes based on the flat slate used for grinding mineral pigment for eyepaint, but made much larger and carved with scenes commemorating special events, bear images of towns or settlements surrounded by battlemented walls. The excavations at sites like Nagada and el-Kab show that ancient towns were provided with fortifications in the form of mudbrick walls with bastions and gateways. Originally round or oval in plan, such walls gave rise to the hieroglyph for 'town' which shows two principal streets crossing within a circular wall. Later fortifications were built to a rectangular or at least straight-sided plan with substantial mudbrick walls which had a panelled façade like those of the Second Dynasty 'fort' or 'castle' of Khasekhemwy at Abydos. The surrounding walls of this structure, which may have been a ceremonial building associated with the King's jubilee, survive to an impressive height of more than 10 metres. The city walls at Kahun in the Fayum, built as a home for the builders of the pyramid of Senusert II, were 3 metres thick and probably twice as high. This wall was not a defensive feature but marked the boundaries of the built-up area.

Ancient bricks were made in much the same way as mudbricks are still made in Egypt. The most important ingredient was Nile mud which naturally contains clay and sand in varying proportions. The clay content determines whether the mud will be sufficiently cohesive to form bricks without the addition of a binding

Figure 11 *Brick-making*: The mud is mixed and blended then carried in buckets to the brickfield where rows of rectangular bricks are shaped with a wooden mould.

agent such as chopped straw or animal dung. If the mud is too rich in clay, the bricks will dry out slowly and tend to shrink and crack. The process of making bricks is shown in the tomb of Rekhmire at Thebes. The earth mixed with water, and the vegetable binder if necessary, is worked into a smooth mud. This is then formed into bricks by being pressed into a rectangular wooden mould and tipped out on to the ground to dry in the sun (fig. 11). Rows of these bricks may be seen in brickfields today, though the modern blocks are likely to contain cement powder to add strength and to accelerate the hardening process. Many bricks intended for important buildings were marked with impressions from a wooden stamp usually bearing the name of the King who commissioned the building. The majority of bricks were not kiln-fired or baked, as was the custom in Mesopotamia at the same time, since the climate of Egypt was much drier and there was no significant problem with rain or wind erosion. Occasionally 'burnt' bricks were used to pave streets or ceremonial ways where sun-dried bricks would be quickly worn away by use or eroded by water. In general building use, damaged bricks or those which had crumbled with age could be 'recycled' by being crushed and mixed with water and fresh mud to start a new batch.

Bricks were set in place with clay mortar. Door and window sills and lintels were of wood in peasant houses, but even the owners of modest town houses could afford limestone features. Roofs were usually flat, made of reed and grass thatch over wooden or reed-bundle rafters. The fibrous nature of date palm trunks makes them unsuitable for woodworking but they were useful as roofing beams. Acacia wood seems to have been the timber employed most often for building purposes. The builders of the grander royal or public buildings employed imported wood, especially cedarwood from the Lebanon and northern Syria. The thatch could be strengthened with layers of mud plaster and overlaid with woven matting to turn the roof area into a usable second storey. A mudbrick staircase, often outside the house, gave access to the roof which became a storage and work area and probably a sleeping area for hot summer nights. Inside and outside the walls of the house were rendered with a mud plaster and in many cases also whitewashed. In the principal room the walls were sometimes decorated and in the mudbrick palaces of Malkata, built by Amenhotep III, walls, ceilings and floors were painted with elaborate geometric patterns, figures of popular deities and scenes of wildlife along the riverbank. Kitchens were usually open courtyards where, perhaps, an awning would have protected the cook from the weather. A cool cellar provided room for storing valuable and perishable goods.

The collection of models in Meketre's tomb included several houses ranging from a simple hut to a fine two-storey villa with its own garden pool and sycamore trees. In paintings like that from the tomb of Nebamun at Thebes, sloping sections of roof may be identified as the tops of staircases or vents to catch the breeze – a primitive form of air-conditioning (fig. 12). Although most roofs were flat, arched and vaulted ceilings could be built using bent reed supports which would be removed once the bricks and their mortar had dried enough to hold the shape required. A series of brick vaults may still be seen in the remains of the administrative buildings surrounding the Ramesseum. These are thought to have been store-rooms, possibly for grain. Windows were usually placed high up in the wall to take advantage of the cleaner air above street level. They were latticed with the stripped central ribs of palm fronds or could be filled with wooden or stone window grilles, some of which could be highly decorative. Doors were made from planks and were fitted into wooden frames. They were most commonly hinged on tenons inserted into stone sockets in the sill

Figure 12 *An Elegant Abode*: This country house has a papyrus stem column in the window above the door and woven matting window blinds. The two sloping sections of the roof may be air vents or the tops of staircases.

and lintel (fig. 13) as is shown quite clearly in the hieroglyph for 'door'. The commonest type of door fastening was a bar which slid through staples in both leaves of a double door. Doors and windows were provided with rolled matting curtains or screens to keep out dust and sand, as is clearly shown in the model hut from Meketre's tomb where a rolled blind can be seen above the window.

Mudbrick was used for most secular buildings throughout the Dynastic Period. Even at the major temple sites, and especially in the forts in the southern Nubian territories, brick was the preferred material for temenos and defensive walls. Early mastaba tombs built for royalty and the most important court officials, were lined, partitioned and faced with mudbrick. The exterior walls of the superstructure of such tombs were plastered and painted to represent the woven reed patterns of houses or palaces. The Third Dynasty tomb of Hesyre at Saqqara had wooden panels carved in delicate relief set into niches in the exterior mudbrick walls. The practice of imitating one building material in another was an enduring feature of the Egyptian builder's art.

According to the Egyptian historian Manetho, it was Imhotep, the architect of the Step Pyramid, who invented the techniques of building with stone. Imhotep was revered as a healer and man of wisdom long after his death. His tomb at Saqqara, close to the

Figure 13
Closing the Doors:
Sennedjem seals the
double doors to his
tomb. They are
suspended between
hieroglyphs for the
sky and the hills and
are pivoted rather than
hinged.

pyramid built for his patron King Djoser, became a site of pilgrimage for ordinary Egyptians seeking divine blessing or advice, especially on medical matters. Subterranean galleries in the vicinity of Imhotep's tomb have been found to contain thousands of mummified ibises, the ibis being the sacred bird of Thoth, the god of wisdom with whom the architect was associated. These pitiful relics were offered by pilgrims rather in the same way as a Roman Catholic might light a candle to draw attention to a prayer or plea. In the Late Period, Imhotep achieved demi-god status and was included in the divine triad worshipped at Memphis. He is shown as a seated scribe, with a papyrus unrolled on his lap, and wears the skull-cap of his divine father Ptah, the 'Master Craftsman' of the Egyptian pantheon, who was both smith and sculptor (fig. 14). The workmen at Deir el-Medina who built the royal tombs of Thebes, worshipped both Ptah and Imhotep as patrons who would understand and appreciate their needs and requests.

The Step Pyramid represents a startling development in building methods. Striking forms which thenceforward became standard in Egyptian architecture were clearly based on mudbrick and organic originals. The six-stepped construction represents the final stage of a plan which was changed several times before its completion. The base is a rectangle measuring some 125 by 110 metres, the original height was almost 62 metres. The pyramid complex covers an area of more than 150,000 square metres. The outer surface of the pyramid was originally faced with the finest white Tura limestone to create a clean-edged stairway to heaven, but the buildings around it and the subterranean galleries beneath, give much more

Figure 14
The Master Craftsman: The god Ptah of Memphis, enthroned in a primitive shrine, holds a sceptre composed of the hieroglyphs for life, stability and dominion. He is given the title 'Lord of Maat'.

information about the work of the Egyptian builder. Like the pyramid itself, the perimeter wall was constructed of limestone blocks with a panelled facing of Tura limestone and was made to resemble the mudbrick surrounding wall of nearby Memphis, the city whose nickname was the White Wall.

Spaced around the wall were bastions made in imitation of towered gateways with double doors. Only one of these bastions was a real entrance and the wall around this gateway has been reconstructed to show the nature of the original. Doors complete with hinges and bolts were carved as if opened and folded back against the inner walls of the dummy gateways. Similar imitation closed doors are carved in the niches between parallel corridors beneath the pyramid. Each is carved as if set in a frame and is provided with a rolled blind, the wood and reeds being represented in stone and glazed tiles. The ceiling of the entrance passage through the main gateway is carved with cylindrical beams representing timbers. The columns of the hall beyond the entrance are massive stone representations of reed-bundle roof supports (fig. 15), and the dummy chapels which flank the ceremonial courtyard are imitations in solid masonry of ancient shrines with arched roofs and prominent corner posts. In the underground corridors, walls are decorated with panels of blue-green glazed tiles which formed a non-perishable version of the ornamental woven reed hangings which would have

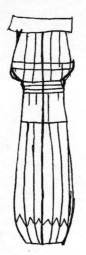

Figure 15 *Column Design*: This drawing of
a reed-bundle column based on a vertical line
of symmetry has been corrected by the artist
or architect. It shows the proportions used for
columns in the Nineteenth Dynasty.

adorned the walls of the King's palace. Similar patterns were painted
on the walls of the burial chambers in later pyramids, or carved on
the sarcophagus itself, in order to provide a real 'home' for the
deceased in the next world. The rectangular enclosure known as the
serekh in which one of the King's names was written, was supported
by a stylized representation of a palace façade.

The façades of the two national sanctuaries were decorated with
engaged columns representing the heraldic plants of Upper and
Lower Egypt, the lily and the papyrus. The papyrus stem shape
became the classic bell-topped column of temple halls, notably the
Hypostyle Hall at Karnak. The papyrus stem hieroglyph was used
to mean 'column' and columns continued to be made in imitation
of single plant stems, or bundles complete with cord bindings,
throughout Dynastic history. The two plants of the North and
South are represented on the square columns which supported the
roof of the hall erected by Tuthmose III before the sanctuary of
Amen at Karnak. The architects of the Ptolemaic era adapted the
idea to classical forms by decorating their column capitals with
bunches of papyrus or lotus heads, or stylized palm fronds.

There was little precedent for the working of stone for such
dramatic building purposes before Djoser's time. Roughly dressed
limestone slabs had been used in tombs of the Archaic Period for
paving and lining burial chambers, and stone lintels, sills and door
jambs were included in mudbrick structures. Egypt had a reputation for the production of fine stone wares such as vases, bowls

and fancy offering vessels, themselves sometimes imitations of baskets or reed trays, carved from a variety of stones, some very hard like diorite, or difficult to work, like schist. So the principles of stone-working were understood and the locations of sources of suitable materials were known from a very early period.

The Palermo Stone records the 'stretching of the cord for the temple called the Thrones of the Gods, performed by the priest of Seshat', during the reign of a First Dynasty king whose name is lost. Seshat was the goddess of writing, the archivist who kept records of all the King's deeds, primarily his military successes and his benefactions to the gods. The building of a major temple would have warranted inclusion in the catalogue of the King's good works, hence the presence of the priest of Seshat. The expression 'stretching the cord' is a literal translation of the term describing the laying out of the plan of the building. Surveyors armed with measuring rods and cords defined the area to be used and marked the principal features of the building on the prepared surface.

The unit of measurement used in ancient times was the cubit, originally the length of a human forearm from the point of the elbow to the tip of the middle finger. This measurement obviously varies from person to person and although a cubit was the recognized unit of length in several civilizations, the actual length it represented varied from culture to culture. The ancient Egyptians used two standard cubit measures: the royal cubit which was a little over 52 centimetres, and the short cubit of approximately 45 centimetres. Buildings were measured by the royal cubit which was subdivided into 7 palms and each palm of about 7.5 centimetres consisted of 4 fingerbreadths or digits. Measuring rods marked with these divisions and others such as the span – the distance covered by the outspread hand measured from the tip of the forefinger to the tip of the thumb – were an essential part of the tool-kit of the Egyptian architect or surveyor. Examples have been found from the tombs of several important builders including Kha, who lived at Deir el-Medina during the reign of Amenhotep III, and Maya, the overseer of the building works on the west bank of the Nile at Thebes in the reign of Tutankhamen. For surveying purposes a cord knotted at cubit intervals was used. This was commonly 100 cubits long and land area was measured by the *aroura*, a square of side 100 cubits. The cord was made of palm or flax fibres which were likely to stretch in use, leading to errors in measurement. However, the lengths of the four sides of the square base of Khufu's pyramid vary only by a little over 20 centimetres at most in a side length of over 230 metres, an error of less than 0.09 per cent showing that the Egyptian surveyor or architect was able to take the inaccuracy of his tools into account in his calculations. The lines of the architect's plan could be marked out with pegged cords or by plucking a taut cord which had been dipped in red paint to slap a line on the stone surface, hence the term 'stretching the cord'.

The area to be built on was cleared down to bedrock and then the surface was levelled. A temporary dyke or dam was built around the building site which was criss-crossed with shallow interconnecting trenches. When the area was flooded the trenches were excavated further so that their floors were all at a constant depth below the water level. When the area had been drained, the intervening areas of stone were removed to the same depth as the bottom of the trenches. Herodotus recounted the legend of how Menes, the first king of the united Two Lands, had built his new capital city: 'On land which had been drained by the diversion of the river, King Menes built the city which is now called Memphis. . . . In addition to this the priests told me that he built there the large and very remarkable temple of Hephaestus [Ptah].' The folk tale about the diversion of the Nile by means of damming it and forcing it to flow in man-made channels could have been an elaboration on the builders' techniques employed in laying the foundations for the new capital. For large areas such as the base of a pyramid it was not necessary to level the whole site. The Giza pyramids are built on natural knolls in the plateau which added to the stability and strength of their superstructures.

The King himself attended the foundation laying ceremonies for major religious monuments. Building texts from the Ptolemaic temples of Denderah and Edfu describe how the alignments of walls were defined according to astronomical observations performed by priests. The senior priest involved in the alignment ceremony represented the god Thoth, the patron of scribes, architects and scientists. Foundation deposits were often laid at important points in the planned structure, many in stone- or brick-lined pits sunk beneath the corners of walls. These were filled with offerings to the gods, miniature tools and samples of the building materials to be used in the construction, and many amulets or lucky charms in the form of sacred symbols and inscribed scarabs. Such foundation deposits beneath the pyramid and mortuary temple of Amenemhet I at el-Lisht contained bricks, plaques of copper, alabaster and faience, pottery and alabaster vases and saucers as well as the skull of an ox. The name of the pyramid is given on the plaques as 'the abodes of Sehetep-ib-Re are shining'. At Deir el-Bahri, the mortuary temple of Queen Hatshepsut, foundation deposits included several inscribed jars, which had contained valuable unguents, bearing the queen's names and titles with a text explaining why they were there: '. . . she made it as her monument to her father, Amen, on the occasion of stretching the cord over Amen-Djeser-Djeseru [the name of the temple meaning Amen, Holy of Holies], may she live, like Re, forever!' Similar foundation deposits have been found in other royal monuments, for instance the unfinished mortuary temple of Ramesses IV. Many of the glazed amulets from such deposits represented food offerings, principally joints of meat and loaves of bread, or symbols of renewal or rebirth associated with the cult of the Afterlife, such as the lotus flower and the *bulti* fish. Engraved tablets of stone, glazed ware or metal usually bore the King's names and the designation of the temple itself, since each building had its own name.

Once the foundations were laid, the building materials had to be brought in. Limestone quarries were opened up at or near every major building site. The bulk of the core material for the Giza pyramids of Khufu, Khafre and Menkaure was quarried on the Giza plateau itself. The remaining artificial cliff face, into which later private tombs were excavated, shows that good quality stone was available there in a bed as deep as 27 metres in places. The limestone quarries of Beni Hasan extend for over 5 kilometres along the eastern cliffs. Quarrying techniques for limestone developed from the experience of builders excavating burial chambers into the bedrock and were the same as those employed for other 'soft' stones such as alabaster and sandstone. Quarrymen used saws, chisels, adzes and axes of the same design as those used for woodworking (fig. 16), together with picks and spikes, all made of copper

Figure 16 *Man at Work*: A stonemason with his hammer and chisel was captured in this caricature sketch by an artist with a sense of humour.

in earlier periods before bronze was introduced in the Middle Kingdom, though some implements would themselves have been made of harder stones. Hammers and mallets were of wood or stone, some being simply conveniently-sized natural rocks used to pound the stone surface. Trenches were cut outlining the block to be quarried on four sides and once these were the required depth, holes were made horizontally from the base of each trench so that wooden wedges could be hammered in. The wood swelled when soaked with water, causing the stone to split along the line of holes, and so the block was freed from the living rock. In the ancient quarry faces at Aswan, rows of wedge slots, like the perforations on postage stamps, remain to show how blocks were separated from the mass.

Hard stones like the prized granite of Aswan were quarried in a similar way, but digging the trenches around a block took much longer. The rock was pounded with stone hammers or natural dolerite nodules which have been found at the Aswan quarries. The process was accelerated by lighting fires over the area being worked, then quenching the flames quickly so that the rapid expansion and contraction weakened the surface layer which could be easily pounded and chipped away. This cycle of heating, cooling and pounding was repeated time after time to reduce the rock layer by layer. Granite was not as easily worked as limestone, even with bronze tools, and most Egyptian stone-working implements were made of the softer copper. Flint and other hard stones were used as chisel points and as bits for drills and were probably used with an abrasive agent, the most likely being quartz sand of which there was an unlimited supply. The action of rotating a drill or sawing caused grains of sand to become embedded in the points of these tools, creating an edge which was much harder and sharper than the copper alone. Petrie suggested that granite was cut by jewelled saws which had been deliberately set with emery points, though he also stated that: 'There is no doubt that sawing and grinding with loose powder was the general method.' The marks of a saw can be seen on the granite sarcophagus of Khufu which is still in the King's Chamber of the Great Pyramid. A tubular drill was used to cut cylindrical pillars of stone which could then be broken off at the base. In this way stone blocks could be hollowed out as was necessary for the huge royal sarcophagi and even complete burial chambers. One such is the yellow quartzite burial chamber sunk into the bedrock beneath the pyramid of Amenemhet III at Hawara. Quartzite, a crystalline form of sandstone, was the hardest stone to be worked by the Egyptians. When Petrie excavated the pyramid, he found the chamber to be a rectangular, lidless box measuring 6.7 by 2.4 by 1.8 metres. It was so finely cut and polished that, until he examined it more closely, he thought the sharply defined corners must have been jointed. Instead he realized the whole chamber had been carved from a single block of quartzite which, in its original state, would have weighed about 112 tonnes.

Min, the fertility god, was also the patron of miners, quarrymen and travellers. His cult centre at Coptos, modern Qift, was the meeting point of several important caravan routes through the Eastern Desert, including the Wadi Hammamat which links the Nile Valley with the Red Sea coast. The earliest known map in the world is a late Twentieth Dynasty papyrus which marks some of the mines and quarries in the region of the Wadi Hammamat and the places where miners and travellers might find water.

By taking advantage of the high water levels during the season of Inundation, stones were transported to their building site as far as possible by water. Canals were dug from the river to the site and special quays and strengthened embankments were built for loading and unloading the stone from barges. The barge which carried two obelisks from Aswan to Karnak for Queen Hatshepsut's coronation is depicted in her temple at Deir el-Bahri. It was over 60 metres long and was towed by three rows of nine boats. Overland stone was carried on wooden sleds pulled along on rollers over solid ground, but where the surface was looser, as over sand or soft soil, trackways of timber sleepers set into mudbrick or packed clay were laid. The rollers or tracks were lubricated with water which also reduced the heat caused by friction. The ceremonial causeway which served the Great Pyramid was probably built over the line of the track along which the building stone for the pyramid itself was hauled. A colossal statue, shown being transported in this fashion in the Middle Kingdom tomb of Djehutihotep at el-Bersheh, apparently weighed over 60 tonnes. The average weight of the 2,500,000 or so limestone blocks used in the Great Pyramid is over 2.5 tonnes, though granite slabs used to roof the burial chamber average over 45 tonnes and some of the largest slabs used in Menkaure's pyramid have been estimated at 200 tonnes each.

Experiments in recent years have shown that quite large stones may be moved efficiently and effectively by gangs of no more than ten men. Herodotus wrote that 100,000 men were employed in building Khufu's pyramid. Close to the pyramids were the barracks or living quarters for the labourers which would have housed the permanent skilled labour force of as many as 4,000 architects, surveyors, engineers, stonemasons, carpenters and bricklayers. The vast majority of workers would have been peasants conscripted from the fields during the period of the Inundation when the land was unworkable. They would have lived in temporary camps around the plateau and were paid a subsistence wage while they were performing their duty to the royal corvée. This was unpleasant work, but while they were employed by the state the men were fed at the state's expense. A bakery has been identified where bread was produced on an industrial scale to supply the daily needs of the pyramid builders. A set of texts known as the Reisner Papyri, thought to date from the reign of Senusert I, is a series of official registers from the workshops and stores of the necropolis at Naga ed-Deir. This includes rosters of workmen, both conscripted and members of the permanent workforce, and names foremen and men appointed to each work gang. Accounts listed the delivery of cargoes of cattle, fish and fowl which may have been intended to feed the labourers, but were more probably intended for the officials and administrators.

Among the mathematical calculations in the Reisner Papyri are those used to work out the volume of stone blocks and the number of men needed to handle them. Other examples show how logistics scribes calculated the volume of stone which had to be excavated for a temple. The working implies that each conscript was expected to work 10 cubic cubits of stone per day. Scribes were on hand with their measuring rods to check the quarried stone arriving on site and the volume of floors, trenches and corridors excavated, to see that the workers were keeping to the agreed schedule. It was a crime to evade this work deliberately and criminals were punished by being permanently attached to quarrying and stone-hauling gangs. Certain professions were exempt from the corvée and wealthier citizens could remit some of their dues in kind rather than labour. Peasants, however, formed the largest part of the workforce until, in later times, vast numbers of prisoners of war were drafted in as forced labour. Herodotus recorded what he was told about the building of Khufu's pyramid: 'To build the pyramid itself took 20 years. . . . it is of polished stone blocks, beautifully fitted, none of the blocks being less than 30 feet long. The method employed was to build it in tiers, or steps. . . . when the base was complete the blocks for the first tier above it were lifted from the ground level by cranes made of short timbers.'

There are no contemporary pictures or models showing such 'machines' in use, though the Egyptians did employ wooden scaffolding. The most commonly accepted method of raising stones to higher levels, whether for pyramids or temple pylons, was a combination of leverage and the use of ramps made of rubble and mudbrick. The remains of several ramps exist around monuments at Giza and even behind the First Pylon at Karnak. In the brick-making scene from the tomb of Rekhmire, a ramp constructed from the bricks is shown. Another is described in a Nineteenth Dynasty papyrus in the British Musuem. The ramp's measurements are given as about 380 metres long and 30 metres wide, with a maximum height allowing for a slope of 1 in 12. This would require a total volume of material of over 180,000 cubic metres. The ramps built for the construction of the Giza pyramids were huge, perhaps equalling more than 60 per cent of the volume of the pyramids themselves. These ramps were almost certainly constructed of stone chippings discarded from the shaping of building stones and excavated from underground chambers. Once a pyramid was completed, the ramps were dismantled and the rubble dumped in the worked-out quarries, if not required for the ramp for the next monument.

Different methods were employed by the builders of pyramids for the Twelfth Dynasty Kings. Amenemhet I plundered Old Kingdom tombs and temples, both private and royal, to accelerate the construction of his pyramid at Lisht. The tomb built for his son Senusert I was formed by a framework of stone walls making compartments which were then filled with rough-cut stones, sand and rubble. The rough interior construction of the core was concealed behind the smooth white casing layer. Later pyramids of the Dynasty were built using mudbrick to fill in the compartments of the superstructure. Unfortunately, once the Tura limestone was removed, much of it robbed for modern buildings in Cairo, the core disintegrated quite quickly so that the pyramids of Illahun and Dashur are almost unrecognizable. Much ancient Egyptian building was on such a monumental scale that the size and weight of the stones used meant that they stayed in place where they were put and there was little need for mortar. However, gypsum mortar was used, partly as a lubricant so that one stone could be slid in place over another. The smoother the faces in contact the closer the joint between the stones. The remaining casing stones on the lowest course of the Great Pyramid are so accurately cut and placed that it is impossible to insert even a razor blade between them.

Huge ceiling slabs were used in the columned halls of the great temples, but there is a limit to the distance that can be spanned by a stone before it cracks under its own weight. Therefore, larger, unsupported ceilings were laid on wooden joists fitted in sockets in the stone walls. Ramps and platforms of mudbrick reinforced with stone would have been built wherever it was necessary to raise stone to any height. Levers, wedges and rockers were used to move the stone from these ramps to their final position. Slots for the insertion of levers may be seen in some unfinished casing stones. Sockets for stone posts could have been filled with sand so that the weight of the upright pressing down forced the sand out of a plug hole so lowering the stone into position. This method was used for lowering in place the last ceiling block of the burial chamber of King Khendjer of the Thirteenth Dynasty, at Saqqara.

From the simplest reed shelters erected by the poorest peasants to the magnificent royal tombs and temples, the builders of Egypt demonstrated their ingenuity and great technical skill in working with a wide range of materials, using only the most primitive of tools. The results they achieved are still amongst the most remarkable monuments in the world.

Hieroglyphs associated with the Builder

shrine

plan of building, 'house', 'building'

heker knot, 'decoration', 'ornament'

flowering reed, alphabetic ';'

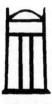

reedbed 'marshland', 'peasant'

swt-reed, symbolic of Upper Egypt, 'King'

papyrus stem, 'column', 'sturdy', 'green', 'fresh'

village with cross-roads, 'town', 'place'

door

door bolt, alphabetic 's'

wall with bastions, 'wall', 'fortification'

pick excavating a pool, 'to found', 'establish'

CHAPTER 3

Women and Children

•

THE ANCIENT EGYPTIAN civilization supported one of the most humane societies of all time, a society based on the family unit and the institution of legal marriage which was considered to have been ordained and sanctified by Osiris and Isis who were, according to legend, Egypt's first king and queen (fig. 17). Egyptian women enjoyed a degree of freedom and independence which would have been envied by their counterparts in other civilizations of the Middle East, in Classical Greece or even in Medieval Europe. The rights of an Egyptian woman to own and inherit property were better than those of married women in Victorian England. Though there was no formal codification of the society's moral laws, the rule of Maat compelled all Egyptians to uphold the rights and respect the needs of the weaker members of their society. They believed that when the deceased presented themselves before the scales of Maat in the Hall of Osiris, they would have to justify their right to everlasting life by making a statement known as the 'Negative Confession', in which they denied a catalogue of offences against the gods and against society. The strikingly simple phrases of this statement eloquently express the attitude of the Egyptians towards their fellow citizens:

> Behold, I have come before you. I have brought you truth. I have foresworn falsehood. . . . I have not impoverished my neighbours. I have done no wrong in the Place of Maat. . . . I have not deprived the orphan of his property. I have done nothing that is detested by the gods. . . . I have caused no pain. I have made no one hungry. I have caused no one to weep. I have not killed nor have I commanded to kill. I have caused no suffering. . . . I have not taken the milk from the mouths of children. . . . I am pure!

Figure 17 *Husband and Wife*: The enthroned Osiris is supported by his sister-wife Isis who wears the throne sign as her crown, and his sister Nephthys, whose symbol is her name which means 'Mistress of the Mansion'.

In the Great Harris Papyrus, a detailed record of the reign of Ramesses III, the King made a claim which says much about the Egyptians' belief in the equality of women:

> I planted the whole land with trees and greenery allowing people to sit in the shade. I caused every woman of Egypt to go with head held high to any place she desired for no stranger nor any traveller upon the road would molest her. I kept alive the whole land, whether foreigners, commonfolk or citizens, all people both male and female.

The family was all-important and it was considered a man's duty to marry and start a family while he was still young. Life expectancy in African countries has always been low in comparison with Europe. In the first quarter of the twentieth century, the average life expectancy for men and women in Egypt was only 31 and 36 years respectively. By the third quarter of the century these figures had risen by nearly 20 years in each case, but were still another 20 years behind the life expectancies of men and women in Western countries such as the USA. In ancient times, men of the privileged classes in Egypt could hope to live for between 45 and 50 years. An examination of human remains in the Turin Museum has provided an estimate of 36 years for the average age at death of Egyptians from the Dynastic era. A study of the royal mummies in the Cairo Museum has demonstrated that the better quality of life enjoyed by the nobility could considerably increase life expectancy. Ramesses II, who probably came to the throne in his late teens, is known to have reigned for more than 65 years. The examination of his mummified body has confirmed that he was at least in his seventies when he died. Women were not so lucky. Thirty-five would have been considered a good old age for a middle-class Egyptian woman, but, since pregnancy and childbirth were so dangerous, many of her less affluent countrywomen died before they reached the age of 20.

The apparent large size of the average Egyptian family as portrayed in tombs is misleading. In a funerary context all children, whether living or dead at the time of the completion of the painted scenes, would be included in them as members of the family (fig. 18). Since all children were portrayed as miniature adults, with no indication of relative age, there is no obvious way to distinguish between those who may have died as infants or in childhood and those who had survived to achieve puberty. A wife's role in society as the manager of the household and mother of the heirs to the family property was highly valued and respected. Family life was idealized in the literary compositions known as *Wisdom Texts* which have survived from several periods. These expounded on the acceptable code of conduct for all Egyptians and were commonly used as teaching material for student scribes who, it was hoped,

Figure 18 *Happy Families*: Anherkau and his wife receive funerary offerings from their son while surrounded by their favourite grandchildren.

would absorb the good advice as they practised their handwriting. The text known as the *Wisdom of Ptah-hotep,* purportedly written by a Vizier in the latter part of the Old Kingdom, includes recommendations on suitable behaviour for all occasions. A man was advised that it was his duty to take a wife and that he should provide her with every comfort: 'When you prosper and establish your household, love your wife dearly. Feed her well, clothe her in style and provide precious ointments for her body. Keep her happy as long as you live. . . . Thus will you make her stay in your house.'

According to Ptah-hotep, children were to be cherished, but were also a responsibility. Children were a man's insurance for the afterlife. The oldest surviving son would be in charge of his father's funeral and would be required to make the funerary and mortuary offerings to perpetuate the memory of his parents. A prudent man, according to Ptah-hotep, would raise his children to behave well and to have respect for their elders if he hoped to be supported by them in his old age: 'If you are a man of substance and by the grace of the gods you have a son; if he is honest, taking after you, and cares for your possessions, then do for him everything that is good for he is your true and worthy son, your spirit gave him life. Do not withdraw your blessing from him!'

It seems to have been the nature of children throughout history to rebel against parental authority and family arguments or feuds were not unknown. Ptah-hotep advised children to heed the advice of years: 'If a man's son accepts his father's words, his plans will not fail. Teach your son to be a listener . . . a son who hears is a follower of Horus and all goes well for him as long as he continues to listen. When he is old and respected he will speak likewise to his own children, renewing the teaching of his father . . . he will speak to his children so that they in turn will speak to their children. Set an example, do not give cause for rebellion. If Maat is upheld then your children will live . . . a dutiful son is a divine gift.'

The only respectable way to start a family was within a marriage which, in ancient Egypt, was a monogamous relationship. Only one woman at a time was recognized as Mistress of the House, *nebet per*, a title which might be equated with 'Mrs'. In a love

poem dating from the Middle Kingdom, a girl expresses her wish
to be married:

> O thou, the handsomest of men! My only wish is to look after all
> your possessions by becoming the Mistress of your House. Oh that
> your hand might always rest in mine. My love is at your service!

There is little evidence for the recognition of a formal wedding
ceremony, either religious or civil. After discussion and negotiation
between the families involved, a marriage was arranged and sometimes an agreement was drawn up in the form of a legal document
which may have been registered or at least lodged in a temple or
administrative archive. The marriage contract was largely a means
of allocating rights to property. Marriages between cousins, or even
between generations, seem to have been popular since the property division was less complicated if it was all kept in the family.
Amenemhet, a granary accountant at the Temple of Amen in the
Eighteenth Dynasty, was married to Baketamen who, as she is
described as 'the daughter of his sister', was clearly his niece. It
was not uncommon for uncles and nieces or aunts and nephews
to be of approximately the same age within the large families of
ancient Egypt. Dowries and bride prices were agreed but some may
have been notional, payment being demanded only if the marriage
failed. The woman retained ownership of any property she brought
into the marriage and kept her rights of inheritance to her parents'
estate. She was also entitled to a one-third share in any property
acquired during the marriage. This was her inheritance should she
outlive her husband. The remaining two-thirds would be shared
equally between all children, boys and girls alike, after any special
bequests had been made.

The occasion of a marriage was marked by the woman moving
out of her father's home and into that of her husband. The procession of the families through the streets with a parade of the wedding
gifts of household goods and furniture was a public display which
set the formal seal on the union. The couple was thus married by
public acclamation. The woman, who may have been as young as
12 or 13 years, had become the responsibility of her husband who
was probably only two or three years older than his bride. Only
if she was widowed or, gods forbid, divorced, would she return

to her father's house, but it was more than likely that she would die before her husband. Where a man portrays more than one wife in his tomb it is almost always a case of his being widowed and remarrying. This was a consequence of the high mortality among women of childbearing age. Sennefer, the Governor of Thebes during the reign of Amenhotep III, is depicted in his tomb in the company of no less than three wives. They are named as Senet-nay, Senet-nefert and Meryt (fig. 19), the last-named appearing only on the walls of the burial chamber itself, which was the last part of the tomb to be excavated and decorated. This would imply that after losing two wives, Sennefer took a third spouse in the latter part of his life, by which time his tomb was almost complete. The scenes in the tomb, corroborated by inscriptions on statues and in the tombs of relatives, indicate that Sennefer's first two marriages produced no sons. A grandson, the son of his daughter, is shown presenting the funerary offerings to Sennefer and his first wife Senet-nay. However, in the burial chamber Sennefer and Meryt

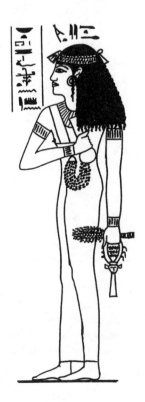

Figure 19 *Mistress of the House*: Meryt, the third wife of Sennefer, is named as Mistress of the House and Chantress of Amen. She carries the *menat* necklace and sistrum as symbols of her priestly rank.

receive libations and offerings of incense from their son, showing that the Governor was finally given a male heir by his third wife.

The New Kingdom sage Any had advice to offer about starting a family: 'Take a wife while you are young so that she may bear a son for you. She should bear children while you are still in your youth. It is proper to increase the population. Happy is the man whose family is numerous, he is respected on account of his children.'

Any also advised his reader to have respect for his mother: 'Give to your mother double the food she gave you. Support her as she supported you. You were a heavy burden to her but she did not abandon you. When you were born after your months in the womb she was still tied to you, her breast in your mouth, for three years . . . she kept watching over you daily. . . . When you take a wife and are settled in your own home pay attention to your children. Bring them up as did your mother. Do not give her cause to criticize you.'

Figure 20 *The Great One*: Taweret, the hippopotamus-goddess and protector of women in pregnancy and childbirth, rests a hand holding the *ankh* sign of life on the symbol for 'protection'. She wears the horned sun's disc crown of Hathor.

This extract is particularly interesting for its statement concerning the length of time for which an Egyptian child was breast-fed. Three years seems excessive by modern standards, but there are several possible reasons for this. Waterborne diseases such as dysentery and typhoid resulting from poor sanitation, and diarrhoea caused by bacterial contamination of food, were all dangerous to infants and a delay in weaning a child away from the breast may have given a degree of protection from these problems in the most vulnerable years. Goats kept in most villages and rural communities could have supplied a substitute for human breastmilk, but not everyone could afford the upkeep of these beasts and milch-cows were out of the question, so mother's milk was the cheapest food for infants. Breast-feeding also temporarily decreases the fertility of the mother and, although not a foolproof method of birth control by any means, this could have increased the length of time between pregnancies and so allowed the woman to recover her own health and strength. If all babies survived and were fed for three years by their mother, in theory she could have been feeding three children at a time while being pregnant with a fourth, but so many babies died at or soon after birth that there were always wet-nurses available. Upper class ladies would employ such women, who would perhaps continue in the service of the same family for a lifetime, their role changing to that of nanny, then governess or chaperone as the children grew up. Sennefer's first and second wives, Senetnay and Senet-nefert both bore the title Royal Nurse. It is difficult to define precisely the capacity in which either lady served the Court, but clearly it was an honourable profession and the charges of such ladies were taught to respect their nurses as members of their immediate family.

Several goddesses were associated with childbirth and motherhood. Hathor, the cow-goddess, was often depicted suckling the infant King as in her chapel at the Deir el-Bahri temple of Queen Hatshepsut. At certain auspicious births, a group of goddesses known as the Seven Hathors were thought to appear like fairy godmothers to predict the future for the child. In the Luxor Temple reliefs illustrating the story of the divine conception and birth of Amenhotep III, Hathor is shown holding an *ankh*, the sign of life, to the noses of the clay figures of the King and his *ka* that have

Figure 21 *Stand by Your Man*: Even in the afterlife, a man's wife would support him at his labours in the fields of Osiris. Sennedjem reaps as his wife gleans, both inappropriately dressed in their finest clothes.

been moulded by Khnum on his potter's wheel. In the equivalent scene at Deir el-Bahri, Hathor is replaced by the frog-headed Heqet, the midwife of the gods. The ancient mother-goddess Taweret, whose name means simply 'the Great One', is shown as a hippopotamus walking upright on her hind legs, with a frowning expression and teeth more like those of a crocodile since she was a fierce protector of pregnant women. Her leonine front paws rest on the hieroglyph *sa* meaning protection, and tiny faience figures of Taweret were worn as protective amulets by women and children of all classes. On the Papyrus of Ani, a copy of the text known as the *Book of the Dead*, the goddess, portrayed in the form of Taweret, wears the horned sun's disc crown and is named as Hathor (fig. 20), showing the close links between these mother-goddesses, especially in their roles as funerary spirits.

Hathor and Taweret also share the companionship of the dwarf-god Bes who seems to have been introduced, perhaps from Libya or from farther south, during the Middle Kingdom and immediately became one of the most popular household deities in Egypt. The bandy-legged figure of Bes, draped in a lionskin cape with the animal's mane framing his equally shaggy-haired and bearded face, is a common decorative element on household items. He was thought to dance around any house in which there was a woman in labour, scaring away evil spirits by clashing knives together or beating a drum. An amuletic pendant of Bes suspended on a cord or string of beads is painted around the neck of the delightful boxwood statue of a servant girl carrying a perfume jar on her hip, which is in the Oriental Museum in Durham.

Isis was often depicted as a mother suckling her infant son Horus. She was the perfect mother, bringing up her child in hiding, protecting him from his uncle Seth who had murdered her husband Osiris, until Horus was old enough to avenge his father's death. She kept him from harm, according to one legend, by tying her girdle or sash about him, so surrounding him with her considerable magical powers. The knotted sash, always coloured red, was a powerful amulet of protection, especially for women and children but also for the dead. Horus the Child, known as Harpocrates to the Greeks, was shown wearing the plaited sidelock of hair indicating youth and, in the traditional pose of the Egyptian child, with a finger held to his lips. This is one of many artistic conventions adopted for the portrayal of Egyptian culture. Another is the differentiation of skin colour between the sexes. In the best quality paintings, men are shown with terracotta-coloured skin, as if deeply sun-tanned, while women are depicted with a paler, more natural complexion, tending towards yellow in some cases. Peasant women who had to work in the fields alongside the men would have been exposed to the weather in the same way as their husbands (fig. 21), while more privileged ladies would have spent more of their time on household or administrative duties which kept them indoors, but this would not have been enough to account for the dramatic difference in skin tone usually employed. In reality, the artist painted a pale skin as an indication of affluence or status.

Besides raising children, a wife's primary role was as manager of a household which could be large. It was the responsibility of a man to care for any unmarried or widowed females in his immediate family. On the death of his father a son might become the head of a household which included his mother, aunts and sisters as well as his own wife and children. In the tomb of Amenemhet at Thebes his unmarried sister Nefertari is always shown in the company of his daughters (fig. 22) and despite being their aunt, and aunt to their mother, she appears to have been of their age. Elsewhere in the same tomb, Nefertari is named as the daughter of Amenemhet's brother. Clearly, orphaned nephews and nieces

Figure 22 *The Extended Family*: These two children of the family of Amenemhet are named as his deceased daughter Amenemheb and his brother's daughter Nefertari. All children living and dead, adopted or orphaned, were part of the Egyptian family.

would be adopted and brought up as the householder's own children. In larger houses in towns and the villas of the landed gentry, the women and children occupied their own quarters which are commonly referred to as the harem, a word with unfortunate connotations. In Egyptian, the same word was applied to the personal apartments of the King within a palace complex, and to the innermost sanctuary of a temple where the deity was thought to reside. It was not therefore a secluded, guarded semi-prison. In fact, women had the run of the whole house, while as Ptah-hotep wrote, men were warned against intruding on the women's domain: 'If you want friendship to endure, when you enter any house, whether as master or friend, wherever you go beware of approaching the women! Unhappy is the place where this warning is ignored and unwelcome is he who intrudes upon them!'

Women were considered to be under the protection of Hathor, the goddess of love and beauty (fig. 23). Her face was used to decorate toilet articles such as cosmetic pots. On her magnificent sarcophagus, the Lady Kawit, who was a member of the royal family in the reign of Montuhotep II, is shown having her hair

Figure 23 *Hathor*: The goddess of love and beauty, identified by her horned crown, holds out her *menat* necklace to King Seti I as a gesture of protection.

dressed by a handmaiden while holding up a mirror so that she can direct her coiffeuse (fig. 25). The mirror has a round reflective surface which would have been of metal, usually bronze or copper, though superior examples were of silver. The mirror itself was supported on a straight or L-shaped handle which was often decorated with the Hathor head, the face of a woman with cow's ears and horns. The horned sun's disc head-dress worn by Hathor was also adopted by Isis whose popularity, especially among women, caused her cult to continue longer than that of any other ancient Egyptian deity. The Romans included her in their pantheon, building temples and shrines to Isis throughout the Empire, even as far north as Hadrian's Wall. At Philae, the cult of Isis survived well into the Christian era.

The household crafts supposedly introduced by Isis were, throughout Dynastic history, always considered to be the duties of the housewife. In a domestic context it is women who are shown baking, brewing, spinning and weaving, while in the large workshops attached to the temples many if not all these tasks were performed by men. Wealthier ladies would take a supervisory role while

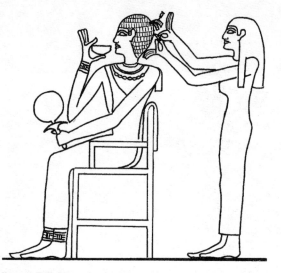

Figure 24 *Coiffeuse*: The Princess Kawit sips a cup of wine as a handmaiden dresses her hair. The lady holds a mirror decorated with the head of Hathor who was patron of the beautician's art.

servants carried out all the manual labour, but the *nebet per* made the decisions on all household matters. She could call upon the assistance of her children, especially her daughters, and any of her unmarried sisters or sisters-in-law who might be living under her roof. Better-off housewives and even the ordinary town-dwellers were able to afford servants, and despite the low wages paid for menial work, peasant girls were able to contribute to the support of their own families by taking such employment. In some cases the wages were almost non-existent, the servants receiving hardly more than their daily food rations. One of the letters in the Heqanakht archive lists the members of his household with the monthly grain rations which he allocated to each of them by way of wages. He also ordered the dismissal of a servant for apparently being impertinent if not actually abusive to his new wife who herself was resented by the children of Heqanakht's first marriage:

> Make sure that the housemaid Senen is thrown out of my house at once. Be sure to do this on the very day that Sa-Hathor arrives with this letter. If she spends one more day in my house be sure I shall hold you responsible for any evil she does to my new wife. I should not have to tell you this. Are you afraid of her? What can she possibly do to five strapping lads like you?

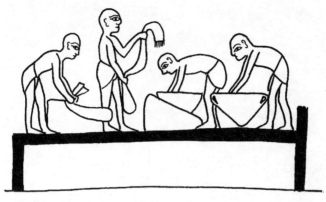

Figure 25 *Laundry*: Some of the better-off citizens could afford to pay to have their washing done by specialist launderers. Linen was soaked and scrubbed with natron and beaten to remove the dirt.

Servants could be hired on an occasional basis, such as the farm-hands employed at harvest time, or on a form of temporary contract or indenture. This was not exactly slavery, more a kind of serfdom, and even these servants had rights. A woman complained to a scribe called Ahmose that her daughter, who had been placed in service in his household, had been 'sold' without her consent. Ahmose wrote to his own superior to pass on her complaint:

> Ahmose of Peniaty says to his master the treasurer Ty, why has the servant girl who was in my care been carried off and given to another? . . . Let her value to me be estimated and taken instead for she is still young and not yet fully trained. Let the work she has been set to do be carried out by another of my master's servants. Her mother has complained to me that I have allowed her child to be taken away while she was still my responsibility as she had been with me since she was a child.

This letter is rather vague as to the details of the case but the mention of the girl's 'value' to Ahmose may represent an exchange of goods between the scribe and the girl's mother, either as a fee for her training or as a payment for her services as a household servant. It may be taken from this that the mother of an inden-tured servant still had a say in the upbringing of her child and could protest about exploitation. At Deir el-Medina servants were provided as part of the wages for the royal Workmen. Housewives were entitled to the labour of one or more of these servants for a

Figure 26
Provisions for the Afterlife: Female bearers with baskets on their heads deliver fruit, bread and beer, the produce of their master's estates, to his tomb.

certain number of days each month, depending on the householder's rank within the Workmen's community. These servants, both men and women, were employed on labour-intensive tasks and heavy manual work such as portering, cleaning, laundering (fig. 25) and the grinding of grain, which time-consuming and back-breaking job had to be done every day to provide the large quantities of flour needed to make bread. Every meal was based on bread and in the poorest homes bread was sometimes the only food available. In the funerary offering lists, bread of many types was requested in vast quantities. The lists of offerings made by Ramesses III to the temples during his reign include loaves numbered in tens of thousands. Bread was the staple diet for all Egyptians as well as for the gods themselves. In the Pyramid Texts the importance of bread is stressed on several occasions.

'What will you live on?' say the gods and spirits to me.
'I will live and have power through bread.'
'Where will you eat it?' say the gods and spirits to me.
'I will have power as I eat it under the branches of the tree of Hathor, my Mistress, who made offerings of bread, beer and corn in Heliopolis.'

In order to make the process of flour extraction slightly easier the corn could be parched, that is dampened then dried in the sun so that the tough, outer layers were softened and began to separate from the grains. The breaking up of the grain was started in a limestone mortar set in the floor. The emmer or barley was pounded with a heavy wooden pole. The partially broken grain was then transferred to a saddle quern, a dished, sloping stone on which it was crushed and rubbed to produce a coarse flour. The miller, usually a woman, knelt at the higher end of the quern and the flour was collected in a trough or basket at the lower end. The resultant flour was likely to contain partly crushed grains, husks and fragments of straw which had to be removed by sieving. Since sieves were made of woven reeds or grasses they were not very efficient and the flour used for baking could never have been as fine as modern bread-making flour. Further contamination in the form of sand and grit particles introduced during storage and the various processes was also difficult to remove and bread made with this flour must have been harsh-textured and difficult to chew as revealed by the severe wear on the molars of Egyptian mummies.

The fuel for cooking fires was predominantly animal dung and waste plant material such as straw. Peasants in Egypt today also use dung and the stripped leaves and stems from maize or sugar cane. Only in the largest kitchens would the fires have been fed with wood since the cutting of trees for firewood was strictly controlled. Most kitchens had a simple cylinder oven of baked clay. The fire stoked inside heated up the walls of the cylinder oven enough to cook flat pancakes of dough slapped on to the outside. These loaves of the pitta bread variety were usually unleavened, but yeast-risen bread or bread raised with sourdough was also baked. This required a domed oven with the fire set under a baking floor or shelf. The loaves were cooked either directly on the floor of the oven or in pottery moulds.

Water for all household needs had to be collected from the river or the nearest cistern or well several times a day. This was the sort of task allocated to the lower-ranking household servants. Herodotus remarked on the way in which Egyptian women carried such burdens: 'The Egyptians, in the practice of their everyday life, seem to have everything back to front. . . . Men carry loads on

Figure 27 *Partytime*: Two female guests at the funerary banquet are named as nurses of the family. One refuses the offer of more beer.

their heads while women bear loads on their shoulders.' This was not strictly true as is apparent from the models of female offering bearers from the tomb of Meketre, who balance square baskets on their heads (fig. 26), and numerous other portrayals of servants, male and female, fetching and carrying all kinds of burdens

The preparation of food and drink for the family was the prime concern of every housewife. The brewing of beer was usually overseen by the Mistress of the House, though the Workmen at Deir el-Medina considered the supervision of the household brew to be a legitimate excuse for absence from work. Beer was made by allowing a mixture of partially baked bread and a flavouring agent, commonly dates, to steep in water so that the yeast in the bread worked on the carbohydrates to produce alcohol. The fermented mash was pressed through a sieve and the liquor collected in beer jars. The finished, strained product would have been nothing like modern beers, but rather cloudy, flat and with a good deal of unpleasant sediment. Everyday beer was a mildly alcoholic thickened barley drink and was an important contribution towards the nutrition of the population. The brewing process also produced the liquid yeast or barm which was used to leaven bread, so on large estates the bakery and the brewery were always found close to each other. Stronger beers were produced for special occasions such

Figure 28 *Lady with Cat*: A guest at the funerary banquet is seated on a fine chair beneath which sits a cat, symbolic of sexual attraction.

as religious holidays. The drinking of such brews, whose potency was denoted by colour, was not restricted to men. Drunkenness at a party was considered a compliment to the host. In the banqueting scene from the tomb of Paheri a woman announces her intention to enjoy herself: 'I should love to drink until I am thoroughly drunk. My insides are as dry as straw.' Another more abstemious guest puts up her hand to refuse a servant's offer to refill her cup though her companion is not so reticent: 'Let the cup come to me. It is only right that we should drink to the health of our host.' (fig. 27).

Keeping the house clean was another important part of the daily routine for any Egyptian housewife. Dusty and sandy floors were swept with brooms made either from reeds bound on to a wooden handle like a besom, or from bundles of palm fibres. The dust was first laid with a sprinkling of water to prevent it rising in clouds and settling elsewhere. Evidence of vermin, especially rats and mice has been found in every settlement site from all periods. Rats in particular could gnaw through almost anything and could cause devastation in food stores where goods were not securely protected

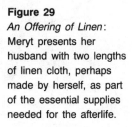

Figure 29
An Offering of Linen:
Meryt presents her
husband with two lengths
of linen cloth, perhaps
made by herself, as part
of the essential supplies
needed for the afterlife.

in stone or pottery containers. Children would be set to tracing
and blocking up rodent tunnels and finding nests so that they could
be destroyed. Noxious compounds were placed in the regular rat
runs and pottery rat traps were used, but the main defence against
rodents was the domestic cat. Most households would have kept
a cat whose sole purpose was to keep the house free from rats
and mice. Only the wealthy could afford to keep cats purely as
pets. In some wall paintings, as in the tomb of Ipuy at Thebes, a
cat is shown sitting under the chair of the Mistress of the House
(fig. 28). This may represent a pet, but the imagery of Egyptian
tomb paintings is very complex and the cat, as a symbol of female
fertility and sexuality, was included to ensure the lady's continuing
allure in the next life. Prince Tuthmose, son of Amenhotep III,
made elaborate provision for the embalming and burial of his
favourite cat called Ta-miw which means simply the Lady Cat.
Snakes were always a problem, but they were also sacred, the coiled
cobra being the hieroglyphic determinative for 'goddess'. In ancient
times, as now, snake catchers or charmers would tour the villages,
removing snakes that had taken up residence in inconvenient places.

There are no identifiable words in Egyptian for 'tailor' or 'seamstress', so it is reasonable to assume that making clothes for the family was another housewifely occupation. Spinning and weaving were largely carried out in specialized workshops, either attached to temples or as part of the business of the larger estates. Women were employed in these crafts which would have been useful skills for the unmarried daughters of a family to acquire. There may have been some sort of contracting out of the work so that spinning at least was done at home as a cottage industry. Woven cloth and spun thread were often part of a workman's wages, if he was employed by the state, or could be purchased from the workshops in exchange for grain or other negotiable commodities. Most ordinary clothing was very simple and required the minimum of sewing. In fact, children of both sexes appear to have gone naked until reaching puberty. There was no feeling of shame or prudery attached to nudity in ancient Egypt and the wearing or not of clothes was seen entirely as a matter of practicality and decoration. For household duties, a simple shift or even a wrap-around skirt was enough for most women. Men wore a knee-length kilt or a loincloth for everyday work. On formal occasions and for parties, clothes for both men and women were of finely woven linen and in styles which changed with fashion as in any civilization and the best festival gowns were decorated with embroidery or applied beadwork. Skilled needlewomen would have been employed by the religious foundations to provide the ritual garments and hangings used in the temples. Bandages for wrapping the body for burial were often no more than torn strips from old or worn clothing and household linen, but the better quality mummies were prepared with purpose-made bandages, some of which had elaborate patterns in the weave. The manufacture of these bandages required only simple hand looms and they could have been made by out-workers (fig. 29).

Apart from the usual household chores and crafts based on the home, there were few professions which were considered suitable for women. Midwifery was a matter of support from other female members of the family and perhaps the village wise woman, rather than a calling. There is very little evidence that women had general access to education which was the first requisite for any professional career. Female scribes were rarities, though evidence from the remarkable community of Deir el-Medina shows that a large proportion of the village population, including the women, could at least read if not also write. If they were fortunate enough to have indulgent parents, the daughters of upper-class families might be allowed to share in the lessons of their brothers and so acquire enough learning to be able to deal with the administration of a home which might also be a business.

Most property owners held lands in several parts of the country and besides personal inspection the management of these properties would require instructions to be relayed in writing. In the absence of the master of an estate, if his sons were too young to carry out his orders, his wife would pass on his instructions to the estate manager. Although the Egyptians clearly accepted the equality of men and women in law, their roles in life and their everyday activities were still governed by gender and class distinction. It would have been demeaning to a woman to have her servant instruct her as to her husband's wishes, so it was almost essential that she should be able to read to maintain her superiority. The more menial task of writing would be left to a scribe or secretary who would write letters from her dictation without the lady herself having to dirty her hands with ink.

It was a mark of rank for a woman to hold a religious post within her local temple. In most cases these women were not strictly speaking priestesses but *hesyt*, the 'favoured ones', a title also used for the female members of the royal household and sometimes translated as 'concubines'. The *hesyt* were singers, dancers and musicians who accompanied the sacred hymns and prayers to entertain the god in the daily rituals. A senior member of the choir or orchestra might hold the title Chantress, while the lady in charge of the female temple personnel was called the Matron of the God's Harem. These ladies were not celibate priestesses like the Vestal Virgins of Rome, nor were they nuns who had dedicated their lives to the service of their god. Many of them were respectable married women with children. As a badge of her rank, a Chantress like Meryt, the wife of Sennefer, is often shown carrying the *menat* and the sistrum. The *menat* was an antique-style necklace of many strings of heavy stone beads which was rattled as part of the percussion accompaniment for the sacred songs. It has a distinctive club-ended counterpoise which was commonly decorated with the figure of Hathor, and the necklace is more often shown being carried than worn. The sistrum, or sacred rattle, was also shaped like the head of the goddess with her horns curved inwards to form the hoop across which metal jingles were hung on wires. Those ladies who are named as priestesses were usually associated with the cult of a goddess, most often Hathor, Isis or Neith. It is not at all clear whether priestesses were required to undergo the same ritual purification, including the shaving of all body hair, as their male counterparts.

A woman's nearest male relative was responsible for her funeral and in most cases this would be her husband since wives rarely outlived their spouses. The Mistress of the House is shown prominently in any man's tomb, albeit on a smaller scale than him, and shares in all the offerings made at the tomb in his name. Children who had died young or unmarried were also buried in their parents' tomb. For the funerary ritual the oldest surviving son was known as 'he who causes their names to live' and through his actions in organizing the funeral, preparing the tomb furnishings and performing the rites, his father and mother would continue to enjoy a pleasant afterlife. The family was so central to Egyptian life that prayers were said for a man to be reunited with his family in the next world.

In some scenes showing the banquet at which all the family gathered together to celebrate the transition of the tomb-owner from mortal to everlasting life, several generations are shown together and no distinction is made between those who were still alive at the time of the funeral and those who had passed on many years before. A prime example of this is the scene from the tomb of Paheri at el-Kab where four generations are depicted, together with close friends and nurses, showing that the term 'family' was interpreted in its very broadest sense. During the reign of Ramesses II, the Foreman Neferhotep at Deir el-Medina adopted Paneb, the son of another Workman, even though both the boy's parents were still living. Neferhotep and his wife Wabkhet were childless, so they decided to give a likely lad all the opportunities they would have provided for their own children, had there been any. Paneb eventually inherited not only Neferhotep's property but also his job. The Foreman and his wife also adopted a household servant Hesunebef, possibly after Paneb had left home to start his own family. Although Hesunebef was originally a very lowly servant, his acquired status as Neferhotep's adopted son gave him a start up the ladder of success and he attained the rank of Workman on the royal tombs. Hesunebef married a girl who may have been a blood relative of Neferhotep and, as a mark of gratitude, he named two of his children after his adoptive parents.

Not all relationships were so amicable, even between parents and their children. Naunakhte, the widow of the Scribe of the Tomb Kenhirkhopshef, had eight children from her second marriage but four of them were a great disappointment to her. She made a will in which these four were barred from inheriting anything which had come to her through her marriage to Kenhirkhopshef as well as her share of the property accumulated jointly with her second husband. The main reason for this seems to have been that her ungrateful children had not fulfilled their filial duties: '. . . I brought up these eight servants of yours and provided them with everything that is customary for those of their situation in life. But see, now I am grown old and they are not caring for me in my turn. Whoever of them has looked after me, to him I will give a share of my property. But to him who has done nothing for me I will not give a single thing of my possessions.'

Despite occasional family disagreements the impression that prevails is of a caring and sociable society in which women and children played an important part. By modern standards, it may be thought that the Egyptian woman was disadvantaged by the general acceptance that her place was in the home and her first duty was to bear her husband's children. However, by the standards of her own time, the Egyptian woman enjoyed rights and privileges which were not available to her sisters in neighbouring countries and her children were cherished rather than exploited. Life was short and hard for most Egyptians, and shorter still for women, but pleasant enough for them to want it to continue for ever.

CHAPTER 4

The Scribe

•

THE SKILL OF WRITING emerged early in Egypt's history and the ability to read and write was essential to the smooth-running of the administration of the country in all periods. The Egyptian scribe, for the most part anonymous, was depicted in scenes of all everyday activities which were, in turn, annotated by other scribes to give a full description of what was being portrayed. Any picture was made more 'real' by its accompanying inscription, however brief. The words were just as important as the picture itself and together they served to encapsulate the essence of an activity or an event, or even the true personality of an individual. Words, both spoken and written, were thought to hold great power.

The Egyptians believed in the latent creative power of every word, as in the myth of the creator-god Ptah of Memphis who had called into being by means of his word: 'that which his heart thought and his tongue brought forth'. It was said of Re, the supreme solar deity, that the gods came into being through his word and the Word of Re was seen as an independent deity called Hu. The concept of spoken language having divine power is implicit in the opening verses of the Gospel according to St John:

> When all things began, the Word already was. The Word dwelt with God and what God was, the Word was. The Word then was with God at the beginning and through Him all things came to be; no single thing was created without Him.

Hu, the Word, was partnered by Sia, the embodiment of perception or conscious thought, who was said to be responsible for carrying the sacred book which recorded all intellectual achievement. Together, Sia and Hu made the most powerful combination of the Will and the Word (fig. 30). The importance placed on

Figure 30 *The Will and the Word*: Personifications of Sia and Hu, the Will and the Word of Re, shown amongst the judges of the Underworld.

words, and in particular on names, is shown by the Egyptian belief that things could be brought into being simply by speaking their names. This power was also thought to be contained in the written word, so that anything that could be put into writing could be controlled. Writing was thus a means of preserving, in physical form, the power inherent in the more ephemeral spoken word. The reading or speaking of these words unlocked that power.

The hieroglyphic script of ancient Egypt was called in the language 'the god's words'. The god in question was Thoth, the ibis-headed god of wisdom and scribe to the gods, who was said to have invented writing and to have passed on the secret to mortal men. Thoth was the embodiment of all scientific and literary attainment. He was in command of all 'the sacred books in the House of Life'. Scribes regarded themselves as 'followers of Thoth' and from earliest times, a man who could read and write was a man to be envied if not actually held in awe. Scribes were taught to pay reverence to their patron deity and invocations to Thoth were often inscribed on the writing palette which was a scribe's most precious possession. This prayer to Thoth comes from a text used to instruct student scribes:

Come to me, Thoth, O noble ibis. . . . O letter-writer of the
ennead. . . .
Come to me and give me counsel to make me skilful in your
calling;
He who masters it is found fit to hold office.

I have seen many whom you have helped who are now among
    the Great.

They are strong and rich through your actions on their behalf.

You are he who offers counsel. Fate and Fortune are to be found
    with you.

Come to me and give me counsel for I am a servant of your
    house.

Let me tell of your valiant deeds wheresoever I may be;

Then the multitudes will say, 'Great are they, the deeds of
    Thoth!'

Then they will come and bring their children to assign them to
    your calling,

A calling that pleases the Lord of Strength and happy is he who
    performs it!

As the god of wisdom and justice, Thoth played an important role
in the mysteries associated with the Judgment of the Dead. In the
Hall of Osiris, as in the vignette from the Book of the Dead of
the scribe Ani, Thoth is shown standing beside the scales of justice
on which the heart of the deceased would be weighed against the
feather of Maat (fig. 31). Everybody's fate was entrusted to Thoth's
impartiality and accuracy in recording the result of the judgment. He
was also believed to record the deeds of men, especially those of the
King, on the leaves of the sacred *ished* tree, the Tree of Life. In
the scene showing the tree at the Ramesseum, the mortuary temple

Figure 31 *Weighing the Heart*: Thoth, the Scribe of the Gods, records the verdict of the
scales in which the heart of the deceased is weighed against the feather of Maat.

of Ramesses II, Thoth is accompanied by the goddess Seshat whose name means 'female scribe' or 'she of the documents'. Seshat was the archivist of the gods who recorded all important events such as coronations and jubilees.

The first true hieroglyphs are found on labels attached to jars and boxes or impressed by cylinder or stamp seals into the damp clay used to seal the knots and lids securing such containers. These inscriptions usually consist of the name and title of the owner, perhaps the name of the King or god he served, and a list of the contents of the container. Other information such as a date might be conveyed by means of a picture accompanied by small groups of rudimentary hieroglyphs. Despite the sparsity of hieroglyphs from the early dynasties, it is clear that hieroglyphic writing and the short-hand version of the script which developed from it, and which is known as hieratic, were developed side by side. Where writing was in use there must have been scribes.

Within ancient Egyptian society, the scribe was always well respected. People of all ranks up to and including the King divulged information of the most sensitive and personal nature to the scribe who committed it to writing. They entrusted every aspect of their lives to the scribe's discretion, from legal documents to laundry lists, from invocations to graffiti. Every piece of writing, however humble in nature, was a demonstration of the scribe's privileged status. Even the apparently mundane labels on funerary offerings and tomb and temple furnishings had magical properties. By fixing a description of a basket's contents in writing and assigning ownership, that basket and its contents would belong to that person forever, or at least as long as the words survived, and regardless of whether or not the contents themselves rotted away. In lists or charts of offerings requested at tombs or in temples, recitation of the words ensured the continuity of the offerings so listed because, by means of the Word, they were made real. Many inscriptions in both royal and private tombs are simple requests for the repetition of the tomb-owner's name, and wishes for his or her eternal existence.

Many jobs were open to the trained scribe within the ancient Egyptian system. At the lower end of the salary scale were the clerks and letter-writers who worked as community scribes or as secretaries to businessmen. Successful or ambitious scribes might advance into local or regional government or into the administration of a nobleman's estate or of a religious foundation. Further education could lead to a professional career, but whatever his calling, however ordinary his job, every scribe had to undergo the basic scribal training. Education was the key to advancement, as student scribes were constantly reminded in instructional texts used as copy material. The tone of these writings was supposed to instil in the student a desire for learning and a commitment to the education system through which they would acquire status (fig. 32). The text known as the *Wisdom of Duauf*, sometimes called the *Satire of the Trades*, was almost certainly composed by teachers. It compares the lot of workers in a variety of professions with that of the scribe and is introduced as if by a father giving advice to his son who is just about to start his education:

> I have seen many beatings – set your heart on books! I have watched those conscripted for labour – there is nothing better than books!

Figure 32 *Mark of Education*: A bearer carries his master's prized scribal equipment consisting of a palette and writing board, to be included among the tomb furnishings.

Read to the end of your instruction book and there you will find this saying; 'A scribe at whatever post in town will never suffer in his job. As he fills another's needs he will not lack rewards.' I know of no other calling of which the same might be said. I will make you love scribedom more than your own mother, I will cause its advantages to become obvious to you. It is the greatest of all callings, there is none like it in all the land.

The scribe is always described as being better off than anyone with whom he is compared. In exaggerated phrases the work of every other trade is condemned as being dangerous, dirty or degrading:

The reed-cutter travels as far afield as the Delta to get arrows. When he has done more than his arms can take, mosquitoes have half-killed him and gnats have eaten him alive. He is quite worn out . . . The weaver in his workshop is worse off than a woman; working with knees drawn up against his chest he can hardly breathe. If he misses a day of weaving he is beaten fifty strokes. He bribes the doorkeeper with food to let him see the light of day. . . . See there is no profession without a boss, except for the scribe; he is his own master. Hence if you know writing it will do better for you than all these other professions which I have described, each more wretched than the last.

In contrast a teaching text from the Nineteenth Dynasty paints a rosy picture of the life of the scribe:

The scribe directs the work of the people. For him there are no taxes for he pays tribute in writing and there are no dues for him. . . . Put writing in your heart that you may protect yourself from hard labour of any kind and be a magistrate of high repute.

Even allowing for the biased point of view of the authors of such works, it is obvious that becoming a scribe could lift even the most lowly-born boy out of poverty and having a scribe in the family was a mark of status. The prospects for an educated boy were, in theory, boundless. In practice, literacy was very much a privilege of the middle and upper classes. With most peasants living at barely a subsistence level, few households had the surplus income necessary to support a student during his training. Without sponsorship, peasant boys were inevitably and irrevocably tied to the land. The student whose family had made personal sacrifices in order to pay for his education was under an obligation not to abuse their generosity. Letters expressing concern that a student was neglecting his studies were also used as copy material. They were written as if by worried parents and several such letters are preserved in a series of Nineteenth Dynasty papyri in the British Museum. In one, a father tells his son that he was supported during his years at school by his family: 'I was immured in the temple while my father and mother, and my brothers too, worked the land.' In another admonition, the father of a student scribe paints a dire picture of the life of a peasant and finishes with a warning from the heart: 'If you have any sense at all you will be a scribe. If you have once experienced what it is like to be a peasant you will not want to be one. Take heed of this!'

A formal education was available in one of the schools attached to the temples. During a seven year training food and clothing were supplied by the students' families. The daily deliveries of such supplies also provided opportunities for the exchange of letters and progress reports. Boys from wealthy homes received private tuition and were often groomed to follow in the footsteps of their fathers. Although the hereditary principle was strong in Egypt, a son had no automatic right to inherit a post from his father. If, however, he had been educated properly, instructed from an early age in the running of the family business or the requirements of a particular profession, and had gained experience from working with his father, he could become the obvious successor to the job. Even a village scribe would train his son to take over his work when he died or when the workload became too heavy. With the prevailing high infant mortality rate in all classes, it was not unusual for a man to have no surviving son to whom he could pass on his knowledge and expertise. In such cases it was not unknown for a scribe to adopt a successor and train him accordingly to fill his post. In the atypical community of Deir el-Medina the leader of the village was the Scribe of the Tomb who was directly responsible to the Vizier in Thebes and who had to make regular reports on the activities of the Workmen and their progress on the royal tomb. One such Scribe was Huya, the son of a quarryman, who came to the notice of the practising Scribe when he was a youth, and was trained to fill the post in his turn. In the early Nineteenth

Dynasty the Scribe of the Tomb was Ramose who adopted a boy called Kenhirkhopshef when it became apparent that he would have no son to succeed him. Kenhirkhopshef was trained by Ramose specifically to become Scribe of the Tomb, a post which he held for more than fifty years, dying when well into his eighties. He too was childless, but he had trained several promising scribes to carry on his work, and to take on some of the burden of his job in his later years, so that the appointment of his successor from among them was left to the Vizier.

Later at Deir el-Medina a painter called Amen-nakht might have expected to follow his father as Chief Workman in charge of one of the two gangs working on the royal tomb. However, he was deemed unsuitable, possibly because he was too young at his father's death, to take on the Foremanship which was the most important appointment in the village next to that of the Scribe of the Tomb. The job passed out of Amen-nakht's family, but he married the daughter of the other Foreman, Hay, and had some very influential friends. It was by direct appointment of the Vizier himself that Amen-nakht became Scribe of the Tomb in year 16 of the reign of Ramesses III. He even named one of his nine sons after the Vizier Tua in gratitude. The post of Scribe of the Tomb thereafter remained in Amen-nakht's family for five generations, passing each time from father to son, growing in authority and influence all the time. Scribal training, however it had been acquired, paid dividends for all the family.

Wherever scribes received their training, the teaching methods seem to have been much the same. Improving literature was provided as copy material, so that the student might practise his handwriting. Standard texts, including liturgical books, poetry and works of fiction, were studied and copied as illustrations of classical literary forms. Students learned how to compose letters, contracts and accounts which also required a basic knowledge of arithmetic. There would have been lessons in the theory of record-keeping, filing and labelling, so that any half-competent scribe could perform that most essential of all Egyptian scribal functions, the making and updating of lists. Exercises in note-taking, summarizing and writing from dictation would have been included in the syllabus to prepare scribes for their duties as clerks or secretaries.

Text books were available for reference. These included 'ready reckoners', like the Rhind Mathematical Papyrus which contains useful tables to help in calculations involving multiplication and division and the combining of fractions as well as worked examples of the sort of problems the scribe might come across in the course of his work. Egyptian 'dictionaries', giving lists of both hieroglyphic and hieratic signs, were not arranged in alphabetic order since the Egyptians did not recognize an alphabet in the modern sense of the word. Instead, the symbols were categorized, a technique at which

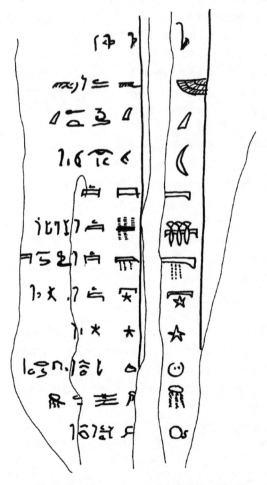

Figure 33 *Dictionary*: Part of a reference work detailing hieroglyphic and hieratic equivalent signs. The entries in the righthand column are largely in Gardiner's category N, Sky, Earth and Water.

the Egyptians were highly skilled, so that signs were grouped according to type rather than phonetic value. One such 'dictionary' or 'sign list' was found by Flinders Petrie at Tanis, in the collection of papyri belonging to a scribe named Bakakhuiu. His library included legal and religious texts as well as working documents associated with the planning and building of a temple. The Sign Papyrus is a continuous roll which was divided into thirty-three narrow pages. Although damaged by fire, enough remains to see that the scroll was a reference work in which some 462 hieroglyphs are listed in columns beside their hieratic equivalents (fig. 33). A third column indicates alternative 'spellings' or groupings of signs and the name by which each sign was commonly known, at least in Roman times when the papyrus is thought to have been written. The way in which this syllabary is organized seems to be a traditional form for scribal reference or teaching texts and the Tanis Sign Papyrus may have been adapted from a much earlier original, perhaps dating from the New Kingdom.

Another reference book from Bakakhuiu's library, the Geographical Papyrus, takes the form of a gazetteer or almanack. It includes calendars of important religious festivals and a province by province list of important towns, with details of their temples, lakes, cemeteries and local feast days. This, too, is of a late date, but part of the dedicatory text names Khufu, the builder of the Great Pyramid at Giza, so it may be a copy or at least an updated version of an Old Kingdom original, or, more probably, the last in a long series of copies. Such documents would have been invaluable to any scribe working in the taxation service.

Scribes were probably encouraged to copy out their own versions of the texts required in their everyday work. Besides giving them practice in the application of their skills, the purity of the text could be maintained if every scribe copied his book from the same original, which was kept in the scribe school or House of Life. Scribes were also expected to be able to prepare their own writing materials. There were no handy stationery stores where pens and ink could be bought. To make a pen, the scribe chewed the end of a reed to splay the fibres and create a brush point, the thicker the reed the broader the brush tip. Some of these brush pens were so fine that the handiwork of the Egyptian scribe rivals the results achieved by use of modern drawing pens. The reeds cut for making pens were stored in pencases which were hollowed rushes with stoppered ends. More elaborate pencases were carved or painted to imitate a column, usually with a palm tree capital, and some were even more intricately decorated, like that from Tutankhamen's tomb which is inlaid with gold, semi-precious stone and coloured glass.

The scribal palette, the badge of the scribe's profession (fig. 34), was a narrow rectangle of wood, ivory, or even metal, with a slot for holding the pens in use and at least two depressions for ink which was used in solid block form. It was made by mixing the pigment – charcoal or soot for black, ochre for red – with a light vegetable gum such as that obtained from acacia pods. The paste was formed into round or oval cakes or pressed into the hollows in the palette, and allowed to dry. The scribe took ink on to his brush by dampening the surface of the ink block and swirling his wet brush over it, in the same way that modern artists use solid watercolours or poster paints. Part of the essential equipment of the scribe's trade was a water bowl or saucer. This was usually of clay, but the water bowl in the basket of writing paraphernalia found at Deir el-Bahri by Howard Carter was a small tortoise shell

Figure 34 *Scribe at Work*: The scribe supports his work on a board, his palette within easy reach by his side.

which, unlike unglazed pottery, would not leak. The pencase, palette and water bowl, or a bag containing the bowl and other accoutrements, became the tools of the scribe's trade, by which he may be recognized in pictures. The three items strapped together form the hieroglyph for 'scribe' and 'writing'. In the version of the *Book of the Dead* belonging to the scribe Ani the tomb-owner asks to be provided with this equipment by which his status is proclaimed:

> O you great one who see your father, keeper of the Book of Thoth, see I have come, spirit and soul, mighty in the knowledge of the writings of Thoth. . . . Bring me a water-pot and palette from the writing kit of Thoth together with the mysteries which are contained in them. For I am a scribe. Bring me the ink of Osiris that I may write with it and that I may do what the great and good god says. . . . I will do what is right and I will report to Re daily.

The manufacture of the papyrus used for the most important documents and especially for the best quality funerary texts, was also a craft with which scribes had to be familiar. It is most likely that papyrus sheets were produced in workshops attached to the schools. The earliest example of papyrus being prepared for use as a writing material was found in the First Dynasty tomb of Hemaka, a court official c. 2900 BC. The Greeks used the word *papuros* to describe the plant from which the creamy white sheets were made and called the writing material itself *bublos*. The hieroglyph depicting a roll of papyrus tied with a cord was used as the determinative for 'writing', 'learning' and abstract ideas. Each sheet was made by pressing together two layers of thin slices of papyrus stems, one laid at right-angles to the other. Papyrus was the most expensive of writing materials available to the scribe and it is thought that the Greeks adapted their name for the plant from an Egyptian phrase meaning 'that belonging to Pharaoh', indicating a royal monopoly on the manufacture of papyrus sheets, at least in the Ptolemaic Period. From *bublos* is derived a wide range of words in many European languages indicating association with writing or books, the most obvious being Bible and the various versions of 'library' – *bibliothèque* (French), *biblioteca* (Spanish), *Bibliothek* (German). Most scribes would have used more mundane materials, the most common being ostraca, stone flakes which were the by-product of the excavation of tombs and the quarrying of stone in the limestone cliffs. These flakes varied in size from those used for simple notes and memoranda to the largest used for extracts from works of literature. The biggest ostracon so far discovered is now in the Ashmolean Museum, Oxford. It is covered on both sides with the *Story of Sinuhe*, a tale originally written in the Middle Kingdom but which became so popular that it has survived in many copies from much later periods.

Daily records of correspondence, reports and visits received by the government departments, temple administrations and the offices of the large estates were often transcribed on to leather rolls which were more durable than papyrus for everyday handling. One such leather scroll was used by the scribe Tjaneni who accompanied Tuthmose III on his campaigns into Canaan and Syria. In his tomb at Thebes he recalls what his job entailed. 'I followed the . . . King of Upper and Lower Egypt, Menkheperre [Tuthmose III]. I witnessed the victories of the King which he won in every country. . . . I recorded these victories which His Majesty won in every land, putting them down in writing according to the facts.'

The introduction to Tjaneni's *Annals of Tuthmose III*, inscribed around the sanctuary of the Karnak Temple, includes a description of how the scribe completed his task: 'Now everything that His Majesty did to this city, to that wretched foe and his despicable army, was recorded each day as it happened under the heading of the date, upon a roll of leather which is in the Temple of Amen to this very day.'

Tjaneni obviously made a more detailed record than was finally committed to stone, for in the *Annals* a description of the supplies provided for some of the Palestinian harbours during the campaigns is dismissed as irrelevant to the purpose of the inscription: 'They may be found in the daily register of the palace, the statement of them not being given here, in order not to multiply words [to save space].'

A scribe at work is usually depicted sitting cross-legged on the ground with his scroll open on his lap, the classic pose of the Egyptian scribe as used in statues. The linen fabric of his kilt drawn taut across his knees was enough to support the papyrus since the pressure exerted by a brush pen was very light. Less formal portrayals show that the scribe often used a board on which to

Figure 35 *Everything to Hand*: The scribe has tied his pencase to his palette which rests on a makeshift 'desk' with his water jar and document tubes. He has tucked his spare pens behind his ear.

rest his writing material (fig. 35). This board might be leaned against a document case or box to give a sloping work-surface, or a smaller version might be used like a modern clip-board while the scribe was standing. Documents were kept safe in compartmented boxes or pottery jars and could be transported in stiffened leather tubes with drawstring tops. Much of the everyday business of the land was conducted out of doors. Tomb paintings show scribes present at the harvest, at the cattle census and at the vintage. The Egyptian scribe had to be adaptable and willing to travel.

A scribe skilled in accountancy and arithmetical calculation would readily find employment in the finance services. The state economy depended on taxes which were paid in kind, much of it in grain. Surveyors were needed to measure the fields, to estimate the expected yield and to calculate the amount of tax due. Once the harvest was in, the grain was stored in granaries which employed scribes of all grades from the humble ledger clerk to the Overseer of the Granary. To become a granary official a scribe would have to display honesty and competence in dealing with the wealth of the Two Lands. Documents surviving from the archive of the sun-temples of the Fifth Dynasty at Abusir show how the daily deliveries of tithes and donations were carefully recorded so that the income of the temple over one year could be estimated. This annual income was divided by 365 to reach the notional 'temple day', the unit of income on which the pay for all employees of the temple was based. Some would receive a fraction of this, others would receive a multiple of the 'temple day', according to rank, expertise and responsibilities. Similar methods were employed in calculating the wages for workmen involved in royal building projects, soldiers and boatmen of the armed services, and other state employees. Such financial details were overseen by specialist scribes, some with responsibility for a particular department giving rise to titles such as Scribe of the Herds and Scribe of the Sacred Offerings. The treasuries in the temples and royal palaces were the strongrooms in which the real valuables were kept, in particular the metals which were used to value more expensive goods. The rate of exchange between grain and copper varied over time, but as a rough guide, between one and two *deben* of copper would buy 10 *hekats* of grain, the *deben* being a weight of about 91 grams and the *hekat* a unit of capacity approximately equivalent to 7.8 litres. The exchange rate between copper and silver was 100:1 and between silver and gold it was 2:1. Keeping the account ledgers in order was a complicated task which required specialist training in the use of weights and measures, knowledge of the relative values of raw and processed materials and the ability to assess accurately the initial worth and depreciation of a wide range of objects. Measuring rods, scales and weights were considered part of the scribe's tool-kit. A treasury was called the House of Silver and employed scribes in many capacities. Maya, who served Tutankhamen as Treasurer, continued to hold the purse-strings of

Figure 36 *How to Build an Arch*: This architectural sketch gives the relative proportions for uprights over which an arch of the desired curvature may be built.

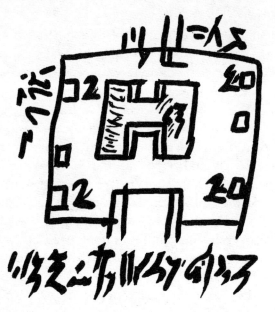

Figure 37 *Builder's Plan*: This rough sketch on a scrap of pottery shows a simple shrine in plan with doorways in elevation. Hieratic notes give details such as measurements and the orientation of the building.

Egypt until the end of the Eighteenth Dynasty. In the list of his titles which surround the wooden funerary effigy he donated to Tutankhamen's burial, Maya also describes himself as King's Scribe, the simplest but most prestigious title for any scribe.

Architects, artists, lawyers, doctors and priests would all have required further education. Lawyers dedicated themselves to Maat, the goddess who represented truth and justice, while architects and engineers (figs. 36 and 37) were under the patronage of the Great Artificer Ptah of Memphis. Doctors paid homage to Sakhmet, the lioness-headed wife of Ptah who was both healer and bringer of disease. There was very little invasive surgery practised in ancient Egypt. Physicians treated their patients according to the symptoms exhibited. Surviving medical texts list groups of symptoms giving for each a diagnosis and in most cases a treatment. The Edwin Smith Medical Papyrus contains 48 typical 'case studies' of this sort:

> Instructions concerning a break in the column of the nose: If you examine a man having a break in the column of his nose, his nose being disfigured and having a depression in it while the swelling

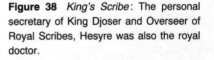

Figure 38 *King's Scribe*: The personal secretary of King Djoser and Overseer of Royal Scribes, Hesyre was also the royal doctor.

that is in it protrudes and he has lost blood from both nostrils, you may say concerning him: 'He has a broken nose, this is an ailment I can treat.' You should cleanse it with plugs of linen then place two more plugs of linen saturated with grease inside his nostrils. . . . You should apply a stiff roll of linen by which his nose is held fast.

Such treatments were the result of a long tradition of clinical observation and experimentation in the use of plant, animal and mineral remedies, all carefully recorded by the scribe-physicians. Most remedies were of a sensible and practical nature which had been shown to work by generations of doctors. Hesyre (fig. 38), a prominent court official of the early Third Dynasty, was a physician in the household of King Djoser, but his portraits show him simply dressed and carrying the scribe's equipment, the tools of his trade to which he owed his success. Amongst other titles, Hesyre was Overseer of Royal Scribes, indicating that he was possibly the most important scribe in the King's service, rather like being the King's private secretary, as well as being a doctor. Only a literate man, skilled in all the arts of the scribe, could become a medical doctor and several famous scribes were remembered for their skills as physicians, such as Imhotep, who was probably a contemporary of Hesyre, and the architect Amenhotep, son of Hapu. One of Egypt's earliest monarchs, King Djer of the First Dynasty, was said by Manetho to have written an anatomy text which was still available to doctors in the Ptolemaic Period. Rather than considering scribedom demeaning for a nobleman, the Egyptians respected and revered their men of letters.

As the Egyptian state grew, the need to co-ordinate the various activities associated with running the country also encouraged the development of specialized administrative skills. The scholar king was more the rule than the exception, but even the King had neither the time nor the inclination to deal with every aspect of government personally. There is evidence that the principal members of the royal family – including, in some instances, the women – were involved in political matters and diplomatic exchanges between the Egyptian King and his fellow monarchs in neighbouring states, but in dealing with foreign correspondence scribes trained in languages other than Egyptian would have been essential. It is difficult to identify any scribe who had responsibility for the translation of foreign texts. This may be because the 'god's words' were considered the only legitimate form of writing for any decent Egyptian to study and yet, by necessity, some were forced to prostitute their skill by taking up the degrading task of reading and writing foreign languages. From the New Kingdom onwards letters exist both to and from the Egyptian court and the other principal states of the Middle East. The *lingua franca* of the ancient world at that time was the Mesopotamian language Akkadian. It was written in the cuneiform script, formed by a series of wedge-shaped indentations made with a reed pen on clay tablets which were then baked to preserve the text. Letters written in Akkadian reaching the Egyptian court would have been translated by specialist Foreign Office clerks and then transcribed on to papyrus or leather rolls for filing and presentation to the relevant court officials for appropriate action

to be taken. Replies would have been drafted, perhaps from dictation, in Egyptian and then translated and copied on to the clay
tablets which were delivered by messengers or diplomatic envoys.
The originals would remain in the files for reference. During the
Amarna Period an official called Dudu or Tutu, probably a diminu-
tive of the common name Tuthmose, is named in correspondence
concerning the politics of the Canaanite region.

During the Ptolemaic Period, the language of the court was
Greek, and Egyptian texts, even secular monumental inscriptions,
were written in a yet more short-hand version of hieroglyphs called
demotic. Fewer scribes were trained in the true ways of the 'god's
words' as more and more were required to learn Greek and eventually Latin. Cleopatra VII, the last ruling queen of the Ptolemaic
Dynasty, is the only member of her family known to have learnt
the Egyptian language. She was a patron of learning and a scholar
in her own right, but by her time the Egyptian language was being
spoken only by the common people with whom she rarely had
contact. As the usefulness of the language as a means of interna-
tional communication faded, so too did the skills of the scribes
who tried to uphold the old traditions.

In the temples more emphasis was placed on the preservation of
the language for religious purposes. Liturgical texts and books
of hymns, prayers or 'spells', which had been set down in writing in
antiquity, were considered to have been sanctified by age and use.
Scribes whose handwriting was most nearly perfect were employed
to make copies of the texts from which the inscriptions on tomb and
temple walls would be transcribed. As scrolls became brittle with
age, or were damaged, or before the ink faded to illegibility, new versions of definitive texts were made, to preserve the religious wisdom
and heritage of the country. The most coherent explanation of the
theological doctrine propounded at Memphis is to be found on the
Shabaka Stone, dating from *c.* 700 BC and now in the British
Museum. The text has an introduction which reveals the importance
placed on the maintenance of religious traditions:

> This writing was copied out anew by His Majesty in the House of his
> father Ptah-South-of-His-Wall, for His Majesty found it to be a work
> of his ancestors which was so worm-eaten that it could not be under-
> stood from beginning to end. His Majesty ordered that it be copied to

be made as good as new, in order that his name might endure and his monument last in the House of his father Ptah throughout eternity, as a work done by the Son of Re Shabaka . . . so that he might live forever . . .

The 'worm-eaten' original was presumably a scroll of papyrus or leather, which itself was probably not the original version of the text, but the style of language used indicates a very early date for the composition of the work. It is impossible to guess how many scribes over how many generations had faithfully copied this important document to preserve it for posterity.

Scribes who paid their religious dues by caring for the sacred books were able to earn a very respectable living by writing and painting copies of the funerary text now commonly known as the *Book of the Dead*. These were prepared in the temple scriptoria and could have been commissioned by wealthy patrons, or made for purchase 'off-the-peg' with gaps left for the insertion of the owner's names and titles once a bargain had been struck. The palettes used by scribes employed on this work often have eight or more ink depressions holding the colours used for illuminating the manuscripts. The chapters included varied according to the requirements of the owner, but the Judgment of the Dead with the scales of justice before the enthroned god Osiris was the most popular theme.

Several examples of Egyptian fiction survive, often in the form of student copies and frequently damaged or incomplete, but they serve to illustrate the full range of the scribe's skill. Most tales would have been performed by professional story-tellers for the entertainment of guests at parties or on special holidays. In the majority of cases, both the teller and his audience would have been illiterate so there would have been no need to have the story in written form. The scribe responsible for the first written version of any story was not necessarily its author, and even when the writer appended his name to the manuscript, it was only to have the quality of his penmanship acknowledged. The most frequently copied stories were obviously the most popular and most well known. In their literary tastes, the Egyptians displayed a fondness for tales of magic and mystery, of intrigue and betrayal, preferably in a historical setting.

The most complete and skilfully composed story is that contained in the Papyrus Westcar in the Berlin collection. It is now known as the *Story of King Khufu and the Magicians* and is really several stories cunningly woven together. The scene is set in the court of King Khufu who announces that he is bored and demands that his sons entertain him by telling him stories of magic. Two of the princes dutifully tell tales which centre on the best-loved themes of Egyptian literature – an insignificant servant getting the better of the King himself and an illicit love affair ending with the retribution of the cuckolded husband. The story continues when the third son volunteers to present a demonstration of magic rather than to tell a story about it. He introduces Djedi who performs miracles before the very eyes of the King and the assembled Court. Khufu is so impressed that he asks the magician to do something even more spectacular, but then Djedi seems to go into a trance and makes a prophecy which profoundly disturbs the King:

> . . . The wife of a priest of Re of Heliopolis has conceived three children of Re, Lord of Sakhebu, and he has told her that they will exercise this excellent office [the Kingship] in the entire land and the eldest of them will become High Priest in Heliopolis. . . . O King, my Lord . . . I say this to you: your son, then his son but then one of them . . .

Angered by the suggestion that his dynasty will fail within the next generation, Khufu sets out to discover if there is any truth in Djedi's story. The scene shifts to Heliopolis where the priestess gives birth to her triplet sons attended by goddesses sent by Re, the divine father of the children. With future echoes of the story of the Massacre of the Innocents, the text breaks off at the critical point. The whole work is a masterpiece of the story-teller's art. The author hooks his audience with the sort of stories they like to hear, he adds the spice of 'real' magic and the mystery of prophecy and before the listeners are even aware of it they have been fed a hefty chunk of propaganda justifying the rise to power and excessive piety of the Fifth Dynasty. Sadly, the author of this masterful work will for ever remain anonymous, though he deserves to rank among the greatest story-tellers of all time.

In all walks of life there was great advantage to be had through the application of literacy skills. From the preservation of religious beliefs to the mundane laundry list, writing was employed by all Egyptians on an everyday basis, even by those who could not read. The important place of the scribe within this society was established by ancient precedent. He was the guardian of the history, ritual, economy and diplomatic status of the country. The administration of the country was heavily dependent on an army of scribes who worked within a sophisticated hierarchical structure, every scribe having his area of responsibility or expertise, and each knowing his place within the system. The understanding of the 'god's words' gave the Egyptian scribe a pride in his work and a feeling of superiority over all other less fortunate beings.

Hieroglyphs associated with the Scribe

 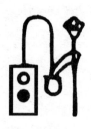

| ibis standard of the god Thoth, inventor of writing | scribe's equipment, palette, bag and pencase | roll of papyrus, 'book' |

CHAPTER 5

The Priest

•

THE CLOSE ASSOCIATION between the Egyptians and their gods is apparent in all areas of their everyday life and yet they did not practise the kind of organized religion recognized in more modern societies. By tradition it was Osiris and his wife Isis who had instructed mankind in the proper rituals and every temple in Egypt had a claim to be the site of the First Occasion, the place where the first moment of creation had occurred. This powerful concept was the basis for the conservatism in Egyptian religious practice, since what had been ordained by the gods themselves at the very beginning of all things was considered to provide the pattern for life for all future generations.

The Greek author Plutarch wrote a treatise in which he rationalized the legends of Isis and Osiris. The style of this version of the myth cycle owes more to Classical mythology than to the underlying Egyptian beliefs. It is, however, a useful compilation of stories which had developed into a relatively coherent form over a period of 3,000 years. Plutarch explained, and to some extent was responsible for, the popularity of Isis throughout the Classical world. He wrote that the goddess herself had decreed the way in which her adherents should worship her: 'In memory of all she [Isis] had done and suffered she established certain rites and mysteries which were to be types and images of her deeds, and intended these to incite people to piety, and to afford them consolation.'

There was no single Holy Book on which the religious system of Egypt was based. In fact, the various cosmogonies developed at the main cult centres, specifically Memphis, Heliopolis and Hermopolis, appear to be in some ways contradictory and muddled. Each version of the Creation of the Universe was subtly different from all others. Viewed overall, the bewildering variety of myths and legends concerning the gods of Egypt was totally incompatible with the development of a coherent system of belief. There were, for example, several explanations of how the sun travelled across the sky. One version explained how Re, the falcon-headed sun-god, was ferried across the sky in his sacred boat, the Solar Bark, whose divine crew the deceased King would hope to join on his resurrection (fig. 39). According to another myth, the sun was born each morning on the eastern horizon to the sky-goddess Nut and travelled across her body which formed the vault of heaven, to be swallowed by her at sunset on the western horizon. During the night the sun passed through Nut's body and was born again the next day, the miraculous rebirth being seen as a sign of the gods' continuing favour. A third explanation of the phenomenon was that a giant scarab beetle called Khepri pushed the fiery ball of the sun up through the horizon at dawn and rolled it across the sky just as a real dung-beetle rolls its ball of dung. The fact that these mutually exclusive schemes existed side by side without arousing the sort of doctrinal conflict or even religious war that has characterized more 'sophisticated' societies says much for the pragmatic and easy-going nature of the ancient Egyptians.

Evidence for the forms of religious observance from the pre-literate age though sparse, indicates the early establishment of a priesthood, or at least that some members of a community were chosen to perform rituals in honour of their patron deities. Even the earliest Egyptians were prepared to support non-productive

Figure 39 *The Solar Bark*: The scarab Khepri, god of the rising sun and symbol of renewal and rebirth, is ferried across the sky on Re's sacred boat accompanied by a crew of lesser deities.

members of their society in order to pay proper respect to their gods. Stone artifacts from the Predynastic era show that the presentation at temples or shrines of ceremonial or votive items was part of this respect. Some of the beautifully carved palettes show human figures participating in ritual hunts or carrying religious emblems as battle standards. Decorated pottery and the most ancient of all Egyptian tomb paintings, that in the so-called Painted Tomb of Hierakonpolis, show primitive shrines and boats like the sacred barges or barks in which the gods themselves travelled.

One easily identifiable emblem in the ancient scenes is the horned female head known as the *Bat* head, which became associated with the goddess Hathor. On a buff-ware jar from the Gerzean Period, which may be seen in the Cairo Museum, a female figure is shown performing what is presumably a ritual dance before a shrine marked with a *Bat*-head standard (fig. 40). The dancer has her arms upraised in imitation of the lyre-shaped horns of the goddess. On the Narmer Palette, a piece made to commemorate the Unification of the Two Lands, the *Bat* head appears twice on each side, flanking the rectangular enclosure, the *serekh*, which contains the King's name. In the scene showing Narmer reviewing war dead, several religious standards precede him, and his personal patron, the falcon deity Horus, is depicted in a rebus or picture sign-group representing his subjugation of the peoples of the marshlands. The worship of the sky-god Horus was well established at the southern city of Hierakonpolis and a permanent shrine of some size had been built there early in the Archaic Period if not before.

According to the tradition recorded by Herodotus, one of the first concerns of Menes, the king of the Unification, was to build a national shrine in his new capital of Memphis. The deity of the Memphite area was Ptah, the creator god who thereafter maintained his position as one of Egypt's national patrons. His temple at Memphis was called *Hwt-ka-Ptah*, the 'Mansion of the Spirit of Ptah', which the Greeks corrupted into *Aiguptos*, the name they gave to the country as a whole. The Palermo Stone records several major festivals, described as 'appearances', of the most important deities, and the founding, building and embellishing of their shrines and temples, as being the most significant events of the years in which they occurred.

Figure 40 *Hathor Dancer*: A female figure who may represent the goddess or one of her priestesses, performs a dance imitating with her arms the shape of the sacred emblem of Hathor seen on the shrine standard.

Religion was a way of life in Egypt and yet for most people the concept of organized religion had no meaning. Since the gods were completely integrated into Egyptian society, living among their followers, overseeing every aspect of daily life, little in the way of superstitious awe was demonstrated in their worship. The gods not only belonged to Egypt, they were Egyptians. As the most important citizens of the land they were accorded the greatest respect and were provided with the best of everything in the way of accommodation, sustenance and entertainment. In return for this VIP treatment, the gods protected the land and its people and provided a stable, safe and comfortable environment for all. The relationship between the Egyptians and their gods was one of mutual appreciation and support.

An essential part of any act of worship is the recitation of prayers or the chanting and singing of hymns. Much about the earliest style of worship has to be surmised from the remaining physical evidence, since the phraseology of ritual must have been transmitted by word of mouth for generations before the written language had become sophisticated enough to deal with such abstract and complex compositions. The development of the hiero-glyphic script and the importance placed on the written word and the skills of the scribe were vital to the evolution of religion in Egypt. The surviving religious literature of the Old Kingdom suggests the existence of priestly colleges or centres of religious learning where the mythologies were developed. The prayers and ritual utterances which were used in sacred ceremonies, especially those associated with funerary rites, were recorded in book form and kept in libraries. The largest corpus of religious literature to survive from the Old Kingdom is the compilation now known as the Pyramid Texts. These were inscribed on the walls of the burial chambers within royal pyramids of the Fifth and Sixth Dynasties. From these evolved the Coffin Texts of the Middle Kingdom which were painted or carved on the coffins and sarcophagi of both royalty and the nobility. In the New Kingdom the same texts under-went a process of democritization and emerged as the funerary work commonly called the *Book of the Dead*. The ancient origin of these texts may be deduced from the style of language employed in them. Even some of the Pyramid Texts were couched in such antiquated idiom that their meaning was already uncertain by the time they were inscribed. According to later tradition some of the 'spells' or magical prayers included in the *Book of the Dead* were discovered, perhaps this means composed, by King Den of the First Dynasty. All the authors of such works were guardians of Egypt's religious heritage which was encapsulated in the concept of Maat, the system of law, morality and ethics which the Egyptians had received from their gods at the First Time.

The sacred texts were read or 'performed' by a very special type of religious functionary known as *kher heb*, the lector priest (fig. 41). The aura of mystery surrounding the written word gave lector priests a powerful position in the superstitious beliefs of the people and they feature in several popular stories, like the *Tale of King Khufu and the Magicians* which dates from the late Old Kingdom. One of the 'magicians' of the title is a *kher heb* who displays awesome and frightening powers in wreaking his revenge on his adulterous wife and her lover. Prince Khaemwase, the son of Ramesses II, is portrayed as a seeker after wisdom in a series of stories from the Late Period. In one tale he comes to hear of a

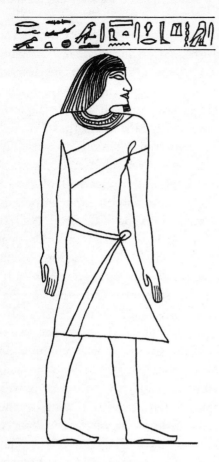

Figure 41: *Lector Priest*: A courtier wearing the priestly stole and who claims to be 'privy to the secrets of His Majesty's documents' is also designated *sem*-priest and lector or reader of the sacred liturgy.

copy of the original sacred book, written by the god Thoth himself. An elderly priest describes the contents of the book:

> The book is that which Thoth wrote with his own hand. . . . Two spells are written there. By recitation of the first you will charm the sky, the earth, the underworld, the mountains and the waters. It will allow you understanding of all that is spoken by the creatures of the air and those of the land. . . . By recitation of the second you will be granted a vision of the true form of Re himself with his divine companions wherever you may be . . .

In a more practical sense the lector priest had a duty to recite the sacred texts, exactly as they were written, in the rituals performed before the cult statue of his deity. Deviation from the ordained words would have offended the god. The lector priest read from the papyrus book held open between his hands. No matter how many times he had performed the ritual, no matter how well he knew the words, he always read them from the book.

The authors of religious works had no responsibility for instructing the people as a whole in the ways of the gods. The same was true for the priests who performed the rituals in the temples and shrines throughout the land. These buildings were of two types. The cult temples were the earthly residences of Egypt's gods and goddesses, where the deities lived among their followers and were treated as the first citizens of their towns or as honoured guests. The mortuary temples were the places where the memory of the deified kings was perpetuated so that the deceased monarchs might continue to exist in the company of the gods forever. Both types of temple employed priests in various capacities, but the most common title which is now generally translated as 'priest' was *hem netjer*, meaning 'servant of the god'. This is a very precise job description. The role of the 'priest' in ancient Egypt was very different from that of the priest in any other society. There was no truly national deity recognized in every part of the country and the local priesthoods saw no need to proselytize, to spread the word about their own god's superiority. Nor was it the job of priests to care for the moral and spiritual welfare of their communities. Their duty was to their gods.

The tombs of many court officials who also served as servants of the principal cults of their day are clustered around the royal tombs, for instance at Saqqara and Giza. Career priests were appointed to each temple, their numbers depending on the importance of the deity and the wealth of the temple foundation. The King himself was effectively the chief priest of every cult in the country (fig. 42), though of necessity he had to delegate his authority to his appointees. The highest ranking priest, known as the First Servant of the God, a title usually translated as High Priest, was often as much a political as a religious appointment and, especially in the case of the First Servitor of one of the major cult temples, the position tended to be held within one powerful local family for several generations. Herodotus remarked upon the hereditary nature of the priesthood in Egypt: 'They do not have a single priest for each god, but a number, of which one is chief priest, and when

Figure 42 *The King as Priest*:
Ramesses III makes offerings of
incense and water to the gods. He
wears full royal regalia including the
White Crown, as well as the broad
shoulder strap or stole and white
sandals of a priest.

a chief priest dies his son is appointed to succeed him . . .' The
situation described by Herodotus may not have applied in all
periods, but evidence from the New Kingdom onwards shows that
becoming a priest was a family tradition. On the stela erected by
Tutankhamen in the Karnak Temple to annouce his restoration of
the cult of Amen, the young king recorded the parlous state of the
temples at his accession. He vowed to make restitution for the
hardship and negligence suffered by the religious foundations during
the reign of his predecessor, Akhenaten, and to re-establish the
priesthood: 'He appointed as priests and prophets, children of the
notables of their towns, each the son of an eminent man whose
name is well-known . . .'

There is Old Kingdom evidence for the acceptance of women as *hemet netjer*, the feminine equivalent of Servant of the God. The wives and daughters of noble families held offices in many cults, usually those of goddesses, as was the case with Tadebet, the wife of the Fifth Dynasty courtier Tjetji. On the monuments from her husband's tomb, which may be seen in the British Museum, she is named as priestess of both Hathor and Neith, the warrior goddess of Sais, evidence which contradicts what Herodotus recorded: 'No woman holds priestly office either in the service of goddess or god; only men are priests in both cases . . .'

It is difficult to assess how significant a part was played by female priests in the daily ceremonies at the shrines of both gods and deified kings. In religious scenes in tombs and temples, only men are shown performing the rites. Women are relegated to the roles of singer, dancer and musician, except in the Third Intermediate Period when the title God's Wife of Amen was bestowed upon a daughter of the royal family who then became the senior ecclesiastic or at least the equal of the High Priest, at the Karnak Temple. The God's Wife, served by a staff of female acolytes, was a celibate priestess herself and designated her successor by 'adopting' another royal lady, often her niece.

The High Priest is sometimes called the First Prophet, though there is no tradition of prophecy evident in the religious literature. He was able to delegate his responsibilities to his immediate subordinates, the Second, Third and Fourth Prophets or Deputy Priests. One such was Aanen, the brother-in-law of Amenhotep III, who served for most of that king's reign as Second Prophet of Amen at Karnak and High Priest of Re-Atum. Aanen was the son of a priestly family. His father Yuya was High Priest of Min at Akhmin. His mother Tjuya was Matron of the Harem of Min, in charge of all the female personnel at the god's temple. Yuya's religious titles included that of God's Father which, in his case, has been interpreted as meaning Father-in-law of the King. However, the term 'father of the god', was applied to the rank of priesthood directly below the High Priest and included his deputies. These Fathers of the God, like the First Prophet himself, were usually high-ranking courtiers or noblemen who had other important duties besides those they exercised in the temples. Yuya, for example, was Master of the King's Horse, in charge of the royal stables and chariots, as well as Superintendent of the Cattle belonging to the temple of Min.

More is known about temple organization in the New Kingdom than in any other period, with most information coming from Thebes and concerning the cult of Amen at Karnak in particular. The majority of senior priests were not permanently resident in the temple. Instead, the priesthood was organized into four phyles, each working one month in three. For eight months of the year the servants of the god carried on their normal profession or business, whether in the political, administrative or commercial sector. Most numerous among the priests were the 'purified ones', a title written with the descriptive hieroglyph of a man with water pouring from a jar balanced on his head. This conveys the importance of ritual purity inherent in the priest's title. Great emphasis was placed on the necessity for cleanliness in all aspects of temple ritual. Each temple had its own lake which provided water for the regular ablutions of the priests and the cleansing of ritual vessels and garments, as well as the libations which were poured over offerings to purify them. Priests were permitted to wear only garments of white linen and sandals made from papyrus. Animal products in the form of leather or wool were forbidden as being 'unclean'. The only exception to this seems to have been the cheetah- or leopard-skin robe which identified the priest who took the leading role in any ceremony. The skin is draped diagonally across the back like a cloak with the animal's head hanging down in front of the priest's right shoulder. Even this robe may have been imitation. An example found in Tutankhamen's tomb has 'spots' made from gilded sequins and the head and paws attached were of carved wood decorated with gold leaf and glass paste inlay.

Bodily cleanliness was achieved by scrupulous washing with natron, a naturally occurring crystalline mixture whose principal constituents were sodium carbonate (washing soda) and sodium bicarbonate (baking soda). This all-purpose cleanser was used for everything in ancient Egypt from household crockery to sacred vessels, from linen clothing to the people who wore the clothes. Natron was considered to be so necessary that bags and bowls of it were offered to the gods and requested in funerary offering lists. Pellets of natron were chewed to freshen the breath and clean the teeth. When used on the human body it has a strong degreasant action, so moisturising oils and lotions were needed to counter the drying effects on the skin. While serving in the temple a priest had to shave all the hair from his body, including his eyebrows. Shaving their heads also rid the priests of lice, which were a problem in all social classes. In the group of mourners towing the funeral bier shown in Tutankhamen's burial chamber, the priests may be identified by their bald heads and their distinctive, sarong-like gowns reaching from underarm to ankles and suspended by a neck strap. Other priests wore a long kilt with a diagonal shoulder sash or stole. Serving priests were expected to abstain from sexual activity during their tour of duty, but for the rest of their time they were able to marry, raise families and carry on their normal business or profession.

Having attained the requisite degree of purity to allow them to enter the presence of the god, the priests were ready to perform the daily rituals. These rites were not for the benefit of a congregation, nor even an act of appeasement or sacrifice performed by the priests on behalf of the people. Their purpose was to honour the god by paying him the same courtesies and providing him with all the comforts that any visiting dignitary would expect. The deity, in the form of a cult statue, was housed in a shrine within the innermost sanctuary of the temple. The statue was not always life-sized and could be made of stone or gilded wood or even solid gold inlaid with semi-precious stones. It was considered to be the receptacle for the spirit or *ka* of the deity, rather than an idol. From time to time a king would dedicate a new cult statue as an act of piety, or would refurbish the shrine or the miniature bark on which the shrine was carried in festival processions. In Tutankhamen's Restoration inscription the King describes his donations to the Temple of Karnak:

> His Majesty took counsel with his heart and searched for any effective measure and every beneficial deed that he could perform for his father Amen. So he fashioned the god's portable bark from real electrum, the sacred statue being wrought of electrum, lapis lazuli, turquoise and every precious stone. . . . He has made great every work of the city temples by increasing two- three- and fourfold the donations of gold, silver and precious stones . . .

There were at least three religious services every day, each corre-
sponding to a meal. At dawn the god was awoken by temple singers
chanting the Morning Hymn. The shrine was usually closed by
means of a double flap door with bolts which were tied and sealed
every night. The breaking of the seals, the drawing back of the
bolts and the opening of the doors were the first acts of the priests
at the Morning Service. The statue was treated to the same purification rituals already undergone by the priests. In addition incense
was burned to fumigate the atmosphere of the sanctuary. The statue
was washed and dressed, had perfumes and cosmetics applied, and
was adorned with jewels in the same way that the King himself
would have been prepared for the day. Jewellers, weavers and seam-
stresses made and maintained the divine vestments. Carpenters,
metalworkers and stonemasons saw to the maintenance of the
shrines, the sacred barks and the ritual vessels, as well as the fabric
of the temple itself. The organization of the temple and the god's
daily routine were modelled on the life of the King in his palace.

The 'meal', in the form of offerings of food and drink representing the best of everything Egypt had to give, was laid out
before the shrine. There was bread in vast quantities, joints of
meat, roasted fowl, baskets of fruit and vegetables and jars of beer
and wine. All the offerings were prepared in the temple kitchens
with ingredients provided from the temple's own farms or by tithe
from tenants of the god's estates. Meat offerings were always of
the most prestigious kind, often whole carcasses of beef and wild
game. These were prepared in the temple abattoir where the
slaughter was overseen by a priest who pronounced the beast pure
and fit for the god's consumption (fig. 43). No beast was dragged
to be killed in the god's sight and no blood was spilt in the god's
presence on a sacrificial altar. The stone blocks which stood before
the shrines, and which are sometimes mistakenly identified as altars,
were in fact resting places for the cult statue in its bark around
which the offerings were arranged on portable stands. Some offering
slabs were carved in imitation of the hieroglyph for 'to satisfy', a
single loaf of bread placed on a reed mat, bread being the basic
need which would satisfy the hunger of anyone, god or human.

In smaller provincial chapels, offerings were on a less lavish
scale, but bread was always included as it was in the everyday

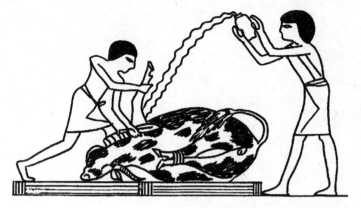

Figure 43 *Meat for the God's Table*: The carcase of an ox is butchered on a reed mat and the leg joint is removed for presentation in the temple. A priest purifies the intended offering with a libation of water.

meals of the Egyptian people. Temple bakeries and the breweries which were often in the same building were staffed with large numbers of the lay workers who were so essential to the smooth running of the temple's daily business. In order to bring to the temple all the goods required for the offerings, the god also employed sailors and porters and kept a fleet of boats and stables full of donkeys. Tribute from the local landowners, sent as a mark of respect for their god, and the produce of the god's own estates arrived daily to fill the temple storehouses, where every delivery and every withdrawal was conscientiously recorded by the temple scribes. The archive from the sun temple of Neferirkare at Abusir includes a detailed list of such deliveries including the origin of each load, the nature of the goods and even the name of the porter who carried them. Lists of support staff of many temples are given in the Great Harris Papyrus in which the largest religious foundation mentioned is the Temple of Amen at Karnak, employing a total staff of over 81,000 personnel, including priests, scribes, farmers, boatmen, fishermen, hunters and all the other craftsmen and administrators required to run a huge business. They were responsible for nearly 250,000 hectares of agricultural land, 433 gardens, 46 construction yards, a fleet of 83 boats and the land-lordship of 65 small market towns the output of which supplied the temple offerings.

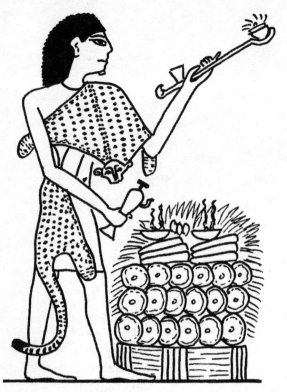

Figure 44 *Divine Scent*: The burning of incense in a spoon-like censer was an important part of any ritual. Pellets of frankincense resin were burned with charcoal and the smoke wafted before the face of the cult statue.

Libations of water were poured over the offerings and incense was burned in saucers or in spoon-like censers. The incense-burning spoons were shaped like a human forearm, often with the elbow carved to represent the head of a hawk. The open palm held the pot in which a mixture of frankincense resin and crushed charcoal was burned (fig. 44). The Egyptian word for incense meant simply 'divine scent' or 'perfume of the gods'. The trees which bear the resin were not native to Egypt, so regular expeditions to the Southlands of Nubia were necessary to fetch the essential temple supplies. Several attempts were made to establish the trees in Egypt, notably in the reigns of Hatshepsut and Ramesses III, when living trees were brought back with their roots packed in baskets of soil. These projects were never successful as, despite copious artificial watering, the trees failed to thrive in Egypt's climate. Perfume was very important in temple rituals where the intention was to stimulate all the senses of the god. Food and drink supplied taste, music and singing added sound, incense and perfumes provided scent and everything was presented in a decorative way to delight the eyes of the god.

Offerings always included floral decorations in the shape of bouquets, garlands and batons bound with flowers and leaves providing both colour and perfume. The larger temples kept flower gardens and employed gardeners and florists to prepare the floral offerings. Nakht, whose tomb in Thebes dates from the reign of Amenhotep III, was Gardener of the Floral Tributes of Amen and at least three of his sons followed in their father's craft (fig. 45).

While the 'meal' was presented to the god and while his *ka* was believed to be absorbing the essence of the offerings, he was entertained with music, singing and dancing. The hymns sung by the temple singers both male and female were little more than statements of the god's attributes and words in praise of his goodness. The style of Egyptian hymn-writing tended towards the repetition of key phrases, especially employing variations on the name or titles of the deity, and the use of puns, double meanings and alliteration. Any metrical form which might have been evident is lost in translation. Some of the earliest hymns are found in the Pyramid Texts, like the Morning Hymn to the sun-god:

> Awake in peace, thou Cleansed One, in peace!
> Awake in peace, thou Eastern Horus, in peace!
> Awake in peace, thou Eastern Soul, in peace!
> Awake in peace, Harakhti, in peace!
> Thou sleepest in the bark of the evening.
> Thou awakest in the bark of the morning,
> For thou art he that hath authority over the gods.
> There is no god that hath authority over thee.

The musical accompaniment was usually in the form of percussion, principally the rattling of the *menat* and the sistrum, together with the clapping of hands. For special occasions a small orchestra was assembled consisting of harps, flutes or oboes, drums and cymbals. The sacred dances seem to have been very sedate affairs with emphatic but elegant hand movements. On festival days, however, acrobatic dancers, dressed only in skimpy, fringed loincloths, performed amazing feats of agility to entertain both the god and the pilgrims who visited his shrine.

Once the god was thought to have had his fill, the food was removed, perhaps first to be placed before the shrines of lesser deities worshipped at the same temple, and then to be returned to the commissaries where it would be shared out and given as wages to the temple personnel including the priests. This was true of all temples whether those of the gods or the deified kings. One of the earliest 'biographies' to have survived from ancient Egypt tells how Metjen, a court official from the reign of Seneferu at the beginning of the Fourth Dynasty, received as part of his reward for service a portion of the offerings made at the mortuary temple of Queen Nemaathap: 'There were conveyed to him as a reward. . . . a mortuary offering of 100 loaves every day from the mortuary temple of the Mother of the King's Children, Nemaathap . . .'

Part-time workers employed by the temples in whatever capacity, including that of priest, enjoyed a better standard of living during their period of service than most would have been able to afford for the rest of the year. They all shared the god's wealth, each according to status and the type of work performed. The success of a religious foundation as a business was reflected in the level of 'wages' paid to its workers. Collectively, the temples were probably the largest landowners and employers in the country. Only the Royal Domain, the King's personal properties, exceeded those owned by any one temple.

After the evening ritual the god's vestments were removed before the cult statue was returned to the shrine for the night, to the strains of the Evening Hymn. On most days the statue would not move outside the innermost suite of rooms in the temple which constituted the private quarters of the god and his immediate family. There were regular feast days celebrated within the temple, such as the First of the Month festivals and the New Moon festivals. On these days, the cult statue may well have been paraded around the temple precincts, pausing for offerings to be made at places designated as appropriate to the particular festival. These were the stations or resting places of the god and some were known by name. According to the story told by Tuthmose III, he was serving as an acolyte in the Karnak Temple, standing at the point known as the Station of the King, when the bark of Amen, borne upon the shoulders of the priests, paused before him in its circuit of the

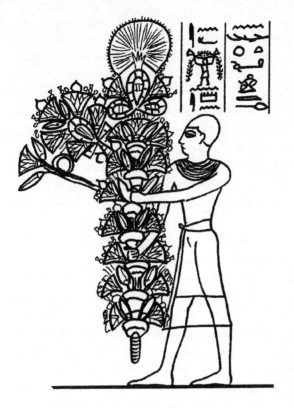

Figure 45
Flowers for the God: A gardener employed by the temple of Amen at Karnak presents an arrangement of flowers. The determinative for his job is a man holding aloft two trailing garlands.

temple and refused to move until it had acknowledged him by 'bowing'. This was taken as a sign that the god had recognized Tuthmose as the true King of Egypt. It is easy to imagine how this miracle could have been stage-managed by the priests, who objected to the rule of Tuthmose's step-mother Hatshepsut, but the story also demonstrates the influence that the gods were thought to exercise through their priests.

The larger religious festivals provided an opportunity for the people to get close to their gods. Since they had no right of entry to the temples, they made the most of the occasions when the gods came out to meet them, the sacred book carried in procession on the shoulders of priests. During the parade around the outside of the temple, the shrine and the statue within were shrouded from the common gaze of the multitude by a gauzy linen curtain. Attendant priests sheltered the god with sunshades which were like huge fans made from woven palm fibres or ostrich plumes. Incense was burned before the bark and offerings were made at significant points around the ceremonial route marked with way stations, some of which were temporary structures erected for the occasion, while others were permanent buildings like miniature temples. At each way station, the bark was set down on a block 'altar' while offerings were made and rites observed. On certain festival days the god was required to travel even farther afield when the portable bark was loaded on to the god's barge from the temple quay. The barge would then be towed along the river, escorted by a small flotilla of boats carrying the important guests including the King and the royal family if they were in attendance, the priests and local dignitaries.

Some festivals were shared between two temples, like the commemoration of the Sacred Marriage of Hathor and Horus. This took place in the third month of summer when the goddess left her temple at Denderah to travel the 70 kilometres to her consort's home at Edfu. In the course of her 14-day journey she would stop at other important temples to pay courtesy visits to her fellow deities, such as the goddess Mut at Luxor. On Hathor's arrival at Edfu on the day of the New Moon, Horus in his barge came out to meet his bride. Pilgrims travelled great distances to Edfu to witness the procession and to share in the free hand-outs of bread and beer which represented the wedding feast. The marriage was consecrated within the temple beyond the gaze of the assembled faithful. On the day of the Full Moon, the goddess started her return journey to Denderah, where she would await the birth of her son, conceived during the honeymoon at Edfu.

So that these festivals were celebrated at the correct times, each temple employed star-watchers, priests who kept the religious calendars by means of astronomical observations. There were several major annual festivals held at most important religious centres and each lasted several days which were public holidays. The people took great delight in celebrating these festivals, not least because they provided a legitimate excuse for over-indulgence in food and drink and time off work. The priests and all the attendant temple workers saw to the gods' needs on behalf of the whole population. In return, the gods played a crucial role in the life of all Egyptians. Their benign presence ensured the upkeep of the rule of Maat, but since their mortal followers were subject to mortal frailties, Maat was easily upset and the wrath of the gods could be swift and drastic.

A story known as the *Destruction of Mankind*, the earliest version of which is inscribed on the outermost of the shrines surrounding the sarcophagus in Tutankhamen's tomb, was a pointed warning about the consequences of taking the gods for granted or neglecting their rituals. It was written that in the time when Re still lived on earth, men became contemptuous of his rule, declaring him to be old and senile. They failed in their duty of care and departed from the ordained pattern of worship. To punish mankind for this show of insolence Re sent forth his Eye, a being which could exist independently of the god, as an avenging angel to show mankind that he was not to be thwarted. The Eye, which is sometimes seen as the uraeus serpent on the brow of the King, in this instance took the form of a lioness who is called Sakhmet or Hathor in different versions of the story. The Eye raged across Egypt in an orgy of slaughter until Re, seeing that the lesson had been well and truly learned, recalled her. Hathor, however, had acquired the taste for human blood and would not obey. The killing continued until Re feared that soon he would have no worshippers left at all. Taking immediate action Re ordered the High Priest of Heliopolis to have a vast quantity of beer brewed and coloured with red ochre so that it resembled human blood. Overnight the blood-red beer was poured out on to the fields in the area where Hathor was sleeping off the slaughter of the previous day, covering the land around to a depth of three palms. When the Eye awoke to see this lake of 'blood' she drank deeply and became so drunk that she fell asleep again. When she awoke, with what must have been a hangover of mythical proportions, she promised Re she would never repeat the experience. The people of Egypt were thus saved, but Re felt he could no longer live among them. He took his entourage into the heavens, leaving only Thoth as his regent on earth to bring education and enlightenment to his followers. Re also ordered that the salvation of mankind by means of beer should be celebrated every year at Hathor's cult centre of Denderah. At New Year, people flocked to the temple which was known as the Place of Intoxication to share in the bounty of the goddess who was called the Mistress of Drunkenness. Whether or not this equivalent of the Biblical

Flood had any foundation in historical fact, the New Year Feast of Hathor became one of the most popular religious festivals on the calendar.

The aspect of religion with which every Egyptian would inevitably be concerned was the ritual associated with death. As part of the Negative Confession the deceased had to confirm his blameless behaviour towards the gods. The statements made indicate some of the ways in which the ordinary people may have been involved in religion, either as lay priests or simply as members of the god's community:

> I have not done that which the gods detest. . . . I have not deprived the temples of food offerings. I have not destroyed the loaves belonging to the gods. . . . I have not trapped birds from the preserves of the gods. I have not caught fish from their marshlands. . . . I have not neglected the dates for offering choice meats. I have not withheld cattle from the gods' offerings. I have not opposed the passage of any god in his procession. . . . I have not reviled the gods. . . . I have not blasphemed any god in his own city.

The funeral rites, including the Opening of the Mouth, were carried out by the closest surviving male relative of the deceased, preferably the eldest son, who wore the priestly leopard-skin robe for the occasion. He was assisted by other priests, who may have been his brothers or cousins (fig. 46), and a priest representing Anubis, the god of embalming, who wore a jackal's head mask. The offerings made at the tomb chapel at the time of the funeral were similar, if on a much smaller scale, to those made in the temples. The prayers accompanying the oblations were intended to ensure that the provision of such offerings continued for ever. Inscriptions on the tomb walls and on the stela set up in the offering chapel repeated these requests, and pictures, lists and the very contents of the tomb reinforced the wishes of the deceased.

It was hoped that anyone visiting the tomb would read aloud the prayers and recite the lists in order to renew the offerings. Of course, since no one could be sure how often a tomb would be visited, nor whether the visitors would be able to read the inscriptions they found there, a prudent man would make special arrangements for the celebration of his mortuary cult, for the rituals which ensured the perpetuation of his memory and the continual

Figure 46 *Reading the Rites*: A member of the family in the role of priest reads the funeral liturgy. He stands beside a table bearing the implements, incense and natron required for the Opening of the Mouth ritual.

presentation of offerings. These arrangements usually took the form of a donation, rather like an investment for the afterlife, to the local temple, or an endowment of land from which the revenues would be used to pay professional priests to carry out the ritual. Such priests were called *ka*-priests because they were the guardians of the spirits of the dead. There were groups of *ka*-priests associated with each necropolis, responsible for the daily rites in the temples of funerary deities, especially Osiris, Anubis and the hawk-headed Sokar. *Ka*-priests were guaranteed an income as long as people were prepared to pay for their services, and though endowments might lapse or funds become exhausted so that the rituals ceased to be performed at some chapels, they would always be replaced by others as people continued to build their tombs in the necropolis.

In rural areas most people would have had very little to do with the major state cults. Their personal beliefs and concerns were centred on their homes and families and on the success of the harvest. Statues of local patron deities or popular household gods such as Hathor, Isis and Bes may well have been a common feature in peasant homes. Painted relief 'icons' were sometimes set in the external wall or gateway of a shrine or temple, so that the local populace had an opportunity to commune with the god on a personal basis. Certain statues were reputed to have magical powers, as is shown by the story of the Princess of Bakhtan, a tale of Late Period composition, but possibly based on events in the latter part of the reign of Ramesses II. The King had married a Hittite princess whose younger sister fell dangerously ill. The Hittite King begged Ramesses to send the healing statue of Khonsu, the moon-god son of Amen, so that his daughter might be cured. The statue was duly sent and the princess was made well again, perhaps by the power of the god working through the doctors who accompanied the statue to the land of Hatti, called Bakhtan in the fictional account. The workers on the royal tombs at Thebes considered the deified King Amenhotep I and his mother Queen Ahmose-Nefertari to be their particular patrons, since they had been the first members of the royal house to commission tombs in the Theban hills. Each year the villagers of Deir el-Medina celebrated the Festival of Amenhotep I, when the elders of the community acted as priests in the ceremonies paying honour to their very own gods who were worshipped nowhere else in Egypt.

Religion was so much a part of life in ancient Egypt that in one sense every Egyptian had the potential to be a priest, even if only in making a simple offering of bread at the family tomb. An examination of the lists of titles claimed by some noblemen will show that most held both priestly and administrative offices at the same time. Religion and life in ancient Egypt were almost synonymous. The Egyptians took comfort from the knowledge that rituals were performed daily for the gods in all their temples. They were horrified by the notion of a god-less society. In a letter of warning to a schoolboy, a father wrote of the perils of over indulgence in beer: 'Beer will turn men away from you and send your soul to perdition. You are like a broken rudder on a ship, obeying commands on neither side. You are like a shrine without its god, like a house without bread.'

The thought that the gods might desert them was too awful to contemplate. For that reason alone, it was important that there should always be priests, not to mediate between gods and men but to keep the gods content, so that they would never want to leave the country where the people pampered and honoured them so well.

Hieroglyphs associated with the Priest

| reed mat with loaf of bread, 'offering', 'to satisfy' | man receiving purification, 'clean', 'pure' | 'priest', literally, 'servant of the god' |

CHAPTER 6

Craftsmen

•

,THE GRAVE GOODS from Predynastic and Archaic tombs in
the great necropolises of Abydos and Nagada, which grace museum
collections throughout the world, are so skilfully executed that it
is difficult to believe that some are more than 5,000 years old.
Even in the production of everyday and household items, the
craftsmen of ancient Egypt demonstrated a high degree of artistry
and a thorough technical competence in the working of many
different materials. Artifacts from the pre-literate age are often
items made specifically for the tomb and so of the highest quality,
made to last for eternity. The craftsmanship displayed in decorative and ceremonial pieces, whose ritual significance is no longer
understood, is nevertheless admirable. Their shapes, patterns and
the context of their discovery give further insight into the society
which demanded such prestige wares, both as personal possessions
and as donations to the gods.

Simple Predynastic graves dug into the desert bedrock usually
included some sort of food offering contained in a pottery or stone
vessel. Pottery was one of the earliest crafts developed in Egypt
and, in the absence of any written evidence, the distinctive pottery
remains from Predynastic excavations have been classified by shape
and design to provide a means of dating the sites. Two basic materials were used in Egyptian pottery. The ubiquitous Nile silt from
the riverbanks and the cultivable plain, fires to a dark rust-red
colour due to its iron oxide content. Marl clay, which is found on
the fringes of the desert, produces pottery varying in colour from
buff to pale grey through shades of yellow and green, depending
on the type of limestone in the region of its origin. Both clays were
quite dry and hard when dug from the earth and had to be worked
into a malleable state by mixing with water. Other materials, such

Columns, imitating roof supports made of reed-bundles (Temple of Luxor)

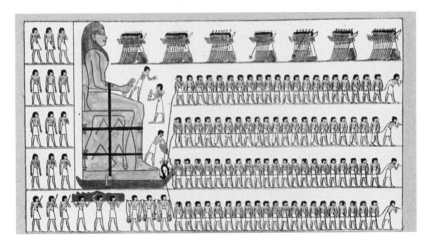

Dragging a colossus based on a painting in the tomb of Djehutihotep, el-Bersheh (derived from Wilkinson)

Bearers bringing food offerings to Nebamun's tomb, including wild game in the form of desert hares and a gazelle (painting now held in The British Museum)

Heap of food offerings for the tomb, including a haunch of beef and an ox's head (Eighteenth Dynasty wall painting from Thebes)

Relief carving from the chapel built by Hatshepsut at Karnak, depicting musicians, singers and dancers taking part in the sacred rituals in the Temple of Amen (red quartzite block now in the Open Air Museum, Karnak)

King Thutmose IV makes offerings to Amen (lower register) and the ithyphallic Min (above) behind whom stands a trough planted with lettuces (part of a wall reconstructed from blocks recovered from the First Pylon at Karnak, now in the Open Air Museum)

Boxwood statuette of a servant girl carrying a jar on her hip. She wears the sidelock of youth and a pendant of the god Bes hangs at her neck.

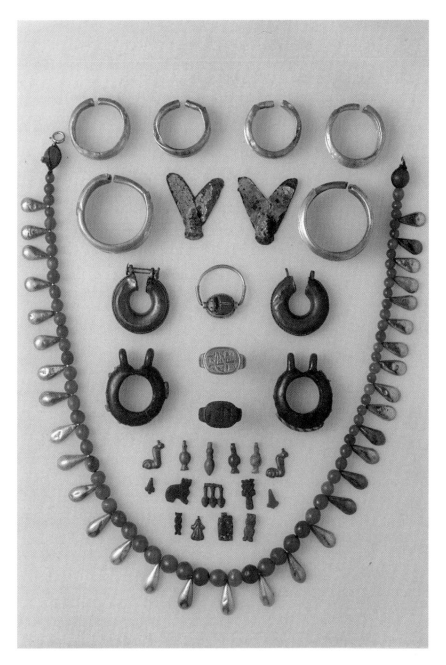

Collection of jewellery and amulets, including pieces made of gold, semi-precious stones, faience and glass

Marsh Arab reed house (Iraq), which was built by the same methods and using the same materials as in Ancient Egypt

Cosmetic or perfume vases made of coloured glass. The deep blue colour was much in demand as a substitute for lapis lazuli.

Fragment of painted plaster, including a sky border with stars, a multicoloured ribbon
banding and the base of a heker frieze showing that this was once at the top of a wall
(now in The British Museum)

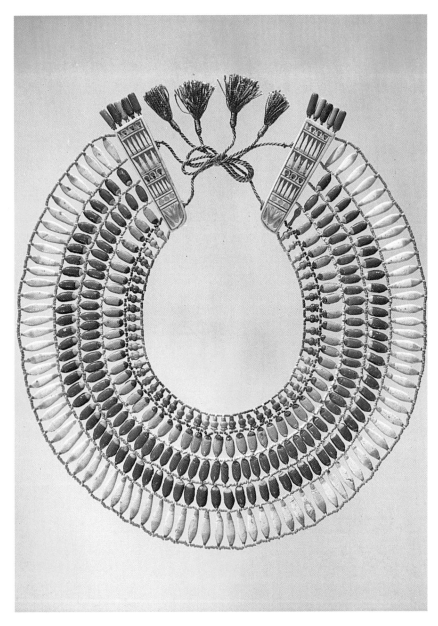

Beaded collar composed of floral elements in multicoloured faience or glazed composition ware

Block statue of Maa-nakht-ef from Medamud. This pose provided ample space for the necessary inscriptions. (The Louvre, Paris)

A scribe sitting on a heap of grain helps to record the harvest (from the Theban tomb of Menna)

Archers in the army of Ramesses III shown on the First Pylon of the Temple of Medinet Habu

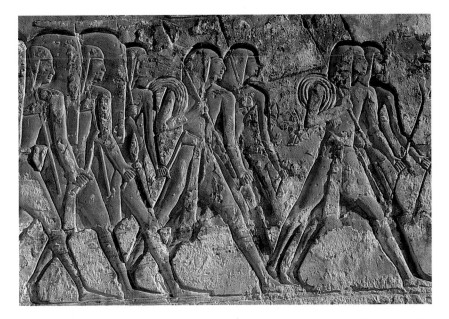

Marching soldiers with shields, spears, axes and throwsticks (Temple of Ramesses III, Medinet Habu)

Kneeling statue of Paser, vizier in the latter years of Seti I and during the first twenty-five years of the reign of Ramesses II

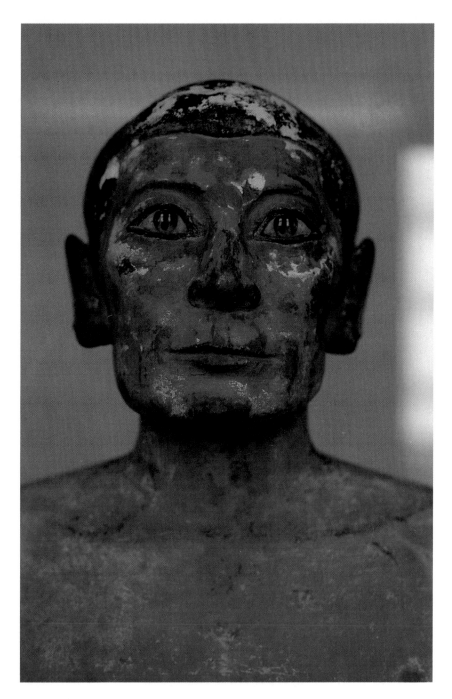

Painted limestone statue of the scribe Kay, showing inlaid eyes with rock crystal corneas which give the face a very lifelike appearance (The Louvre, Paris)

Ramesses III wearing the yellow and blue striped *nemes* headcloth, the simplest of all royal crowns (Tomb of Amenhirkhopshef, Valley of Queens, Thebes)

Horemheb, the king's True Scribe, shown in his capacity as Scribe of Recruits.
This was only one of the many titles held by this official who eventually became king
in his own right.

Columns representing the heraldic plants of Upper and Lower Egypt, erected by Tuthmose III at Karnak

Preparing the ground and sowing the seed (fragment of wall painting in The British Museum)

The two cartouche names of Ramesses II as shown on the King List from his temple at Abydos. The *nesubit* name (He of the Sedge and the Bee) is User-Maat-Re Setep-en-Re which gave rise to Shelley's 'Ozymandias'. (The British Museum)

Ramesses III embraced by Isis. The king wears the Blue War Crown. (Tomb of Amenhirkhopshef, Valley of Queens, Thebes)

as sand or straw, were often added to strengthen or harden the
resulting wares, a process shown in several scenes of pottery manufacture. In the Eighteenth Dynasty tomb of Qenamun a potter is
depicted treading the clay in a pit or trough, kneading the mixture
with his feet in the same way that bread dough was kneaded in
the larger bakeries. Herodotus commented on this Egyptian practice: 'Dough they knead with their feet, but clay with their hands
– and they even handle dung.' The last reference is probably to
the use of animal dung as a binding agent in mudbrick, or perhaps
to the moulding of dung into manageable 'coals' for fuel. The
author of the *Satire of the Trades* also described the clay mixing
process and clearly considered the potter's craft to be most
unpleasant. 'The potter is buried in earth while he is still among
the living. He grubs about in the mud more than any pig. . . . His
clothes are caked with clay. . . . The only air to enter his nostrils
comes in a hot blast from his kiln. . . . He treads [the clay] with
his feet just as he himself is trodden underfoot.'

Small pottery vessels, including some fanciful shapes like animal
and human figures, were shaped by hand. Some were made in
sections cut from a rolled sheet of clay or formed in solid moulds,
which were 'glued' together with semi-liquid clay. Lips, handles,
spouts and applied decoration were also added. During the
Predynastic Period from *c.* 4000 BC, two styles of painted decoration were employed. The Amratian potters painted their red or
brown silt-wares in white or cream with simple geometric patterns
or scenes of animals set against rudimentary landscapes. The marl
pottery of the Gerzean workshops was painted with red, brown
or deep purple scenes which often included boats, shrines and
human figures which might represent deities. Simple kitchen wares
like bread-baking pots were moulded over solid wooden cores so
that the inside was smooth enough to release the finished loaf,
while the outer surface remained rough, sometimes still showing
the marks of the potter's fingers. Finer pots were shaped on a stand
before which the potter knelt or squatted. The turntable top of the
stand was swivelled by hand. In the New Kingdom, a taller version
allowed the potter to sit on a stool, but still, as he turned the platform, he had only one hand free to shape the pot. Only in the
Late Period was a foot-operated wheel developed, allowing the

potter to revolve the turntable at a steady speed by means of a kick pedal or flange on the base of the rotating column. Some very large pottery vessels were produced including, in the Archaic Period, huge lidded coffins which, like the amphorae for wine and oils and heavy water jars (fig. 47) must have been built up in stages, since they are too tall to have been thrown in one piece. Kilns were either domed or shaped like a slightly waisted cylinder and made of mudbrick. The fire fuelled with brushwood, dead reeds and other easily available plant materials, was stoked under the floor of the kiln. The firing floor was formed like a grating so that heat could rise up through, around and between the pots. Known as an up-draught kiln this was perfectly adequate for firing the types of clay used in ancient Egypt. The pottery was never glazed, so only one firing was needed for most wares. Some vases were burnished by rubbing the unfired clay, in its leather-hard stage, with a smooth pebble, or by applying a slip or paint of liquid clay. The black-topped jars known as Nagada wares, seem to have been inverted in a reducing medium, perhaps simply a bed of ashes, immediately after firing.

Pottery was, for most of the Dynastic Period, a purely utilitarian craft. There were always other materials available which were considered more suitable for sacred vessels, more prestigious for luxury wares or more easily worked within the household context. The tradition of working in stone was so ancient that some pottery jars and wooden dummy pots were made in the same range of

Figure 47 *The Streets of Memphis*: Town houses with lanes between them are shown in a combination of plan and elevation. Household furniture is shown consisting mainly of boxes and pottery storage jars set in stands.

shapes and styles as stone vessels and then painted to imitate hard stones like granite. Surprisingly, considering its hard, dense and crystalline nature, basalt was one of the first stones to be used for high quality vases. Locally-quarried basalt was used by the neolithic settlers of the Fayum, and sources throughout the country were exploited continuously, especially in the Old Kingdom when basalt was favoured for temple pavements and sarcophagi. Pottery jars were often painted to resemble breccia with its mottled patterning in contrasting colours. The red and cream variety was popular and made into some amusing forms like the frog-shaped vase dating from the beginning of the First Dynasty or before, which is in the British Museum.

Stone vessels were produced in the greatest numbers during the early dynasties. Beneath the Step Pyramid of King Djoser nearly 40,000 stone vessels varying in design and size were collected together, many having been donated originally to the funerals of preceding kings whose tombs had then been robbed. The great majority of early stone vases, bowls and jars were of alabaster or limestone. Egyptian alabaster, more accurately called calcite, is a compact, translucent form of calcium carbonate. It varies in colour from white through cream to a yellowish tone, often with attractive veins or banding in yellow and brown. Alabaster was so much in demand for decorative storage vessels that it was included in the standard list of funerary offerings. It was also used for pavements where European civilizations would have used marble, and for statues, canopic chests and jars, and sarcophagi. The prize exhibit in Sir John Soane's Museum in London is the calcite sarcophagus from the tomb of Seti I. All but three of the stone vessels found in Tutankhamen's tomb were of alabaster, including exquisite shapes and decorative forms such as the tapering vase decorated with inlaid floral garlands, the lotus flower 'wishing cup' and the funerary boat with a dwarf steersman. Alabaster was used for the finest of Tutankhamen's ornamental lamps, which has three oil reservoirs shaped like the blooms of a waterlily emerging from a common base with lilypads on either side. When the floating wicks were lit, the alabaster would have been illuminated from within and any coloured veining in the stone would add to the beauty of the piece.

Limestone was commonly used for everyday items such as mortars, hearth-stones, bowls and troughs, but was also popular for decorative wares, especially in its coloured forms. Delicate bowls made from yellow and pink limestone, found by Emery in a First Dynasty tomb at Saqqara, at first glance could be mistaken for fine porcelain. Many canopic jars, the containers made to preserve the embalmed viscera of the deceased, were made of limestone which was sometimes painted in imitation of more valuable stones. Although the harder stones like granite, breccia, dolerite and others were carved into vessels of all sizes and shapes, from small cosmetic pots to huge sarcophagi, alabaster and limestone were always more widely used because they were easier to work.

The principles of stone-working were the same whatever the size of the vessel being made. The basic shape of the jar or vase was carved from a solid block and the outside was finished, except for a final polishing or painting, before the vessel was hollowed out. Shallow or broad-necked vases were hollowed by use of cylindrical drills, chiselling and pounding. Narrow-topped jars were drilled out using crescent-shaped bits of flint or metal held in the forked end of a drill shaft. Bits of different sizes and curvatures were used to hollow out cylindrical, conical and spherical sections below the narrow neck, tapering and flaring the hollow to match the external shape of the vessel. A heavy weight at the top of the shaft, or two counterbalancing weights suspended from it, provided the pressure required for the drill to bite into the stone. The drill was operated by means of a crank handle, or by swinging the weights round while pressing down on the drill cap. An abrasive such as damp sand would have been added to speed up the process and to dissipate some of the heat produced by friction. The hieroglyph showing this tool was the sign representing the word 'craft' or 'art', indicating that the production of stone vessels was considered to be the epitome of Egyptian craftsmanship.

Hard stone objects could be given a high polish by using rubbing compounds of increasing fineness. Most items made from the 'great' or 'precious' stones, required no further embellishment, though some may have had gold leaf applied to a lip or rim. Some of the most spectacular examples, found in the tombs of the First and Second Dynasties at Saqqara, include dishes shaped like leaves, an example of which is in the Petrie Collection of University College, London. Other vessels were carved to resemble originals made from other materials. A rectangular schist vessel in the Cairo Museum is clearly a copy of a reedwork tray. Another fantastically-shaped dish, dating from c. 3100 BC and now in Cairo, looks like a baking ring-mould with three 'petals' cut from the rim and apparently bent inwards. The resulting dish is so perfectly circular, the rim so narrow and the curve of the petals so graceful that the whole gives the impression of a dish beaten from metal, and yet it is of slate. Egyptian craftsmen worked difficult stones such as schist and slate, both of which split and crack easily into thin layers, with apparent ease and modern stone-workers would be hard-pressed to achieve comparable results, even with the precision tools at their disposal.

The forms chosen by the makers of stone vessels show what other crafts were well established by the Archaic Period. The most primitive of containers were bags, hardly more than nets, plaited from grasses, leaves and plant fibres. Such bags were imitated in the criss-cross decoration of Predynastic pottery and the practice of carrying pots in such a way was commonplace. More closely-woven basketry was also used to hold grain, fruit and other food supplies and sturdy baskets were used in place of buckets. A basket with a single loop handle was the alphabetic hieroglyph for *k*. Without a handle it was used to mean 'all' or 'every' as well as 'lord' or 'lady'. The ancient patron goddesses Nekhebt and Wadjet were shown as a vulture and a cobra respectively, each perched on this basket which gave them the collective title of the Two Ladies. In their most decorative forms, these basket hieroglyphs are shown with a chequered design indicating the woven style of their manufacture. A round dish of blue-grey schist, from the collection of stone vessels found beneath the Step Pyramid, is carved in the form of a basket made by coiling and stitching. Baskets could be strong enough to hold heavy loads. *Shabtis*, the human servant figures included in the tomb to provide manpower for all the tasks that the deceased might be ordered to do in the next world (fig. 48), were often shown holding agricultural tools including the all-purpose basket which could be used to remove sand or rubble from construction works or for transporting goods. Household

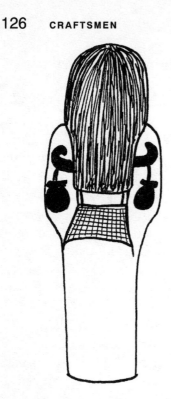

Figure 48 *Jack of All Trades*: The rear view of a *shabti* figure reveals the water pots suspended from a yoke and the basket which were essential equipment for a multitude of agricultural tasks.

baskets were made in a wide range of shapes, some with coloured patterns in the weave and many with lids, and were used often in preference to wooden chests to store personal possessions including clothing and domestic linen.

Mats made by stitching reeds together in the same way that roller blinds or beach mats are still made, served many practical purposes. Made from thicker reeds, they could be as rigid as wooden trays and were used to display and present food offerings in temples and tombs. The female offering bearer figures from the tomb of Meketre carry on their heads rigid reedwork baskets, like flaring boxes with a square section, in which are packed jars of beer and loaves of bread. These baskets could have been made of the same materials as the box in the British Museum which is woven with the stripped outer rind of papyrus stems over a stiff framework of reeds (fig. 49).

Since no scenes of basket manufacture as such are known, it seems likely that this was largely a household craft. The raw materials were abundantly available and a skilled basketworker would be able to barter her wares in the marketplace. The production of

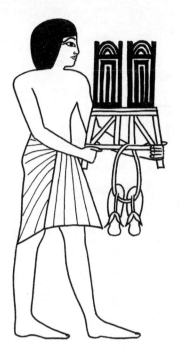

Figure 49 *Products of Papyrus*: The two green-striped containers carried by this bearer are probably *shabti* boxes. Their colour indicates that they, like the sandals, were made from papyrus.

sandals woven from papyrus was a more specialized craft and, since priests were required to wear such footwear as an alternative to leather, they may have been made in dedicated temple workshops. Other specialized forms of basketry were employed by furniture makers as in the weaving of chair seats (fig. 50).

Most households would have had a minimal amount of furniture. Although chairs, stools, beds and storage boxes were regularly included among funerary goods, many pieces were specifically made for the tomb and were often of a different quality and sometimes different designs from those made for everyday use. Queen Hetepheres, mother of King Khufu, builder of the Great Pyramid, was provided with an elegant suite of furniture including a bed, a chair, a canopy frame with matching curtain box and a carrying or sedan chair. In the Fifth Dynasty tomb of Ti at Saqqara, carpenters are shown finishing off various items of furniture including a bed and in the tomb of the Eighteenth Dynasty Vizier Ramose at Thebes servants bearing funerary furniture are depicted in the parade of mourners.

A decorative theme in furniture from all periods was the use of animal features in the design. The legs of chairs and beds were

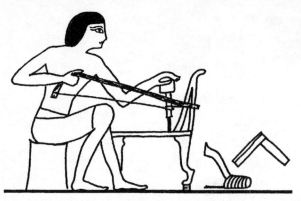

Figure 50 *Bow Drill in Action*: A carpenter drills one of a series of holes through which the basketwork or thonging seat of the chair will be woven. An adze and a set-square lie on the ground beside him.

usually carved with the hocks and hooves of a bull or the paws of a lion. Great attention was paid to detail so that the back legs of a chair were carved in a more angled shape to differentiate between the hind and forelegs of the animal. The feet were often gilded or, in the case of smaller boxes or stools, were carved separately from ivory. A set of ivory bull's hoof chair legs was found in a royal tomb of the First Dynasty at Abydos.

The principles of ancient Egyptian woodworking appear to have been much the same as modern practice. Tools were very simple and most were made of copper though the earliest edged tools were made from flint. Mallets and chisels, axes, saws (fig. 51) and bow drills are shown in several scenes of woodworking, as in the

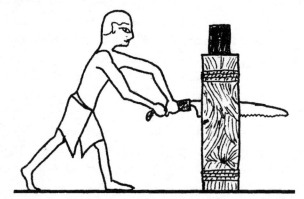

Figure 51 *Saw*: A workman saws a plank which is lashed to a vertical support post. A wedge knocked into the top holds the cut open to prevent the saw from sticking.

Figure 52 *The All-purpose Tool*: The workman sits on a tripod stool using an adze to shape a plank of wood which rests on a primitive carpenter's bench.

model of the carpentry workshop from the tomb of Meketre, but the most common tool of all was the adze (fig. 52). This tool has an angled wooden haft with a metal blade bound on to the vertical head with tough cord or leather thonging. It was used with a chopping motion to shape and plane wooden surfaces. Narrower blades were used for more delicate work and, despite its primitive nature, the adze was used to great effect and was recognized as the characteristic tool of the Egyptian woodworker. The author of the *Satire of the Trades* clearly perceived the adze to be the distinguishing mark of the carpenter's trade, just as the scribe was identified by his palette: 'The carpenter who wields an adze, he is wearier than any field labourer. His field is the timber and his hoe is the adze. . . . His labour is never-ending.'

Sections of furniture were fixed together by means of a variety of joints such as mitre, dovetail and butt joints, by mortise and tenon, or by pegging. Glue made from rendered animal bones and hides was used to attach veneers of decorative or valuable hard wood on to a carcase of native acacia or sycamore. A drum-shaped box from a First Dynasty tomb at Saqqara was inlaid in a chequerboard pattern with plaques of ebony. Ivory and bone were also used for inlay, as in the chairs from the tomb of Yuya and Tjuya, on one of which the couple's grand-daughter Princess Sitamen is shown seated on a chair with lion's paw feet. The very best furniture might be overlaid with gold foil or inlaid with coloured stones and glass paste. A fine example of this sort of work is the so-called State Throne from the tomb of Tutankhamen which is covered overall with gold and has arms in the shape of winged serpent goddesses. The back of the throne is decorated with a polychrome inlaid design of stylized floral borders surrounding the figures of the King and his wife. Tutankhamen is shown seated on another chair of a design similar to a cedarwood example also found in his tomb. The seat and back of his chair are made more comfortable with a cushioned seat pad, which was probably covered in soft leather or kidskin, and his feet rest on a foot-stool. Openwork patterns were popular and often featured plant or animal designs or a frieze of hieroglyphs. The fretwork on a boxwood and ebony chair in the Metropolitan Museum, New York, includes the figure of the god Bes between the *djed* pillars of Osiris and *tyet* knots of Isis. Less opulent items of furniture had simpler designs or plain bars and struts which strengthened the structure as well as adding style.

Plywood was being manufactured as early as the Third Dynasty as shown by the remains of a coffin made of five-ply timber found in the Step Pyramid. Wood was bent and shaped into graceful curved lines by steaming and clamping and surfaces were smoothed with sandstone rubbers (fig. 53). A shine was given to finished pieces by application of a clear varnish comprised of oil and resin. A thick black varnish, like a bituminous paint, was used from the Eighteenth Dynasty to disguise the uneven and open grain of poorer quality timber. White paint, like a thin wash of gesso, was used as adornment, perhaps in imitation of ivory, but also served to cover any unevenness of colour where wood from different sources had been combined in one piece.

Some furniture was made to fold so that it could be easily transported. This was important for any businessman who would want to take some home comforts with him when visiting his various properties, or for the army officer on campaign. Tutankhamen owned several folding pieces, including a camp bed with a base woven from cords. The bed folded in two places by means of copper hinges, which demonstrate that the principle of the hinge was well understood by the ancient furniture makers, though pieces with vertically hinged doors are rare. The Egyptians preferred easily

Figure 53 *Caution, Men at Work!* One man sands the roof of a shrine as another chisels fine details. Their tools, including a saw, are kept in a basket. Another man seems to have dropped his mallet on the overseer's foot.

portable furniture, rather than massive cupboards, so the most appropriate form for storage units was the ordinary box. Boxes came in all shapes and sizes, with flat, arched or sloping lids, pedestal bases or small feet, curved, flat or coved walls and sometimes handles or staples for the insertion of carrying poles. The toilet box belonging to a nobleman named Kenem, which is now in the Metropolitan Museum, New York, has a specially shaped compartment for holding a mirror and a drawer for storing other toilet articles. Tutankhamen's 'toy chest' is partitioned in a very complicated way with several drawers and spaces with sliding lids. Other boxes might have lift-out trays or secondary lids. Box-making must have been one of the best sources of income for the ancient Egyptian carpenter.

Stone-working and carpentry tools are among the earliest metal objects manufactured in ancient Egypt. The stone vases of the Predynastic Period were carved with metal tools which were made by open-cast moulding, but little is known about how the knowledge of metallurgy spread throughout the country, nor where it originated. By the beginning of the Dynastic Period, tools, weapons and household utensils made from copper were in common use. The tomb of King Djer contained over 800 copper items, ranging in size from sewing needles to agricultural tools such as hoes. The ore from which most Egyptian copper was extracted was malachite, the same bright green copper carbonate used for eyepaint.

The temperatures required to smelt copper from malachite are achievable within kilns of the same type as those used for pottery, though the most primitive method of smelting was to roast a mixture of charcoal and crushed ore in a pit lined with mudbrick or earth. The metallic copper sank to the bottom of the pit where it solidified into an irregular-shaped ingot which may be the origin of the hieroglyph used to indicate 'metal'. The slag which floated on top of the molten metal could be drawn off through a channel in the pit wall. Blow pipes were used to increase the temperature of the furnace, as shown in scenes of metalworking in the Fifth Dynasty tomb of Ti at Saqqara and the tomb of Rekhmire at Thebes where foot-operated bellows are also shown. These were made from two dishes of wood or pottery, one inverted over the other, placed within a tube or bag of soft leather. The operator stood with his feet on two pairs of these dish bellows, holding strings attached to the top of each. By raising his feet alternately and pulling up on the strings, air was drawn into the skin bags. By pressing down on each bellows in turn, air was expelled through a reed tube fitted with a clay nozzle and directed into the fire (fig. 54).

The extracted metal could be melted again in a crucible made from rough clay strengthened with sand or ash. The molten metal

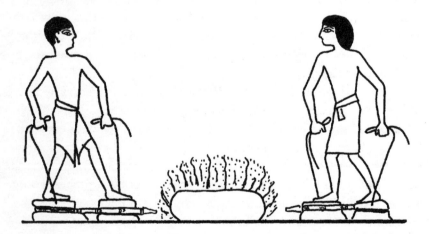

Figure 54 *Turning up the Heat*: By moving the bellows up and down with their feet the men pump air through the nozzles into the base of the furnace hearth to increase the heat so that metal may be smelted.

was then poured into moulds made from pottery or stone. Solid copper items like pickaxe heads, axes and chisels were cast in moulds and hammered whilst still hot to remove any roughness and irregularity of shape. Lighter tools such as knife blades and razors were hammered and sharpened when cold. Copper vessels, such as the basins, vases and ewers used in purification and libation rituals, were made from sheet metal which was hammered from the basic ingots. A set of miniature ritual vessels and an offering table, all made from copper, and now in the British Museum, were found in the Abydos tomb of Idi, a lector priest of the Sixth Dynasty. They were made with cast spouts, pedestal bases and handles attached to bodies which were hammered over a curved shaper or anvil made from wood or stone. To avoid the copper becoming brittle, it was tempered or annealed by a process of reheating to make it ductile before hammering again. The sections of copper vessels were fixed together by simply hammering flat seams, or sometimes by riveting, but from at least as early as the Fourth Dynasty, hard solder consisting mainly of silver, was in use. This was discovered in the copper sockets of the canopy poles from the suite of furniture belonging to Queen Hetepheres. Soft solder consisting of lead and tin was not used until the Ptolemaic era.

Egyptian copper was rarely pure but contained impurities like arsenic, nickel and tin, all of which would have hardened the metal. The dark colour of the ancient metal artifacts seen in museums is such that it is impossible to distinguish copper from bronze by sight. From about 1500 BC in Egypt, bronze was being produced by mixing tin with copper in varying proportions. The addition of tin lowers the melting point of the alloy and makes pouring and casting much easier. It also lessens the shrinkage of a cast object due to the contraction of the metal on cooling. A tin content of about 4 per cent strengthens and hardens the copper and allows blades and weapons made of bronze to keep a sharp edge.

Iron minerals like haematite and red and yellow ochres were found throughout the eastern desert and in Sinai, but there was no early tradition of iron smelting in ancient Egypt. The tomb of Tutankhamen contained several iron objects, the most spectacular being a dagger with an inlaid gold hilt on an iron blade, but most were very small and were included for their ritual significance. Iron was the traditional 'magical' material used for the blades and points of the various sacred implements used in the Opening of the Mouth ceremony. These were almost certainly made originally from meteoric iron, metal from the sky which was considered to be the magical gift of the gods. Before home production began in earnest, most iron in Egypt would have been imported from northern regions such as the land of Hatti, modern Anatolia. Not until the Third Intermediate Period was iron as commonly used as bronze.

Egypt was famous throughout the ancient world for the vast gold-bearing regions it controlled, especially in the southern lands known as Nubia. Native Egyptian gold, containing around 16 per cent silver on average, was found both as alluvial nuggets and as veins in quartz rocks which were crushed to extract the metal. Pictures from the tomb of Sobekhotep, an official at the court of Tuthmose IV, now in the British Museum, include parades of Nubian offering bearers carrying basketwork trays heaped with gold dust or nuggets, and chains of cast gold rings which were standard volume annular ingots. Gold was being used for decorative purposes from the Predynastic Period. The Nagada Diadem, found on the head of a female body dating from about 3200 BC, is made of single strands of coloured stone chips alternating with quadruple strings of gold beads. The remains of a coffin found in a subsidiary burial beneath the Step Pyramid include the gold rivets by which a gold foil or plating was attached. Items of gold jewellery from the tombs of royal ladies buried beside the Middle Kingdom pyramids of Illahun and Dashur demonstrate the height of the goldsmith's art. Tutankhamen's solid gold coffin, weighing more than 110 kilograms, shows the sort of quantities of gold available to the Kings.

Gold, being softer than either copper or bronze, may be worked with tools made from flint, bone or even wood. Sheet gold was beaten out on a stone block with a wooden mallet or polished stone hammer, heated or annealed to make the metal ductile, and beaten again so that very thin gold foil or leaf could be produced. To cushion the jarring effect of hammering stone against stone and to prevent the cracking of the thinnest leaf, the goldsmith placed a soft leather cover over the anvil under the gold sheet. Patterns were pressed into the sheet to be decorated, which was held in a firm bed of a yielding substance like damp clay, resin or wax. Blunt-pointed tools or round-ended punches and hammers were used to create a raised design on the underside. When the raised pattern is considered to be the 'right' side this is called *repoussé* work. When the indented pattern is on the obverse this is called chasing. The two processes can be used together, working from both sides of the sheet, to give a rounded effect and depth to the design. Sharp-pointed engraving tools remove swarf from the surface and so weaken the structure of the object being decorated. For this reason the Egyptians rarely engraved delicate goldwork. Some patterns of jewellery may appear at first sight to be engraved but are usually found to have been chased. Sections were cut by scoring their outlines with a sharp point, perhaps a flint blade, and bending the metal backwards and forwards until it cracked along the required line. Sharp edges were easily smoothened. Voids with more complicated outlines in openwork gold ornaments were cut out by means of a hardened copper chisel struck with a wooden mallet.

When many pieces of the same shape and design were required a die was cut from hard wood or stone or fired from pottery and then used repeatedly as a stamp to cut out as many elements as necessary. A collection of jewellery from the tomb of three lesser wives of Tuthmose III includes a set of wig ornaments in the shape of marguerites. Larger shapes could be hammered over a positive die. Gold wire was made by cutting narrow strips from a thin metal sheet. This would normally have a triangular or square cross-section. The sharp corners could be smoothened by rolling short lengths of wire between two hard, flat surfaces or by threading the wire through a stone bead and rubbing the bead up and down the wire. In the New Kingdom, wire with an almost circular cross-section was produced. Longitudinal twisting of a fine strip of gold sheet resulted in a spiral or thread effect which, being already rounder than the original strip, was easier to smooth into the desired shape. Chains were made by winding a wire about a core, perhaps a fine reed, and cutting it along the length of the core to produce a series of loops which were then linked into chains with various decorative twists. Some Egyptian chains are so elaborately linked that they have the appearance of being plaited.

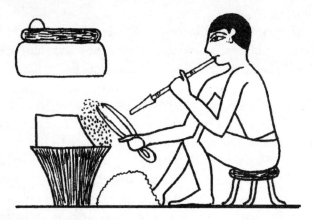

Figure 55 *Goldsmith at his Brazier* : The craftsman holds a metal object, perhaps a piece of jewellery, in tongs and uses a blow-pipe to direct the heat of his brazier.

Amulets of the highest quality were cast in moulds or were made in sections to be soldered together. When dealing with very small or detailed pieces of goldwork, where excessive solder would have been unsightly, the jeweller used colloidal hard soldering. A vegetable gum was mixed with a powdered copper compound, usually malachite, and used to stick the pieces in place. The item held in a pair of tongs was heated in the goldsmith's brazier and the jeweller used a blow-pipe to direct the heat (fig. 55). The burning off or carbonization of the glue caused a thin film of metallic copper to form on the joined surfaces and as this cooled it formed a type of weld. This form of soldering was used most effectively in the jewellery technique known as granulation. Tiny beads of gold were fixed in place in a decorative pattern, as in the diamond shapes and chevron banding on the hilts of the two daggers found in Tutankhamen's coffin. The gold jewellery from the Twelfth Dynasty tomb of Princess Khnumet at Dashur includes an exquisite butterfly pendant on which the insect's body and the veins of its wings are outlined with gold wire and the compartments filled with granulation.

The characteristic Egyptian polychrome inlay work was made with wire-outlined compartments on a gold base, each filled with carved pieces of coloured stone. The finished work is very similar in appearance to *cloisonné* enamel, but the coloured sections in Egyptian jewellery were cut to fit each *cloison* exactly rather than being melted in like enamel. The most desirable colours were the red of carnelian or jasper, the light blue of turquoise and the deep blue of lapis lazuli. Amethyst, feldspar, obsidian and chalcedony provided colours like purple, green, black and white, but the blues were always the most popular. This led to extensive mining of turquoise in the Eastern Desert and particularly in Sinai, where the goddess Hathor was revered by the miners as Lady of the Turquoise. Lapis lazuli had to be imported because it does not occur naturally in Egypt. In fact, the nearest source to Egypt is in Afghanistan, so the stone must have reached the country only after a succession of exchanges involving a wide variety of commodities. Lapis was being imported in the Archaic Period and was so much in demand that Egyptian craftsmen developed an artificial substitute. This was the material now commonly called Egyptian faience. From the period before the Unification, small amulets and beads were being manufactured with a glazed surface, the most common colours for the glaze being the blue-green range of turquoise. By the Fourth Dynasty a dark blue glassy substance coloured with copper-calcium-tetrasilicate, an artificially produced frit, was used as a substitute for the expensive and rare lapis lazuli, and some of the inlay in coloured jewellery from the Middle Kingdom is of this man-made material. By the New Kingdom a soda-lime-silicate glass in the full range of colours was available and was used extensively in the jewellery buried with Tutankhamen. The dark blue stripes of the headcloth on the famous funerary mask are of this opaque glass-like substance.

While ceremonial and funerary items were made in elaborate styles, heavy with symbolism, the jewellery worn in life tended to be simpler. Egyptians of all social classes wore a simple bead amulet made from a polished pebble threaded on a linen cord or a leather thong. Even the humblest burials usually included a pendant or necklace made from shells, natural stone chips or pebbles, or faience beads. The *Book of the Dead* specifies a charm consisting of a barrel-shaped carnelian bead flanked by two round or cylindrical green beads to be hung about the neck of the deceased. This was called the *sweret* amulet, a name meaning 'that which causes [the wearer] to be great' (fig. 56). Multiple *sweret* amulets or strings of beads became the typical broad multicoloured necklace or collar

Figure 56 *Jewellery Box* : Bearers carry a large jewellery chest with samples of its contents displayed on the lid – two multi-stranded collars, a flower counterpoise and a *sweret* amulet.

used almost as an item of clothing to enliven the plain white linen worn by most Egyptians. Some funerary collars were cut from sheet gold in the shape of a vulture or hawk with outspread wings curving around the neck of the wearer. Collars made with stripes of vertically strung beads often have terminals carved, cast or moulded in the form of falcons' heads. The scene of jewellers at work from the tomb of Sobekhotep shows a craftsman threading strings of spherical, cylindrical and teardrop-shaped beads and putting them together with spacers to form a multicoloured collar.

Bead manufacture was an important part of the jeweller's trade. Sobekhotep's jewellers are shown using three or four drill bits at once with a bow drill to pierce stone beads which are held in a tray of packed sand or clay (fig. 57). Modern experiments have shown that it is perfectly possible to drill three beads at once and presumably with practice this could be extended to the five shown in some ancient scenes. Beads were produced by the tens of thousands to be used in jewellery and for appliqué work like Tutankhamen's beaded foot-stool, which bears the figures of bound captives so that the King kept his enemies symbolically underfoot.

Figure 57
Bead-making:
A jeweller pierces
stone beads set in a
sand tray using a bow
drill with three drill
shafts. Strings of his
finished product are
shown to the right.

Networks of beads were made into shrouds and even decorative overgarments like the newly-restored example in the University College Collection in London.

Cheaper and easier to produce than individually pierced stone beads were those made of faience. This Egyptian equivalent of ceramic material is more accurately called glazed composition ware. The core material of Egyptian faience is a mixture of crushed quartz or sand with some lime and an alkali which was usually plant ash or natron. Though not as easily worked as clay, once moulded and dried one firing only is required to obtain a solid, hard product with a glazed surface. The commonest blue-green colours were provided by copper compounds and the glaze was created by one of three methods. In the earliest faience the colouring substance was mixed with the core material and, combining with certain salts from the plant ash, during drying the glazing agent migrated to the outer surface of the object. On reaching a temperature of between 800° and 1000° C this layer melted and fused with the quartz from the core to a shiny soda-lime-silica glaze. The second method was to bury the moulded item in the powdered glaze mixture. On heating, the powder in contact with the core reacted with the quartz to form the glaze, leaving the rest of the powder unchanged and reusable. The third method was to apply the glaze as a thick liquid paint or slip. Relief detail could be added by carving or incising any item in its dried state before firing. Paint, based on a manganese or iron compound, was used to pick out features and to add decoration and inscriptions to pieces, especially to the classic bright blue faience. The development of glass in the New Kingdom provided more colours to the faience-worker's palette. By adding powdered glass to the core material it became possible to make red, yellow, green, purple, black and white faience. Some of the finest examples of this sort of work come from Amarna where glass- and faience-making workshops produced multi-coloured tiles for decorating floors, columns and walls. In the small palace attached to the mortuary temple of Ramesses III at Medinet Habu, faience floor tiles were shaped with vividly-coloured figures of Egypt's traditional enemies and wall friezes were made up with rosettes, flowers, leaves and bunches of grapes, all moulded in coloured faience.

One of the most widespread uses for faience was the manufacture of costume jewellery and cheap trinkets. Beads were made by forming the core material around a thread, straw or grass stem which would burn away during firing. Beads were also formed in fired clay moulds so that the same shape could be reproduced over and over again. The original was probably carved from stone or bone and pressed into the damp clay to form a negative image. A faience collar in the Metropolitan Museum, New York includes elements shaped and coloured in imitation of leaves, petals, flowers and fruit. Amulets, seals, scarabs and finger rings were all made in quantity and in the Late Period *shabtis*, divine figures and small cosmetic bottles were being mass-produced and traded all round the Mediterranean. Faience seems to have been the very first souvenir of Egypt. The electric blue colour which was so popular came to be known as Egyptian Blue.

In any collection of Egyptian artifacts, whether they come from royal tombs or from urban settlements, the high quality and in-genuity of craftsmanship is immediately apparent. It is impossible not to be impressed by the achievements of the Egyptian craftsman in whatever material, from the humble weaver of baskets to the royal jeweller. The paintings in the tomb of the Vizier Rekhmire perhaps display the widest range of scenes showing craftsmen at work; carpenters, metalworkers and sculptors, leatherworkers cutting hides to made sandals, rope-makers twisting cordage for boats, and master bakers making a variety of fancy breads and pastries. Life was enriched by the attention to detail and the pride in quality of workmanship displayed in the exercise of any craft however mundane. Egypt was extraordinarily well served by the craftsmen who provided both the essentials and the luxuries of life.

Hieroglyphs associated with Craftsmen

jar carried in net

basket with loop handle, alphabetic 'k'

basket, 'lord', 'lady', 'all'

Nekhebt and Wadjet, 'the Two Ladies'

stoneworker's drill, 'craft'

mer-chisel

chisel

adze resting in block of wood, 'chosen'

drill piercing stone bead

ingot, 'metal'

collar of beads, 'collar', 'gold'

pectoral of glass or faience beads, 'faience', 'glass', 'to sparkle'

CHAPTER 7

The Artist

•

IN THE COMPOSITION known as the *Wisdom of Ptah-hotep* the advice offered by the Vizier to his reader is rather pompous and the language is often very difficult, but some statements still ring true:

> Do not be big-headed about your own knowledge. Seek advice from the ignorant as well as from the wise for there is no limit set to art and no artist is ever a complete master of his skills.

The word translated as 'art' in this case is written with the symbol of the drill used for hollowing out stone vases. This is usually rendered as 'craft'. There is no distinct word for 'artist' in the Egyptian language, the nearest equivalents being 'scribe of the drawings' and 'draughtsman'. The word meaning 'to write' was also used for the verbs 'to paint' and 'to draw'. An appreciation of this close association between writing and drawing is essential to a comprehension of the nature of Egyptian art. In the modern sense of the word, art did not exist in ancient Egypt. Paintings, reliefs and statues were seen as two- and three-dimensional determinatives of the inscriptions that accompanied them, and the same stylization and emphasis of certain features were required in art as in the drawing of hieroglyphs.

The beautiful painted and carved scenes in tombs and temples were created for a very specific purpose. They were never intended to be purely decorative. Their creators were not given, nor would they have expected, total freedom of expression. Artistic composition, like hieroglyphic writing, was governed by strict rules of form and conventions of shape and colour and, together with a very precise canon of proportion, these make Egyptian art immediately recognizable and different from any other artistic style. Most tomb paintings were never meant to be seen by human eye again, once the tomb had been sealed. The scenes of everyday life on which so much of modern understanding of Egyptian society has been based, were not snapshots, pictures of events frozen in time, but idealized views of the sort of life the tomb-owner hoped to enjoy for eternity. The sun always shines, the harvest is bountiful and the store-rooms bulge with food, fine wines and luxury goods. The tomb-owner and his family are always shown dressed in their finest clothes, even when ploughing the fields or hunting in the marshes. No one is ever shown old or infirm. A sense of continuous action is conveyed by means of a series of scenes, like cells in a strip cartoon but without the outlining boxes to separate one cell from the next. The relative importance of figures within the scene is established by their size, the owner of the tomb being the tallest figure with his wife and children portrayed on a slightly smaller scale, though still taller than their servants who in turn are shown taller than the nameless peasants who carry out all the menial tasks.

To the casual observer who sees only a picture, a 'work of art', the inscriptions which are such an important part of any scene appear to be incidental and no more significant than captions or diagram labels. In the temples, rules governing the composition of relief carvings were even more rigid. The correct way to show the gods had been established by the gods themselves at the beginning of time. To deviate from the divinely agreed format was tantamount to blasphemy. For the same reason, there was little in the way of secular art. No paintings, embroideries or tapestries hung on the walls. Some palaces and the larger villas had painted walls or ceilings, but the designs on these were confined to geometric patterns or simple scenes of birds and animals disporting themselves among the plants of the riverbank.

The same was true of three-dimensional art. A statue was capable of holding the spirit or essence of the subject it portrayed. The word for statue was the same as for 'image' or 'likeness' and a sculptor was someone who 'caused to live' or 'preserved' his subject. The same verb was used when referring to the funerary ritual in which the eldest son perpetuated the memory of his parents by 'causing their names to live'. Egyptian portrait sculpture was almost exclusively funerary in nature. Statues of kings and deities served various religious purposes, but all statuary, including depictions of ordinary Egyptians, was bound by the same constraints as two-dimensional art. The Egyptian sculptor would not have dreamt of portraying his subject 'warts and all'. The portrait, a vessel for the spirit which would last for eternity, had to be perfect, radiating authority, wisdom, tolerance, piety and all those other traits which made a person fit to enter the Realm of Osiris. Even royal portraits were idealized and stylized because they were made to an accepted pattern for representing the King. Any similarity of facial features between statues is not always a guide to family relationship. A superficial resemblance is more likely to relate to the kingship rather than the kinship of the two rulers. Age, stature and physical condition were rarely accentuated. The only concession to age in some statues is the subtle indication of rolls of fat at the midriff which implies prosperity since only a wealthy man could afford to eat well enough to become fat (fig. 58). In contrast, the King, whatever his age, is always shown in the prime of youth and strength. Portraits of Ramesses II made in his early years as King, when he was in his late teens or early twenties, are almost indistinguishable from those made in the latter part of his 67-year reign.

Egyptian sculpture was more of a craft than an art. The sculptor plied his trade in the same way as the carpenter or jeweller. Styles of art were changed very little throughout the Dynastic Period as artists seem to have been unwilling to experiment or to refine their techniques. This could be said to indicate a stagnation or at least a deeply entrenched conservatism on the part of the Egyptian artist, but this is to misunderstand completely both the purpose and the nature of Egyptian art. It was not that the artist was incapable of change; the Amarna Period shows that he could adapt traditional styles to new ideas when directed to do so. Nor was he unwilling to change; certain Amarnan artistic features survived the return to the traditional forms because the artists found them more appropriate or satisfying to their need to portray 'truth'. For the most part the Egyptian artist saw no need to change. His methods served the purpose of his craft and his craft fulfilled the requirements of those who commissioned his work. He expected no more.

The artist was an accomplished craftsman, using materials, tools and techniques developed in other crafts, such as those of the

Figure 58 *Prosperity Personified*:
The delicate indication of rolls of fat
at the midriff was the artist's way of
portraying a prosperous gentleman.

carpenter or stonemason, together with the precision and keen powers of observation required of the scribe, but the Egyptian artist was not employed to be creative or imaginative. He followed plans and sketches set down for him by a designer whose principal training was as a scribe and who would check to see that his instructions were being followed exactly at every stage of the work. The designer was responsible for correcting errors in proportion or alignment. He took decisions about aesthetic changes of composition or form which might be dictated by lighting conditions or the scaling up of his original design. He proposed solutions to problems such as an unexpected fault in the rockface being prepared for relief carving and was ultimately responsible for the accuracy of the hieroglyphic inscriptions that were an integral part of any piece of work. The artist who transferred the hieroglyphs to the wall or statue was unlikely to be as well educated as the literary expert who composed the texts. There was no standardized 'spelling' and there was scope in the alternative signs available for the decorative use of hieroglyphs to complement the designer's overall plan. However, signs were often transposed, omitted or replaced by those with similar shape but of totally different meaning, so that, if the designer was not vigilant in his attention to each stage of the work, ghastly errors could be introduced which would be impossible to correct.

The designer was the true artist. The craftsmen who executed the designs of the masters are almost all anonymous, the exceptions being a few of the painters and draughtsmen associated with the community of Royal Workmen at Deir el-Medina. Few works of Egyptian art can be accredited to an individual artist, but the names of several designers are known, though even the designer himself did not 'sign' his work since that would have been presumptuous. The final painting or statue not only belonged to the person who had commissioned it but actually became the person it represented, no matter how stylized the portrayal might be. This mystical transformation from portrait to reality was a form of creation and creation was the prerogative of the gods. No designer would claim that right.

Some designers are known from their own monuments, especially from the tomb stelae on which they listed their titles and, occasionally, brief details of the achievements of their careers. Designers, like all craftsmen, claimed the patronage of the Great Artificer, Ptah of Memphis. In the Old Kingdom, the title of High Priest of Ptah was often held by the Chief Minister of Works who was responsible for designing or commissioning the designs for royal building projects and other artistic projects. Many sculptors or master craftsmen were pleased to claim priestly rank.

Court officials were often rewarded for their work in the royal service with gifts of tomb furnishings produced in the palace workshops by the best craftsmen in the land. Similarly, the King could commission his court artists to make statues or tomb stelae of the very best quality for his favoured servants. An influential nobleman could afford to employ artists as members of his personal retinue. The tomb of Ptah-hotep at Saqqara is decorated with some of the finest and most detailed reliefs of the Old Kingdom, including one scene showing the Vizier watching his boatmen engaged in a waterborne jousting match. An integral part of the scene, but taking no part in the mock battle, is a small reed boat whose sole passenger is being offered food and drink by a servant. The accompanying inscription names this privileged individual as 'the revered Ankh-en-Ptah, Overseer of Sculptors', who was presumably the designer of the tomb decorations, including the very relief in which he had himself depicted (fig. 59). This is as close to a signed work of art as might be found from ancient Egypt. Occasionally, the sculptor of a statue might have his own name and titles included in the inscription on the piece, but this, as with Ankh-en-Ptah's portrait,

Figure 59 *Signed by the Artist*: The sculptor Ankh-en-Ptah had himself portrayed in the scenes he designed for the tomb of his master.

was more a means of promoting his own immortality than a claim to authorship. Scenes from the tomb of Huya, steward to Queen Tiye at Akhetaten, include activities in the workshop of her personal sculptor Yuti who is shown putting the finishing touches to a statue of Tiye's favourite daughter, the Princess Baketaten. Tuthmose, the court sculptor to Tiye's son Akhenaten, had his own impressive villa in the new capital city of Akhetaten. The excavation of his workshop revealed a collection of portrait busts of members of the royal family, in different stages of completion, demonstrating many aspects of the sculptor's art. The most spectacular of these is the painted limestone bust which, though uninscribed, is thought to represent Akhenaten's wife Nefertiti, now one of the prize exhibits of the Egyptian Museum in Berlin. In the same workshop were several plaster casts of masks taken from life, perhaps intended as models for future works or as practice pieces from which apprentices could acquaint themselves with the structure and proportions of the human face.

Egyptian sculpture of all periods shows that the artist was quite capable of representing the human figure in perfect anatomical detail, in any medium from soft wood to the hardest granite.

Musculature and bone structure were rendered faithfully in statuary, with details such as the definition of the collar bone, the joints of the fingers and the muscle attachment around the knee accurately observed, whereas the formal two-dimensional representation of the human form is less convincing. To the eye trained in the appreciation of Western art, the Egyptian painter apparently displays a fundamental lack of understanding of human anatomy, together with a total disregard for perspective. In fact, the Egyptian artist worked within a well-defined scheme for representing the whole of a three-dimensional shape, especially a living being, in two dimensions without having to resort to what he would have considered to be the distortion of perspective. Compared with Michelangelo's figures in the Sistine Chapel, figures in the wall-paintings of the Theban tombs may appear contorted or awkward, but perhaps a better comparison would be with one of Picasso's cubist paintings. Each part of the body was shown in exact proportion in relation to every other part, but the artist chose that view which most perfectly represented each element of the body. The head was shown in profile with clearly defined brow, nose and chin, while the eye was shown as from the front because the eyes gave real life to the face. The torso from shoulders to waist was shown in front elevation, while the arms, hips, legs and feet were shown in profile. The skill of the artist lay in making the points of transition between profile and front view so seamless as to create an Egyptian style as distinctive in its own way as Picasso's.

Hieroglyphs which represent human or animal figures were drawn according to similar rules, or rather the artist employed the same means of defining features precisely as did the scribe. For example, in their simplest outline form, the signs of the swallow and the sparrow are almost identical in profile body shape. The feature which distinguishes one from the other is the shape of the tail, but since this cannot be seen in profile, the artist drew the tail as if seen from above. Shown this way, the forked tail of the swallow is obviously different from the rounded tail of the sparrow. This distinction is necessary when two such similar signs have very different, in this case opposite, meanings. The swallow means 'great', 'senior' or 'elder', while the sparrow means 'small', 'evil' or 'mean'. Even when birds were drawn as part of a tomb painting,

Figure 60 *Geese*: Two fine specimens of red-breasted geese, shown in profile but with tail as if seen from above.

where the artist had more freedom of space and choice of colours, and could alter both the stance and positioning of the birds whose shape was not dictated by their use as hieroglyphs, he still showed their heads and bodies in profile but their tails in plan, as is clearly seen in the oldest wall painting to have survived from Dynastic Egypt, the frieze of geese from the Third Dynasty tomb of Itet at Meidum (fig. 60).

The designer drew out his figures on a square grid so that the pattern could be enlarged when it was transferred to its intended site. From the classical artistic age of the Middle Kingdom to the beginning of the Late Period, the accepted grid for a standing male figure seems to have been one of eighteen squares from the soles of the feet to the hairline. The height from the base line to the knee and to the elbow, was six and twelve squares respectively. The head, from the junction of neck and shoulder to the hairline was two squares, with the nostril being placed just within the eighteenth square. The hips or buttocks were delicately suggested at around the half-way mark in square ten. The greatest height of the foot, where it joined the leg, was one square. The shoulders were six squares wide for male figures and about five squares wide for females. The forearm from the point of the elbow to the tips of the extended fingers, the measurement known as a cubit, was also five squares, and the foot, from the back of the heel to the tip of the big toe was approximately three squares.

Hieroglyphs could be written from right to left or from left to right, the sense determining which direction the figures faced, since all human, animal and bird signs faced the beginning of the text.

Figure 61   *Amarnan Feet*: Left and right feet are here clearly differentiated by the Amarnan artist.

The usual direction for a hieroglyphic text was, like Arabic, from right to left, which meant that figures were defined as facing towards the right as seen by the reader or viewer. The same was true of art. In default, all figures tended to have a right orientation. Male figures were shown with the left leg, that furthest away from the viewer, striding forward. Women were shown standing with feet together, the left or rear foot only slightly advanced so that both feet could be seen. In the majority of cases, both feet on any one figure are shown with only the big toe defined. A subtle change of style introduced during the Amarna Period was the definition of the toes on the foot closest to the viewer, so that the figure did not appear to have two left feet (fig. 61). Some artists continued to use this more realistic representation, even after the classical artistic style had been restored

Certain fashionable features of dress, like the heavily pleated overlap of a man's kilt, would not have been visible if shown in profile like his hips, so the garment is shown partly from the front. The King's kilt was ornamented with a heavily beaded or embroidered apron, suspended from his belt like a Scotsman's sporran. In two-dimensional representations, the apron seems to be hanging to one side over his hip. In several periods, a fashion-conscious gentleman would have had the overlap of his kilt elaborately pleated, or starched and gathered in to the waistband to form a triangular front section which, in paintings and reliefs, was shown protruding in an inelegant way from the front of the kilt, but comparison with statuary of the same period will reveal the reality of masculine fashion that the artist was attempting to convey. A woman was usually shown with one breast in profile even though her torso is apparently turned towards the viewer. The classic sheath dress with two broad shoulder straps, as worn by goddesses was

Figure 62 *Two Viziers*: The Viziers Ptah-hotep (left) and Mereruka (right) face each other to illustrate the right orientation of Egyptian art. Each holds his staff in the left hand and the sceptre in the right.

a simple but none the less modest garment, even by modern standards, but the two-dimensional representation promotes the impression of a very much more revealing fashion.

Important officials indicated their status by the walking staff carried in the left hand and a baton of office held in the right. In the right-orientated figure, the left hand is held forward while the right hangs down behind the body, effectively turning the torso towards the viewer. Since composition demanded that not all figures could face to the right, mirror image figures were drawn, but this caused the artist some problems in depicting his concept of reality (fig. 62). A standing figure facing to the left still holds his walking staff in the forward hand but this is now his right hand, in which tradition demanded that he carry his baton. To correct this anomaly, the artist sometimes showed the hand holding the staff as a left hand, with the back of the knuckles towards the viewer, while representing the fingers of the hand clutching the baton to show it as a right hand. This could only be so if the back of the body was turned towards the viewer and yet the torso is still shown in front elevation. A further element of 'realism' was to cause the horizontally held baton to pass behind the body, as would be seen by the viewer if the figure were indeed holding the baton in his

right hand. The resultant air of distortion is in fact a more accurate portrayal of reality, a more faithful rendering of Maat, than
the simple mirror image solution.

Similar rules applied to the depiction of inanimate objects and
buildings. The ancient royal title known as the Horus Name of
the King was written in a rectangular enclosure called a *serekh*,
which represented the royal residence. The lower decorated section
was the front elevation of the panelled façade of the building and
the open area above was the plan of the inner courtyard. Perched
on the 'roof' of the palace was the falcon symbol of Horus shown
in profile. The King's name, in hieroglyphs, was written in the
courtyard, claiming both ownership and the god's protection. At
Luxor the front of the First Pylon of the temple itself is shown
perfect in every detail, including the flagpoles with their fluttering
streamers, the obelisks and the statues which flanked the gateway.
The pylon is well enough preserved for comparison to be made
between the artist's rendering and the real thing. Immediately
obvious is the fact that one of the obelisks is missing. It was given
to France by Mohammed Ali and was erected in the Place de la
Concorde in Paris in 1833. A more subtle difference is the orientation of the statues (fig. 63). Originally there were two standing
figures and one colossal seated statue on each side of the entrance.
The remaining statues are all placed with their backs to the pylon,
facing out along the axis of the processional way. The relief carving

Figure 63 *The Artist's View*: The façade of the Luxor Temple is shown in relief within
the temple itself. The artist has shown the statues in profile, but in reality they all face
outwards.

shows the statues in their correct positions, but all are facing inwards towards the central gateway, each apparently turned through ninety degrees from its true orientation and shown in classic Egyptian profile.

The conventions of two-dimensional art set everything from human figures and animals to buildings and furniture on a fixed base line. An area to be decorated was often divided into a series of scenes drawn in several registers, each with its own base line, giving the appearance of a page in a graphic novel. A sense of depth was conveyed by suggestion as, for instance, in the case of a row of men standing shoulder to shoulder and facing to the right who were represented with all their feet on the same base line, but each figure slightly advanced in front of his neighbour, so that at least his eye was not obscured by the head of the man to his right. The figure nearest the viewer was drawn in full detail implying that the others in the rank were similarly, if not identically, dressed and performing the same actions (fig. 64). The same applied to animals, though the artist had more freedom of expression when dealing with non-human subjects. In profile, only one of a pair of

Figure 64 *Mourners All in a Row*: Female mourners raise their arms as they weep for the Vizier Ramose. Isolated from the larger scene it becomes clear that there are five heads but only four bodies.

Figure 65 *Your Chariot Awaits*: The artist has hinted at the existence of a second horse by outlining the first. The team of mules is more obviously a pair.

plough oxen or chariot team is usually visible. The second is shown as the merest outline behind the fully-defined animal, sometimes in a different colour to emphasize the fact that there are two beasts involved. This was clearly shown in paintings from the Theban tomb of Nebamun, now in the British Museum. In a harvest scene, two chariots await the officials who have come to measure the fields and assess the crop for taxation purposes (fig. 65). The vehicle in the upper register is drawn by a pair of horses, one of which is black and the other, shown as the hint of an outline behind the first, is brown. In the lower register a less prestigious vehicle is drawn by a well-defined pair of white mules which are shown restlessly tossing their heads.

The use of colour was also governed by convention. Skin colour was used to define nationality as well as the difference between Egyptian men and women. Nubians were shown black, Libyans were an unhealthy yellow and Asiatics a pasty cream colour. Other physical traits were exaggerated, such as the thick lips of the Nubians, the pointed beards and braids of the Libyans and the heavy beards and oiled hair of the Asiatics, and ethnic details of costume and jewellery were emphasized. No offence was meant by this apparent caricaturization of racial types. The artist was simply using his skill and the materials available to him to create an image of a foreigner which would be immediately recognizable to anyone who saw it. Religious artists in medieval Europe used much the same principles when portraying Christian saints, providing them with sacred symbols or animals so that illiterate church-goers could identify them. St John the Evangelist is represented by an eagle, St Peter is recognized by the keys he carries and St James by the pilgrim's hat and scallop-shell emblem of his shrine at Compostela. In tomb paintings, Egyptian gods in human form were often shown with blue-green skin and hair the deep blue of lapis lazuli. Where the same animal or bird represented several distinct deities, extra symbols such as standards, crowns or sceptres reinforced the identification provided by names and titles written in hieroglyphs.

Colour convention also applied to the portrayal of the natural world. The globe of the sun representing the god Re was always red. A wall painting was supported on a horizontal band of yellow, red and black stripes representing the colours of the Egyptian soil, and each picture was surrounded by a ribbonlike border of red, yellow, green and blue sections alternating with white within black outlines. Water was shown blue with vertical zig-zags in white or grey indicating ripples. Ceilings in temples and royal tombs were painted midnight blue spangled with yellow five-pointed stars to represent the night sky.

Even the finely carved relief sculpture on temple walls and columns was originally painted. The outer walls of the temples would have been covered with a whitewash base and the scenes of the kings performing acts of piety or military prowess would have been brilliantly coloured in primary hues. The original colour of such monuments is still visible in areas which have been sheltered from the elements, such as the underside of lintels and the tops of columns shaded by remaining ceiling blocks. Paints were made with finely ground mineral pigments which keep their colour better than vegetable dyes. Red, yellow and brown were made from ochres, though an arsenical compound called orpiment was used from the New Kingdom onwards to provide a more lemony tone. Green and blue were based on copper compounds or on the same artificially produced frits made for colouring faience and glass. Lime provided a clear white, and black was usually carbon based, commonly lamp black or soot. The pigment was mixed with a vegetable gum or animal glue to thicken the paint and was then applied to a dry surface as a form of tempera. Some colours last better than others. The general brown-ness of some paintings is largely due to the falling away of the brighter blue and green colours or the deterioration or oxidation of metallic compounds.

Trial sketches of all sorts, from single hieroglyphs to portrait studies, were drawn on a whitewashed board which could be scrubbed clean and reused. The apprentice practised his drawing and relief techniques on stone off-cuts or ostraca, some of which still show signs of a master having corrected his pupil's work. The designer drew the final version of his composition on a board marked out with the squared grid which enabled him to obey the canon of proportion and gave guidelines for the artist on site. The Vizier Mereruka, son-in-law of the Sixth Dynasty King Teti, had himself portrayed in his Saqqara tomb as an artist seated at his easel (fig. 66). The drawing board is shown fixed to a vertical support on which there is a ledge for resting brushes. Mereruka holds a paint dish in one hand and his brush in the other and in front of him is a stand supporting his water bowl. The board

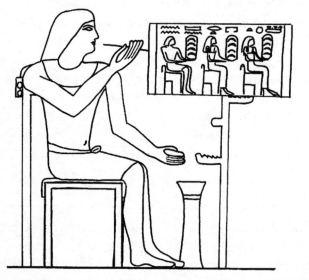

Figure 66 *Portrait of the Artist*: The Vizier Mereruka sits at his easel, drawing an allegorical picture of the Three Seasons.

on which he is painting is turned towards the viewer, revealing his composition as a representation of the three seasons of the Egyptian calendar.

Paint brushes were made of bundles of plant fibres tied on to wooden handles. For fine details reed brushes like those used by scribes were employed. In most cases the designer outlined his picture in black over the grid which was often laid out in red. The largest areas of colour were applied first over a bland background wash of buff, off-white or grey. In some cases, paint was applied over several layers of plaster made from mud, gypsum or lime and strengthened with chopped straw or sand. The designs were usually drawn on to the dried surface, but occasionally the damp plaster was modelled before paint was applied, to produce an effect similar to bas relief. The paintings in the tomb of Queen Nefertari were completed in this way. Probably, the designer's original intention had been to execute the decoration in carved relief, but the rock into which the tomb was cut proved to be so uneven in quality that a thick plaster was applied to the walls to camouflage the imperfections. The resulting coloured drawings of the elegant Queen making offerings to, and being acknowledged by, various funerary deities, are some of the most beautiful examples of ancient Egyptian painting. By modelling the wet plaster, the artist achieved a sense of depth and roundness which is missing from pictures where colour was painted on to a completely flat surface. Shading was rarely used to indicate shape or shadows. Details were drawn in a darker shade over the base colour and finally the outlines were precisely redefined with black or dark brown paint.

The finest type of tomb decoration was the painted relief work as seen in the tombs of Seti I and Horemheb in the Valley of Kings. The chambers nearest the tomb entrance were the first to be decorated, for as soon as the room was completed the tomb builders continued their digging farther into the cliff, while the decorators moved in behind them. The tomb was enlarged and improved continuously throughout the owner's life, so the innermost rooms were often unfinished at the time of his death. On the walls of the burial chamber of Horemheb's tomb the designer had drawn the scene of the Weighing of the Heart in black outlines, but the work had progressed no further. In the tomb of the Vizier Ramose all the stages of the production of painted relief are clearly visible, showing that the work on the tomb stopped suddenly, or was hastily finished, when Ramose died. In the chapel near the entrance, vividly coloured scenes, annotated with inscriptions, indicate what the designer's intention had been for the whole tomb. Farther in, the sculptor had completed large sections of delicate relief which remained unpainted at the time of the tomb-owner's death. With no time to complete the work as intended, the artist picked out in black the outlines and pupils of the eyes of the principal figures, members of Ramose's family, so that the faces had something of life about them. Yet farther into the tomb, the sculptors had not completed some walls and, rather than leave them partly carved, the remainder of the design was finished in incised or sunk relief, which takes less time than bas relief. In the innermost chambers where work had not progressed beyond the levelling of the walls and the drawing in outline of the required scenes, any attempt at improvement in the limited time available before Ramose's funeral was impractical.

The two types of relief were executed by the same methods and with the same tools as for stone-working in general. Bas or raised relief is formed by lowering the background and leaving the details of the scene proud of the surface. In sunk or incised relief, the details are cut out of the surface. Clearly, bas relief required the removal of much more stone than sunk relief, so it took much longer to cover a similar area of design by this method. For carving limestone and sandstone, copper chisels with wooden mallets were perfectly adequate for fine detail. Harder stone pounders were used to remove larger areas of backgound. When carving in granite or quartzite, the process took much longer, requiring hammering and rubbing of the surface to be removed with a series of stone pounders, reducing in size and roughness down to small quartz pebbles. Egyptian craftsmen required great patience.

For large areas of relief, like the outer surfaces of temple pylons, a third type of relief was used. This was relief *en creux*, a combination of the raised and sunk varieties. A figure was defined by cutting a deep outline, then the shape within the outline was modelled and detailed, almost like a shallow sculpture in the half-round. This was ideal for exterior walls such as the pylons of the great temples where the strong sunlight cast deep shadows in the incised outlines, throwing the sculptures into sharp relief.

Errors in relief carving were less easily corrected than those in paintings. The designer had to be vigilant in seeing that his instructions were carried out properly at the drawing stage because any mistakes made by the sculptor, any inaccuracies of line or misstrokes of the chisel, were difficult to repair. The usual means of disguising problems was to cover the affected area with a layer of plaster and recarve it once the plaster had dried. In some tombs, and even temples, where this action was necessary, the plaster has long ago fallen away from the wall and the nature of the original error is revealed side by side with the remains of the designer's restoration. Similar problems with carvings in hard stone were more difficult to solve. The chemical composition of ancient Egyptian plaster was similar to that of limestone and it was not so useful for repairing faults in granite or quartzite. It could be coloured with the addition of finely powdered stone, but it would not bind securely to the surface.

If a fault occurred at a late stage in the carving of a relief or in the production of a statue, a great deal of time and effort would have been wasted. This was possibly one reason why the Egyptian sculptor seems to have been reluctant to free a statue completely from the basic block. The typical Egyptian stone statue is set on a rectangular plinth with a solid back pillar which are integral parts of the statue, the plinth replacing the base line of two-dimensional art and both providing prime sites for the essential inscriptions. Originally the back pillar may have been seen as a means of strengthening the statue by supporting the weak point at the narrowing of the neck, especially on royal statues which tended to have bulky crowns adding to the weight of the head. Long after the Egyptian sculptor had proved that such supports were unnecessary, the back pillar remained a standard feature of portrait statuary. Similarly, arms hanging down beside the body were carved as one piece with the torso, no space was allowed between the open palm or clenched fist and the thigh against which it rested, and the gap between elbow and waist was indicated, but not hollowed out. In a statue depicting a man in the classic right-orientated striding pose, the figure appears to be emerging from the original stone block, the outlines of which are still defined by the

Figure 67
The Finishing Touches:
A colossal statue encased in
wooden scaffolding, is polished
by sculptors as the designer
adds the inscription to the back
pillar. The 'negative space' and
right orientation are apparent.

plinth and back pillar. The rear, right leg is attached along its whole
length to the back pillar and the stone between the right shin and
the back of the left calf is not removed. Viewed in its correct orientation, facing to the right, both legs of the statue are clearly defined
and carved in perfect detail. However, viewed from the other
side, the rear leg is obscured by that stone infill and only the forward
leg is seen. It may have been believed that the removal of the infill
would have put stresses on the statue which might have cracked and
damaged beyond repair a piece on which the artist had been working for months. To avoid this possibility, the sculptor employed a
principle now known as negative space (fig. 67), leaving the viewer
to imagine certain parts of the work to be transparent. This principle, like many aspects of Egyptian art, became enshrined in tradition
and was not a failing on the part of the artist. Egyptian sculptors
were perfectly capable of carving limbs and even finer features in the
round and free from the mass of the base material, as they ably
demonstrated in ornamental stone vessels and wooden statuary.
They were also able to apply these techniques to large portrait statues in hard stone, such as the triad of Ramesses III being crowned by
Horus and Seth in which the figures of the deities are unsupported
by back pillars and their raised arms and striding legs are completely
freed from the block.

Figure 68 *Apis*: A statue of the Apis bull of Memphis demonstrates the principle of 'negative space' with only three of the animal's legs visible from any orientation.

The statue of the Apis bull from the Serapeum at Saqqara, now in the Louvre Museum, is a fine example of this principle. Viewed in right orientation, the bull appears to be striding forward, but only three of its legs can be seen. The left rear is obscured by the solid mass of stone beneath the body. From the opposite side, the right foreleg is totally obscured and the right hindleg is only discernible as a rear profile. The musculature is well-defined and all the elements of the animal's body are there, each so perfectly rendered that it is easy to overlook the fact that the statue is essentially more cuboid than bull-shaped (fig. 68).

One of the simplest poses for human portraiture was the block statue, a representation of a man sitting on the ground with his knees drawn up to his chin and wrapped around in a cloak. This pose reduced the carving of the body to the shaping of the head, the indication of feet under the cloak and stylized hands holding together the edges of the garment. The smooth expanse of 'cloth' provided at least three sizeable areas for the inscription of texts, an important consideration for the designer. Costume or jewellery could be adapted to bear names and titles. The clasp on the belt of a king's kilt was often shaped like a cartouche, the oval enclosure in which was written the royal name. Other cartouches were worked into armlets and bracelets, or were carved directly into the arm or wrist where such jewellery would usually be worn. Clothing could be adorned with bands of hieroglyphs in place of embroidery or braid. The papyrus open in the lap of the scribe was an obvious place for texts, as was the offering mat or votive shrine held by a kneeling priest.

The decoration of hard stone statues was limited to the gilding of some features or the picking out of the hieroglyphs in paint. Limestone statues were almost always painted according to the same conventions of colour that applied to wall paintings. In addition, the eye sockets of many soft stone statues and most wooden statues were inlaid with artificial eyes. These were set in a surround of dark metal, usually copper, representing the kohl-darkened eyelids. The white of the eye was carved from a white stone such as quartz, calcite or crystalline limestone, or from white glass, in which a conical plug of a black material, often obsidian, represented the pupil. The very best quality and most realistic type of inlaid eye had a rock crystal cornea set over a coloured disc of resin or paint with a central bead or depression filled with a black substance, giving the appearance of a coloured iris complete with pupil. The so-called Squatting Scribe statue from Saqqara, now in the Louvre Museum, has eerily realistic eyes which graphically demonstrate the pains taken by the sculptor to create the perfect statue. The Egyptian artist would have understood the idea that the eyes are the mirror of the soul. In his terms, he would have considered this attention to detail his way of keeping faith with Maat.

During the reign of Akhenaten, this emphasis on truth and reality was taken to even greater extremes. The era is known as the Amarna Period, after the modern name for the site of Akhenaten's capital city. His religious reforms led to remarkable and very distinctive changes in art (fig. 69). As part of his official titulary, the King chose the epithet Living in Maat, and he announced his intention to portray all his god's creation as truthfully as possible. Since the Aten was not represented in human form, divine figures in religious scenes were replaced by the royal family who were even shown in private tombs showering the tomb-owners with rewards for their service to the Crown. The basic principles of Egyptian

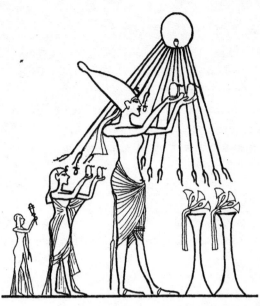

Figure 69 *Icon*: Akhenaten, his wife Nefertiti and their eldest daughter Meritaten offer to the Aten in whose rays they bask. Icons of this sort replaced the traditional cult statue of the god in Aten temples.

art still applied but the canon of proportion was slightly altered. The standing human figure was drawn on a grid of twenty squares instead of eighteen, the two extra squares being added to the upper part of the body. This resulted in a change in the length of the legs compared with the torso and a tendency to elongation of the head. Akhenaten's facial features became the ideal on which all his followers had their own portraits modelled. This more relaxed stance and exaggerations of physical features such as a pot belly, heavy thighs and spindle shanks, made Amarnan art very distinctive. What might be considered a tendency towards caricature, must have been sanctioned and indeed ordered by the King himself in his determination to portray reality. That Akhenaten took an active interest in the style of art developed during his reign is made clear in the words of his court sculptor Bak, carved on a rock stela near the Aswan quarries:

> ... The overseer of works in the red mountain, the apprentice whom His Majesty himself instructed, the chief of sculptors on the many great monuments of the King in the temple of the Aten in Akhetaten, Bak, son of the Chief of Sculptors, Men ...

The Amarnan artist was encouraged in a degree of freedom of expression not enjoyed by his predecessors, but he never broke faith with the centuries of artistic tradition which circumscribed Egyptian artistic style. Art in all periods of Egyptian history was a means of confirming and promoting the nature of Maat. The artist's personal experiences and preferences had no place in official art, but many artists found time to express themselves in a less formal way. Comic sketches, some bordering on the lampoon and others downright scurrilous, and allegorical scenes of animals performing human activities or in role-reversal situations, are perhaps more astute observations on life than the more familiar scenes from tombs. The sketch of the unshaven stonemason now in the Fitzwilliam Museum, Cambridge, and the cartoon of the mouse attended by a cat servant (fig. 70), from the Brooklyn Museum, provide rare insights into the artist's close involvement in the everyday life of Egypt. The reasoning behind most ancient Egyptian art was so different from modern artistic expression that it cannot be appreciated on the same terms as modern art, but the consummate skill of the Egyptian artist must be admired. In his own time and in his own way he was a true exponent of art or, as he would have explained it, a devoted follower of Maat.

Figure 70 *Cat and Mouse*: The mouse master holds a wine cup and a tasty fish bone as his cat servant presents him with a duck dinner.

CHAPTER 8

The Soldier

•

IN THE BRITISH MUSEUM and in the Ashmolean Museum, Oxford there are two pieces of a Predynastic ceremonial slate palette, carved in high relief. The scene on the obverse shows a lion rampaging over a field strewn with human corpses, while crows and vultures scavenge from the bodies. Living captives stand with their arms tied behind their backs, before the tribal standards of their conquerors. From this scene derives the popular name for the artifact, the Battlefield Palette, but this tells only half the story. On the reverse of the palette is an idyllic scene of life in the countryside, with animals and birds in the shade of a palm tree (fig. 71). As the first scene represents war so the second depicts peace. The two sides of the palette combine in perfect balance providing an allegory of the duality of Maat.

By the time the Egyptians had begun to record every aspect of their society, in pictures and later in words, war was already an established fact of life in the Nile Valley. Other Predynastic palettes provide evidence for the sort of organized warfare which could only develop in a society where one acknowledged leader provided protection for his followers and security for their lands and possessions by mustering and leading troops to their defence whenever necessary. The Narmer Palette has the ultimate war-leader, the King, depicted as a bull trampling his enemies beneath his hooves and breaking down the walls of a fortified settlement with his horns. The victorious King is shown reviewing rows of war dead, each decapitated body with its head between its feet. On the opposite face of the palette, the King is shown grasping an enemy chieftain by the hair and with his mace raised in the action of clubbing his captive to death, before the hawk emblem of the god Horus. The King's destruction of his enemies in the

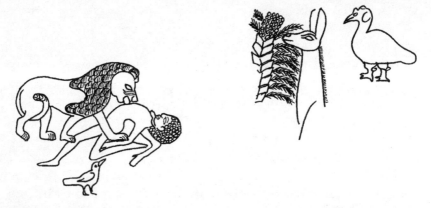

Figure 71 *War and Peace*: Fragments of relief decoration from opposite sides of a Predynastic palette show the horror of war and the tranquillity of peacetime.

sight of the gods, acknowledging the part played by the deities in Egypt's victory, was an enduring theme in monumental art.

The weapon most often shown as the instrument of vengeance is the mace, simple but devastatingly effective. Developed from the primitive wooden club, it took the form of a stone head on a wooden haft. The macehead was either disc- or pear-shaped, the latter becoming the typical weapon of Egyptian infantry troops. In showing himself using the mace to dispatch selected captives, the King was symbolically claiming the destruction of all his enemies. The mace was the principal sign in the word the White One, a name given to the Crown of Upper Egypt, and also a title of the vulture goddess Nekhebt, wearer of the White Crown. Ceremonial maceheads of a size far too large to be considered as practical weapons, were carved with scenes commemorating auspicious occasions to be dedicated as votive offerings to the temples, like the Scorpion and Narmer Maceheads, found at Hierakonpolis.

The army that Narmer raised for his conquest of Lower Egypt must have been drawn largely from his personal following: people from his own tribe or home area, formed around a nucleus of family and friends. The soldiers of Egypt for the most part were not professionals. Threats to Egypt's territorial integrity were met by an army raised specifically for the occasion and then disbanded as soon as the danger was past. Until the New Kingdom, when Egypt entered into a period of military and territorial expansion, there was no standing army. Provincial noblemen, towns and temples maintained their own militias who acted as personal body guards, provided escorts for supply convoys, gave protection to officials going about their lawful but often unpopular duties and generally kept the peace (fig. 72). When the King required an army to repel a possible invasion, or to mount a punitive strike against raiders or bandits, the provincial militias were the first troops to be called up. The bulk of an army of any size would be made up of conscripts. A didactic text recorded on a papyrus, now in the British Museum, and intended for the edification of student scribes, describes conscription:

> All the King's subjects are mustered and the best will be taken. The man is made into a soldier and the youth into a recruit. The boy is born only to be torn from his mother's arms and he reaches manhood only to have his bones battered.

A similar text from an ostracon in Florence describes the lot of the downtrodden soldier:

> His superiors are numerous. There are the general, the commander of auxiliaries, the officer who leads the host, the standard-bearer, the lieutenant, the recruiting officer, the captain of fifty and the leader of the squad. They come and go in their quarters ... saying

Figure 72 *Guard of Honour*: Three members of the military escort sent with Queen Hatshepsut's expedition to the incense land of Punt. They carry battle-axes, shields and spears and a royal ceremonial fan as a standard.

'Get the men to work!' The soldier is awakened after only an hour of sleep and he is worked like an ass until sunset. . . . He is always hungry. He is like a dead man and yet he lives.

The size of an army would have varied according to the circumstances of its muster. During the Sixth Dynasty, to counter an invasion threat on his eastern frontier, Pepi I raised a huge army to send against the *Shasu* or Sand-dwellers. In overall command of the Egyptian troops was a court official named Weni who, according to his lengthy biography at Abydos, had no previous experience as a military leader, but was chosen to command because Pepi had no wish to promote envy among his nobles by setting one of them in authority over the rest.

His Majesty gathered together an army of many tens of thousands from north and south, from both sides of the river, from the fortified towns of Nubia and from the garrisons of Libya. His Majesty set me at the head of this army while the counts, the royal seal-bearers, the sole companions of the palace, the nomarchs and governors of the towns . . . were each at the head of a troop from the stronghold or city which they commanded. But I was the one who planned the strategy. I was the supreme commander. . . . [While I was in charge] not one soldier under my command pilfered from his neighbour nor thieved from the traveller. Not a single loaf of bread was taken from any town nor a single goat from any village.

The fact that Weni praised the behaviour of his troops is perhaps an indication that such self-control was unusual for the army. Weni was successful enough in his first military outing to be appointed as Commander in Chief for four more campaigns against the *Shasu*. His strategy included an out-flanking action which required transport of some of his troops by boat to southern Palestine:

Told there were marauders among the foreigners at the place called the Nose of the Gazelle, I crossed in ships with my troops. I landed behind the ridge to the north of the land of the Sand-dwellers while the enemy army was still on the road. I arrived and caught them off guard, slaying every one of the rebels . . .

Weni's commission from Pepi was for a defensive action only, to protect Egypt's borderlands. An advance into enemy territory was not seen as an occupation or annexation of land. The King of Egypt was content with the size of his realm as defined by its traditional boundaries. Army life was considered less attractive than that of some other more physically demanding trades simply because the job took the soldier away from the Beloved Land. The thought of dying abroad and being buried in foreign soil was anathema to any true Egyptian. In the *Story of Sinuhe*, the exiled Egyptian hero of the tale, having spent many years at a foreign court, begged forgiveness for unspecified crimes, so that he might return to his homeland and end his days there: 'Whichever god decreed this flight, have mercy. Bring me home! Surely you will allow me to see again the place where my heart dwells! What is more important than that my body should be buried in the land of my birth? . . . May his heart ache for the exiled one! If he is truly appeased may he hearken to the prayer of one far away from home! . . . May the King of Egypt have mercy on me, that I may live by his mercy! . . .'

Life for the ordinary soldier was extremely hard and unpleasant, but the duration of most campaigns was limited by the weather and the harvest. Since most conscripts were taken from the mass of peasant workers who were needed in the fields, the army had to be released for the planting and harvest seasons. Officers were the only career soldiers, but even they would hold non-military titles and have responsibilities in the administration other than their army duties. Rahotep, the son of King Seneferu of the Third Dynasty, held a string of appointments, including Controller and Commander of Troops. The royal bodyguard was the only permanent force maintained by the Crown and in many periods this unit performed purely ceremonial duties. At its most professional, the corps was known by a term derived from the word for 'valour' or 'boldness', which might be translated as the Braves.

The weapons carried by the regular troops were the mace, the spear and the axe. Spears and axes had copper or bronze heads mounted on wooden shafts. The handles of maces and axes were bound with cord or leather thongs to provide a better grip. Ceremonial axes, highly decorated and bearing the name of the reigning king, were presented as awards for valour (fig. 73). An officer might carry a dagger with a straight double-edged tapering blade. This was kept in a leather sheath, the best examples being painted, embossed or even gilded, and was tucked into the waist-

Figure 73: *Weapons Rack*: The deceased prepared for all eventualities and provided himself with weapons both for the hunt and defence. The rack holds spears, a pole-axe, a whip, a throwstick, bundles of arrows and bows.

band of the kilt. By its association with authority, the hieroglyphic symbol of the sheathed dagger was used for the word 'chief' or 'first'. Foot-soldiers carried shields made from animal hide stretched on a wooden frame. These were usually arch-topped and covered the body from knee to head. Battle scenes from Karnak show that these shields were used to form defensive structures similar to the Roman *testudo* when approaching the walls of a fortified town, and they were set up as a fence around an Egyptian military camp. Apart from the shield, there was very little in the way of protective clothing. Most ordinary soldiers went barefoot and wore nothing more than a simple kilt or loincloth. In later periods a quilted linen apron was added to the front of the kilt as a loin protector, and officers sometimes wore a padded tunic or jerkin sewn with leather or metal scales. Some officers may have worn close-fitting leather helmets, but these were little protection against the crushing blow of a stone mace. Infantrymen relied on a thick mop of hair.

The army on campaign was provided with only the most basic of rations. Soldiers were expected to supplement these by foraging and, though looting from their fellow countrymen was not officially condoned, as implied in Weni's autobiography, the army's presence in any area, even passing through, was probably viewed by the local people with great misgivings. The author of another instructional text for student scribes had nothing good to say about the life of the soldier:

> Let me tell you how life is for the soldier when he goes on campaign to Syria. He has to march over mountains laden like an ass with his bread and water carried on his shoulder. . . . His drinking water

is stagnant. . . . When at last he reaches the enemy he is as weak as a captive bird with no strength in his limbs. If he returns to Egypt he is riddled with disease like a stick with woodworm.

In early depictions of a king dispatching captives, the nationality of the victims is not always made clear. The curly-headed and bearded dead on the Battlefield Palette could be invaders from what is traditionally called Libya, the desert lands bordering on Egypt's western frontier. Hieroglyphs beside the long-haired chieftain at the mercy of King Den, on the small ivory label from Abydos, show that he represents the people of the eastern regions of the Red Sea coast and Sinai, the homelands of the bedouin Sand-dwellers. These nomadic peoples posed a constant threat to the Egyptians living in the eastern reaches of the Delta and to the important trade routes which passed through the area. The dead on the Narmer Palette are assumed to be natives of Lower Egypt. After the Unification, the peoples of the north and south were all considered to be Egyptians and physical or ethnic differences were no longer relevant, but at the same time the appearance and costume of their common enemies were exaggerated to distinguish friend from foe.

The deserts to the east and west of the Nile provided natural barriers to all but the most determined of would-be invaders. The upper reaches of the river, however, were more heavily populated. The six regions of shallow water and rapids known as the Nile Cataracts impeded waterborne invasion, but persistent enemies would always be able to find a land route around them. The First Cataract at Aswan was traditionally the southernmost border of Egypt – and a permanent garrison was established there from very early times, to provide customs and immigration control as well as a rapid-response force to repel potential invaders – but the Southlands of Nubia were of great value to Egypt because of their natural resources, not the least of which was gold. The King of Egypt had to control those regions, even though he could not colonize the area sufficiently to consider it part of Egypt proper.

The region of Egyptian influence commonly called Nubia is now largely submerged beneath the waters of Lake Nasser. The native tribes were confined by climate and geology to the narrow band of cultivable land along the riverbanks, where they lived by a

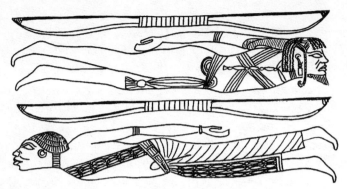

Figure 74   *Fallen Enemies*: A Libyan (above) and a Nubian (below), two of Egypt's traditional enemies, the Nine Bows, bound and helpless before the King.

combination of hunting, herding and crop-growing. They were naturally warlike and famed for their skill with weapons developed for the hunt. The most characteristic of these were the simple longbow and the curved throwstick, similar to the Australian boomerang, both of which feature in the weaponry carried by warriors on the Hunter's Palette in the British Museum. The throwstick became the hieroglyphic determinative for the names of native tribes and the bow was seen as a symbol of a foreign power. The traditional enemies of Egypt were known as the Nine Bows and were represented as bound captives as on the King's footstool or the pavement of the temple over which he walked (fig. 74). The subjugation of an enemy was symbolized by the breaking of the bow.

Though the longbow, or self bow, was considered to be, originally, a Nubian weapon, flint arrowheads have survived from as early as 8000 BC, providing proof that bows were in use throughout Egypt from early prehistoric times. Crossed arrows on a hide shield formed the sacred emblem of the goddess Neith, patron of the Delta city of Sais and one of the national deities of Lower Egypt. The stela of Queen Meryt-Neith, who was possibly the first woman to rule Egypt in her own right, bears the shield and arrows of Neith as part of her name which means 'Beloved of Neith'. A wooden label from the reign of Aha shows a primitive shrine to Neith identified by the symbol of the goddess erected as a standard within the temple courtyard (fig. 75). On her head, the goddess wore either the Red Crown of Lower Egypt or a symbol composed of two antique bows strapped together, giving the appearance of

Figure 75 *Shrine of the Warrior Goddess*: Pictorial 'inscription' from a wooden label showing a primitive shrine, identified as being dedicated to Neith by the standard.

a weaver's shuttle (fig. 76). The bow of this type was made from a solid wooden middle section with curved ends made from the horns of an animal, probably an oryx. This sort of bow was replaced by the longbow as soon as the Egyptians recognized the greater efficiency of the Nubian weapon.

Nubia was a dangerous place for the traders who ventured south to fetch hard woods, ivory, animal skins and incense, and for the miners travelling to and from the gold-fields, but such journeys were necessary to the maintenance of the Egyptian way of life. Many kings started their reigns with military expeditions into Nubia, to remind the tribesmen, who might have considered testing the resolve of a new monarch, that Egypt, even under a change of ruler, was still too powerful to withstand. Some permanent settlements were established in Nubia to serve as trade centres and staging posts for the Egyptian venturers. The longest-established seems to have been the walled outpost of Buhen near the Second Cataract, which may have been founded as early as the Second Dynasty. During the Fourth and Fifth Dynasties, Buhen was a centre for copper smelting but it was also a haven for the tribespeople in times of local unrest. The settlement was enlarged and reinforced during the Middle Kingdom to become a frontier fortress, one of eleven established in the area upriver of the Second Cataract. Senusert III set up a stela to explain the role of the Semna fort:

> [This is] the southern boundary established in Year 8 of the reign of the King of Upper and Lower Egypt, Khakaure Senusert III . . . in order to prevent any tribesman passing by water or by land, with a boat or with herds, except that he be one coming to trade or that he holds a travel warrant.

Figure 76 *Mistress of Bows*: The goddess Neith of Sais, identified by the emblem of two antique bows bound together, worn as a crown.

Communications between the major fortresses were relayed along a chain of lookout posts manned by Egyptian troops, assisted by local informers. Everything that happened in the area, from the movement of people and their animals to more sinister activities like banditry, were reported to the garrison commander at one of the forts, and from there back to the King himself in Egypt. A document in the British Museum, found among a collection of papyri at the Ramesseum, is the collated copy of a series of dispatches from the fortress of Semna, written during the reign of Amenemhet III of the Twelfth Dynasty. The very ordinary details of the everyday concerns of the Nubian garrison show that the King himself was kept informed of everything that went on in the most distant part of his realm. For most of their tour of duty in Nubia, Egyptian soldiers would have acted as armed escorts to the trading and mining expeditions and provided a visible presence to remind the local populace that they were subject to Egyptian authority, however remote that authority might appear to be. When it was necessary to launch a military action against the Nubians, the resident garrisons were reinforced with troops from Egypt, brought south by boat. Native troops were employed as scouts and guides, and the famous archers augmented the Egyptian infantry. The archers in the tomb model from the Twelfth Dynasty tomb of Mesehti at Assyut are shown with the curly bobbed hair, black skin and patterned loincloths of Nubians.

The Nubian longbow was made from a single stave of wood. The examples in the British Museum, and in the collection of archery equipment from the tomb of Tutankhamen, vary in length from approximately 1.60 metres to 1.98 metres comparing with the typical length of around 6 feet (1.85 metres or more) of the English longbow used at Agincourt. The bowstrings used by the Nubian tribesmen for their hunting bows were probably twisted from animal hair. The Egyptians grew flax and so made their bowstrings from linen threads, like the bowstrings used by the English bowmen at Crécy. The power of a bow depends on its draw-weight, the pull required to bend the bow to the length of the chosen arrow. It has been estimated that the draw-weight of the bows in the British Museum was probably no more than 23 kilograms. Longer bows would have had proportionately higher draw-weights, and so would have delivered more power. The arrows fired from the bows were very long and lightweight with shafts made from reeds and points finely carved from hard wood or knapped from flint. The fletching was of feathers from one of the many species of goose native to the Nile Valley. Based on comparisons with medieval weapons of similar size and draw-weight, the Nubian longbow could have had an effective range of well over 200 metres, and despite the lightness of the arrows, they could be fired with sufficient force to penetrate animal or human bodies and lodge in bone. This was vividly demonstrated by the discovery of the mass burial of soldiers who had died in the siege of a strategic border town during the civil war which set the Eleventh Dynasty King Nebhepetre-Montuhotep on the throne of a reunited Egypt. The arrowheads found embedded up to 20 centimetres deep in twelve of the sixty corpses had ebony points. Four of the soldiers were themselves archers, since they wore leather strips bound on their left wrists to protect them from the slap of the bowstring. The collection of archery tackle in Tutankhamen's tomb included more elaborate bracers, and quivers made from leather and linen. Palm patches and finger tabs for the right hand have also been identified. Each of the archers from Mesehti's tomb is shown carrying his arrows in his right hand. Presumably he would stick them in the ground beside him when he reached his fixing position.

The determining hieroglyph for soldier and troops in general was the kneeling archer carrying his bow and a bundle of arrows. The feather in his hair identifies him as a Nubian. From the Second Intermediate Period considerable numbers of Nubians, collectively known by the name of a tribe from the eastern desert areas of Nubia, the *Medjay*, were drafted into the Egyptian army in archery regiments, providing the shock troops in many military campaigns of the New Kingdom. In times of peace, the *Medjay* formed a civil defence force, being employed as guards, immigration officials and bailiffs. As officers of the law, they were often responsible for bringing criminals such as tomb-robbers to justice and administering punishments. The term *medjay* came to mean a peace-keeper or policeman and not every man who was called a *medjay* was Nubian by birth. There was a small guardhouse at the entrance to the village of Deir el-Medina which was the police station of the local *medjay* force. The Chief of Police had his own office in the administrative quarter of one of the major temples on the west bank at Thebes.

The archer came into his own with the introduction of the composite bow at the beginning of the New Kingdom. This weapon was made of layers of horn or sinew over a wooden core and wrapped in bark. Tutankhamen owned a particularly fine example of a composite bow, known as the Bow of Honour, which was sheathed in gold and elaborately decorated with gold granulation and inscriptions. This may well have been a special gift to the King from one of Egypt's ally kingdoms in the north. The composite bow seems to have been introduced by the usurping Hyksos kings and its advantages were immediately appreciated by the native princes of the unoccupied south. Possibly by means of military espionage, or simply by bribing Hyksos bowyers, they acquired knowledge of the construction of the new weapon and trained their troops in its use. Nubian archers were quick to adapt to the new bow, which was more accurate and had double the range of the simple longbow. The kings themselves became proficient in the use of the new weapon and many battle scenes show the King firing his bow from a moving chariot.

The chariot itself was another introduction from the Asiatic region. Horses, though known in Egypt, were not used for draught purposes before the New Kingdom, and then only for pulling chariots. The vehicle was a lightweight platform, with a curved front wall panelled with leather or basketwork to which were strapped weapon cases, and a single pole for yoking a pair of horses. The floor was slatted or woven from leather thongs, its flexibility giving a smoother ride over rough terrain. The wheels were of elaborate construction, with six spokes and rawhide tyres, and were set on a rear-mounted axle which was more than twice the width of the chariot body (fig. 77). This construction made the vehicle light and yet strong and very manoeuvrable. It was also very stable and could execute tight turns without rolling over. The horses were small, wiry animals, similar to the Arabian breed. They were harnessed to the chariot by means of a yoke-saddle with belly and breast girths. The reins passed from the bit and bridle through metal rings mounted on the yoke. Although the King is usually shown in his chariot alone with the reins tied around his waist, the vehicle would normally have carried a driver and a warrior. Horse troops in Egypt were always chariotry and never mounted cavalry. There are a few depictions of Egyptians riding horses bareback, but these all appear to represent grooms or horse trainers or, in dire emergency, messengers.

Amenhotep II claimed to be an expert in the schooling of horses and in chariot-driving. He described his athletic prowess in great detail on the stela erected in front of the Great Sphinx at Giza:

When His Majesty was still a young prince he adored horses and delighted in them. He was tireless in working with them, familiar with their ways and expert in their training, having a thorough understanding of their nature ... the King's Son was charged with the care of the horses of the royal stable. ... he raised horses without

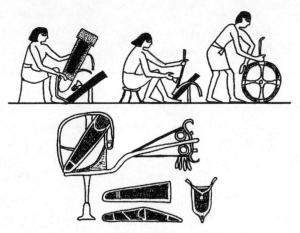

Figure 77 *Fitting out a Chariot*: Craftsmen make the leather fittings for a chariot including quiver, bowcase, yoke-saddle, bodywork and harness. One worker cuts strips of rawhide which another applies to a wheel as a tyre.

equal. They did not tire when he took the reins. They hardly broke into a sweat even at full gallop. . . . He was the one who knew best the management of chariot and team and his like had never before been seen in all the hosts of the army.

Amenhotep was also an archer of some repute, by his own admission:

He drew 300 strong bows in order to compare the work of their craftsmen. . . . He entered into his park where four targets of Asiatic copper, each one palm in thickness, had been set up, each stand separated from the next by 20 cubits. . . . His Majesty in his chariot . . . seized his bow and snatched four arrows all at once. [He shot at the targets] and his arrows emerged from the back of the first as he started for the next. It was seen that he achieved a feat never before witnessed. An arrow shot at a copper target passed right through it and landed on the ground behind [fig. 78].

Even allowing for artistic licence and the usual hyperbole of royal inscriptions, Amenhotep II seems to have been an athlete of considerable prowess. He was buried with his great longbow beside him in his coffin.

Egyptian archery regiments and the chariotry proved their skills in several noted battles, particularly against the Libyans, a modern rendering of *Libu*, the collective term used by the Egyptians when mentioning the disparate peoples of the western desert regions

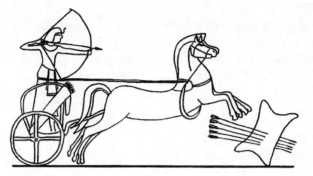

Figure 78 *Archery Practice*: Amenhotep II demonstrates his skill as a bowman by shooting at a copper target from his moving chariot.

beyond the string of oases and along the north African coast. Several individual tribes were recognized by name, such as the Tjemehu and the Tjehenu who inhabited the desert lands bordering Lower Egypt and were considered no better than bandits. There were frequent incursions by raiders from this area who sacked villages and abducted flocks and herds before returning to their semi-nomadic lifestyle. The Libyan homelands were generally arid with sparse grazing, and their arable lands were difficult to irrigate. The lush pastures and constant supply of water enjoyed by the Egyptians were sources of envy, and when crops failed or waterholes dried up, the Libyans turned their covetous gaze on Egypt, particularly the Delta. Personal names in some Egyptian communities show that there were Libyans living in Egypt from at least as early as the Middle Kingdom. A certain amount of trade was conducted across the western borders of the Delta and the Fayum, but these were also the areas most prone to intrusion by bandits and illegal immigrants who sought refuge with their kinsmen.

By the reign of Amenhotep III, the Libyan tribes were considered enough of a threat to be included in the list of the Nine Bows in the tomb of Kheruef, Queen Tiye's household steward in Thebes. Constant movements of the Libyan population led to the establishment of a powerful cattle-herding tribe, the Meshwesh, on the fringes of the traditional Tjehenu territory, posing even more of a danger to the rich northern pasturelands of Egypt. Seti I was the first monarch to record in detail a campaign against the Libyans and had it portrayed in reliefs on the outer walls of the Hypostyle

Hall at Karnak. Seti's son, Ramesses II, established a line of forts along the western edge of the Delta and extending along the Mediterranean coast to el-Alamein and beyond, an indication of how much the Libyan threat had grown. The forts, at intervals of about 80 kilometres, provided a line of communication which enabled news of potential trouble to be relayed by chariot-borne messengers to the seat of government in Memphis, within a matter of two or three days. By the time of Ramesses' son Merenptah, the forts were largely deserted and Libyan infiltration into the western reaches of the Delta had increased alarmingly. Reinforced by warlike immigrants in their own lands, the Meshwesh were emboldened to attempt a full-scale invasion with the intention of settling in Egypt. The incomers who encouraged the Libyans to think they stood a chance of success against the might of Egypt were the so-called Sea Peoples, seafaring warriors displaced from their island homes, who roamed the Mediterranean coast in search of a place to call their own. Several tribes of Sea Peoples were named in Merenptah's list of captives and war dead: for instance, the Sherden who were recognized by their horned helmets, round shields and long, straight swords. The inclusion of such skilled, experienced and well-accoutred warriors in the Libyan host was a significant threat.

The events leading up to Merenptah's Libyan war were recorded at the Karnak temple, beginning with the news of the coalition between the Libyans and the Sea Peoples: 'The wretched chief of the Libu, Meryey son of Deyd, has fallen upon the Tjehenu land with his troops including Sherden, Sheklesh, Akawasha, Luka and Tursha (of the islands of the sea), taking with him the best of their warriors and every fighting man of his own country. He has brought with him his wife and his children ... and all the elders of his tribe, and he has now reached the western border in the fields of Perire.' Merenptah understood the reason for the Libyan invasion and how attractive his land must appear to a people under pressure from food and land shortages: 'They roam the land all day, fighting for food to fill their bellies. They have come to the land of Egypt to find the necessities of life and food for their mouths.'

The presence of non-combatants among the enemy forces proved the Libyans' intention to settle and Merenptah announced the mobilization of his troops to his assembled court: '... The leaders of the bowmen went in front of the army to overthrow the land of Libya. When they went forth, the hand of God was with them, even Amen as their shield. The whole of the land of Egypt was commanded, "Make ready to march in fourteen days."'

When the two armies finally came together, the Libyans were expecting the hand-to-hand fighting at which they excelled. Their only chariots were cumbersome vehicles, not suited for the sort of high-speed manoeuvring that would be needed to match the Egyptian chariotry and the few vehicles they had seem to have been used more as symbols of prestige. The list of spoils includes only twelve pairs of horses captured and these are said to have been the prized possessions of the Libyan chieftain and his sons. When the battle started shortly after dawn, Merenptah had chosen his ground so that the Libyans had to advance into the rising sun. Already at a disadvantage, Meryey was thwarted in his attempts to come to grips with the Egyptians by Merenptah's archers:

> The bowmen of His Majesty spent six hours of destruction among them before they were delivered to the sword. . . . As they fought . . . the wretched chief of the Libyans halted, his heart trembling, then he retreated ... leaving behind him in his haste ... all his possessions. Weakness overcame his limbs and terror flooded through his veins ... all that he had brought with him from his own land, including his herds and his asses, everything was carried away to the royal residence together with the captives. As the wretched Libyan chief fled leaving his people among the soldiers [of Egypt] ... the officers of His Majesty's chariotry set themselves after them, felling them with arrows and carrying off dead and captives.

The six-hour arrow bombardment would have demoralized the Libyan army, and their heavily laden baggage train and accompanying herds must have hindered Meryey's retreat making the slaughter of his remaining troops even easier for the Egyptians. Many of the captured warriors were given the option of changing allegiance and joining the Egyptian army, a practice as followed by Ramesses II, recorded on a victory stela erected at his new capital of Pi-Ramesse, on which he described his victory over the Libyans: 'The Tjehenu are overthrown, trampled beneath his feet. By his slaughtering he has seized them. He has captured the western foreign land and has transformed its soldiery into troops of his following.'

The Egyptian army was reinforced by such new conscripts after every campaign, professional soldiers being placed where they could best be employed, while still keeping them under the close surveillance of their officers and the native Egyptian troops. They were usually stationed at border forts and remote outposts, well away from their country of origin. For seasoned warriors this was an attractive proposition and, having sworn fealty to the King of Egypt, they were able to continue in the only profession they knew, some rising to high rank. Scenes of the Battle of Kadesh show that a band of Sherden warriors acted as personal bodyguard to Ramesses II. Prisoners of war who could not or would not join the Egyptian army were drafted into the national corvée as forced labour on royal building works. The more recalcitrant captives were sent to work in the mines and quarries, under guard of some of Egypt's most hard-bitten troops.

Egyptian military activity in the area generally known as Asia, the lands of Canaan and Palestine northwards into Syria, was conducted on a very different level from that against the poorly organized and primitive tribes of Nubia and Libya. Several major powers in the ancient Middle East were eager to control the resources and trade routes of the area. Occasionally another nation of equal sophistication and ambition, like the Hittites or the Assyrians, started to encroach upon the land known as Retjenu to the Egyptians, demanding tribute from people who had previously paid homage to Egypt. From the mid-Eighteenth Dynasty onwards, garrisons were regularly stationed in the major Canaanite towns, with Egyptian governors and administrators to collect taxes and remit tribute to the homeland. The control of the coastal towns of the Lebanon was vital to the Egyptian economy, since it was through them that most of the essential timber trade was conducted. The goddess Hathor, known as Lady of the Sycamore probably because of her association with trees, was also worshipped as patroness of the city of Byblos. The ports also provided staging posts and supply depots for Egyptian troops on campaigns in the region.

Egypt's first excursion into Asia with the intention of territorial conquest was in the reign of Ahmose, founder of the Eighteenth

Dynasty. In his army was an officer known as Ahmose son of Abana, to distinguish him from the sovereign whose name he shared, who recorded his illustrious military career on his tomb stela: 'His Majesty was besieging Sharuhen [a town in southern Palestine] ... When His Majesty finally took the city, I captured there two women and took one hand. The King gave me the gold of bravery as well as the captives for slaves.' The taking of a hand referred to the practice of cutting off the right hand of every dead enemy body, so that an accurate count could be made of the slain. If the enemy was of a people who, unlike the Egyptians, did not practise circumcision, the phallus was cut off for the same reason. Piles of these gruesome trophies may be seen in some battle reliefs, including those of Ramesses III at Medinet Habu. The 'gold of bravery' was the ancient Egyptian equivalent of a medal for gallantry, usually taking the form of a necklace or collar of gold beads, but for conspicuous bravery a distinctive gold pendant in the shape of a fly or bee was awarded.

Engineers and carpenters must have been included in any host sent to invest a fortified town (fig. 79). Scaling ladders are depicted in battle scenes as early as the Fifth Dynasty, and Middle Kingdom tomb paintings at Beni Hasan and Thebes show a form of battering ram and a mobile siege tower. Tuthmose III besieged the city of Megiddo for seven months, but was able to leave only a part of his army to maintain the siege while he took the rest to continue the subjugation of the surrounding region before pushing on further

Figure 79 *Siege Warfare*: The walls of towns are symbolically demolished by emblems of Predynastic warlords wielding mattocks.

north. He eventually reached the banks of the Euphrates, the river which marked the northern limit of his grandfather's empire and the boundary between recognized Egyptian territory and that of the Hurrian kingdom of Mitanni, known to the Egyptians as Naharin. There was a guarded neutrality between Egypt and Mitanni for much of the early New Kingdom, maintained by several campaigns to emphasize Egypt's supremacy. Mitannian princesses were sent as brides to Egyptian kings, to reinforce a succession of treaties of non-interference if not mutual support. Mitanni was never as serious a threat to Egypt as other Mesopotamian states, but was a useful buffer between Egypt and the far more sinister presence of the Hittites in Anatolia. Tuthmose III was the first king to cross the Euphrates, almost knocking on the door of Hatti itself: 'My Majesty travelled to the furthest limits of Asia. I had many vessels of cedar wood built in the mountains of God's Land [Lebanon] in the neighbourhood of the Lady of Byblos [Hathor], which were placed on carts. Oxen dragged them, travelling before my Majesty to cross that great river which flows between this foreign land and Naharin.'

The Egyptians had no sea-going navy as such. They were, however, expert shipbuilders since boats had provided virtually all their transport needs from the beginning of their civilization. Transport boats were an important element of the Egyptian war machine. Troops were ferried from their mustering stations to staging points near to the battle zone. Military boatyards were established at Memphis and, as seen from Tuthmose's words, in the Lebanon. The crews of the military transports were also fighting soldiers. Ahmose son of Abana was one such as he clearly states in his autobiography:

[I am] the chief of sailors, Ahmose, son of Abana. Let me tell you of the honours which came to me [in my military career]. I was presented with the gold of honour seven times in the presence of the whole land. I was given male and female slaves [from the prisoners of war] and endowed with many fields. . . . I served as an officer in the ship 'The Offering' in the time of the Lord of the Two Lands, Nebpehtire-Ahmose, while I was yet a youth. Then, when I had set up a household, I was transferred to the northern fleet because of my valour. I followed the King on foot when he rode in his chariot and when he besieged the city of Avaris [the Hyksos stronghold] I showed such valour before His Majesty that I was promoted to the ship 'Shining in Memphis'.

The Egyptian army of the New Kingdom was supported by a vast organization of craftsmen who made and maintained the weapons, porters and caravaneers, animal handlers, transport officers, commissariat scribes, cooks and the full range of skilled and unskilled workers necessary to the smooth-running of any army. Under reforms enacted by King Horemheb, the armed forces were organized in two main armies for Upper and Lower Egypt. On campaign, the divisions of the army were named after Egypt's national deities. The divisions that went with Ramesses II to Kadesh were named for Amen, Re, Ptah and Seth, gods who, being associated with specific areas of Egypt, might indicate the region from which each division was levied. A division often had an extra title appended to the god's name such as 'Amen, Rich of Bows', a practice still observed in the naming of British regiments like the '3rd County of London Yeomanry, (Sharpshooters)'. A division consisted of about twenty companies, each made up of five platoons of fifty men, and was supported by specialist troops such as archers, foreign auxiliaries and chariotry. There were heralds and standard-bearers, army scribes and scouts attached to each division and a well-defined rank structure for officers. Overall strategy was dictated by a military council which could be overruled by the King as the Supreme Commander of Egypt's forces.

There was opportunity for advancement through the ranks for a talented officer. Princes of the blood took up careers in the forces after military training, and their army companions were likely to be found lucrative offices at court after retirement from active service. Ameneminet, army buddy and charioteer to Ramesses II, became Overseer of Works in Thebes and Controller of the King's mortuary temple complex, now called the Ramesseum, where most of the government offices were situated. For an educated man, the army life was not as black as it was painted by the authors of those dire warnings to student scribes. However, for the mass of enlisted and conscripted men, life as a soldier was hard and had little reward, apart from the opportunity to travel and this was really the last thing that any true Egyptian wanted to do.

Hieroglyphs associated with the Soldier

mace with pear-
shaped head,
'white', 'silver'

axe

dagger in sheath,
'first', 'chief'

arms holding
shield and battle-
axe, 'to fight'

throwstick,
symbolic of foreign
tribes

two bows tied in a
package, symbol of
the goddess Neith

soldier with bow
and arrows,
'troops'

bowstring

bow made from
oryx horns joined
by a wooden
centre-piece

archaic type of
bow

composite bow
with middle tied to
bowstring when out
of use

arrow

CHAPTER 9

Men at the Top

•

EXCAVATION OF MAJOR cemeteries at Abydos, Nagada and Saqqara has revealed a great deal of information about the social structure of the civilization at the beginning of the Dynastic Age. The impressive funerary monuments erected by the early rulers were surrounded by the equally grand tombs of their families and followers. The kings shown on the first 'documents' such as the Scorpion Macehead and the Narmer Palette are always attended by servants or courtiers whose presence emphasizes the importance of their leader, while at the same time declaring their own superior status. In their tombs this superiority was asserted in inscriptions on their stelae and personal possessions. This demonstration of literacy and the ability to employ the best craftsmen, proclaimed their membership of a very privileged élite. The tombs themselves were arranged according to the rank of their owners. Those closest to the monarch in death were likely to have been those closest to him in life.

This principle seems to have been carried to extremes in the Archaic Period, when First Dynasty royal monuments at Abydos and Saqqara were surrounded by subsidiary burials of personal servants and court officials, who were buried with their masters so that they might continue to serve them in the next world. There is little positive evidence that these were ritual killings, nor even that they all died at the same time. The bodies show no obvious signs of death by violence, nor were the victims buried alive, as was the case in the royal death pits of Sumer or the Nubian royal graves of Kerma. The Egyptians were a highly practical people who would not have wanted to deprive a new king of the experience and expertise of craftsmen and administrators who had served his predecessors. Possibly, the deaths were natural and the corpses were stored away against the inevitable demise of the King. Servants so honoured achieved an immortality not granted to most of their peers. From the rudimentary grave stones which marked many of the subsidiary burials, it appears that only lower ranking officials were chosen to accompany the dead Kings. Their more affluent and influential superiors had their own tombs, some of which were surrounded by their own servant burials. The practice had fallen into disuse by the end of the Second Dynasty, after which the custom of burying real people was replaced by that of preparing reliefs, paintings and elaborate tomb models to serve the same purpose.

The officials of the administration were very proud of their position in the hierarchy which they proclaimed by prefixing their personal names with strings of titles, a custom well established by the beginning of the Old Kingdom. The titles themselves, and the style of language in which they were phrased, varied over the centuries so that, for example, designations which originally indicated agricultural roles were adopted as administrative titles, and those who appear to have been personal and household servants of the King were often far more active in government than their titles might suggest. Some titles represented a degree of prestige not apparent in their literal meaning, with deceptively simple epithets being applied to the holders of some of Egypt's most important administrative posts. Titles declined in significance as others were adapted or new titles invented to accommodate changes in Egypt's circumstances.

Seal stones, each inscribed with an official's name and principal title, were essential for conducting everyday business. The oldest form of seal was the cylinder carved from a soft stone like steatite or jasper, or from ivory, or even cast in metal. The seal impression was made by rolling the cylinder over a layer of smooth clay, such as that used to seal the pottery caps on storage jars, or over the mass of mud used to secure the knots which held lids in place or prevented bolts from being drawn. The pierced seal stone could be suspended on a cord or beaded string around the owner's neck. Some seals were mounted on a wire fixed across a rectangular wooden frame which functioned in the same way as the handle of a paint roller, allowing the seal to be rolled in a single smooth

Figure 80 *Button Seal*: An early form of rubber stamp, this sort of seal would have been used to mark ownership. This example bears the name of Amen-Re, god of Thebes.

movement to form a long continuous band of the seal inscription. Single impressions were made by stamp seals which were small, round or oval, and had a pinch grip like a miniature rubber stamp (fig. 80). This sort of seal is known from the late Old Kingdom and its shape has led to the designation 'button seal', but they were not used as fastenings for clothing. The seal was threaded on to a cord so that it could be firmly tied to the wrist or even round a finger. The form of the signet ring originated in this simple method of keeping the seal safe and available for immediate use (fig. 81). Larger seals with handles were carved from wood and were used for making impressions on mudbricks or in the layer of plaster covering the stone blocks used to seal a tomb entrance (fig. 82).

From the Middle Kingdom onwards, the most common shape for a seal was the scarab beetle. The flat underside bore the incised name or distinctive pattern while the body of the beetle was carved more or less carefully, depending on the importance of the seal and the rank of the owner. Many scarab seals were made in faience, but the best quality examples were carved from stone. The size varied from large commemorative scarabs, like those issued to announce special events in the reign of Amenhotep III, to small seals like those set in signet rings. Most scarabs were pierced longitudinally so that they could be suspended on a neck cord or swivel-mounted on a finger ring. Rectangular or oval plaques carved on both sides were also used in signet rings.

Seal stones, scarabs and the impressions made by them are often the only evidence for the existence of certain officials. The holder of any significant position in the administration would have been presented with a seal as the insignia of his office, a practice

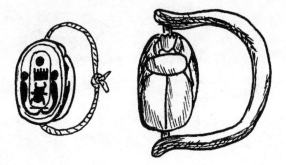

Figure 81 *Development of the Signet Ring*: As a wire replaced the original cord which tied a seal to the owner's finger, the seal stone became the bezel of a ring.

referred to in the Biblical account of Joseph's appointment as Pharaoh's advisor:

> ... 'You shall be in charge of my household, and all my people will depend on your every word ...' Pharaoh said to Joseph, 'I hereby give you authority over the whole land of Egypt.' He took off his signet ring and put it on Joseph's finger. He had him dressed in fine linen, and hung a gold chain round his neck. . . . Thus Pharaoh made him the ruler over all Egypt.

The historical accuracy of this account is questionable, but the presentation of the seal and chain of office was a feature common to many ancient civilizations in the Middle East, and certainly in Egypt where every official wore a seal as a symbol of his rank.

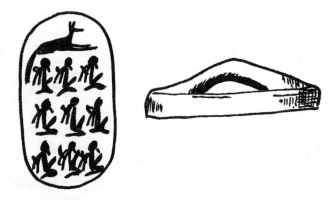

Figure 82 *For Sealing the Tomb*: A large wooden seal with a handle was used to impress the plaster sealing the doors of royal tombs with the symbol of the royal necropolis – the jackal and nine captives.

The sign of a cylinder or rectangular seal stone suspended on a cord was the earliest hieroglyph used for the title which is generally translated as Chancellor, the 'Keeper of the Royal Seal', who was among the most powerful men in Egypt. One of the earliest identified holders of this title was Hemaka, who served King Den of the First Dynasty. The finds from his Saqqara tomb, which rivals in size that of the King himself, comprise the largest single collection of material from the period so far discovered. There, and at monuments of the same reign at Abydos, Hemaka's name and titles feature prominently on labels and jar sealings. He claimed the honorific title 'Ruling in the King's heart', a description of how close he was to the King and therefore of the influence he wielded in the country as a whole (fig. 83). The size of Hemaka's tomb and the quality of its contents imply that he was a man of substance as well as authority. The inclusion among his tomb furniture of a scroll of papyrus, the earliest example of the writing material yet found in Egypt, also indicates the importance placed upon literacy and the recording of information in writing. The ebony tag used to label a jar of oil bears a scene of the King celebrating his jubilee, an event in which Hemaka would have officiated over the receiving and storing of gifts and the release of supplies for the festival. Although little more is known about Hemaka, since he left no formal biography in his tomb and even the papyrus scroll was blank, the principle of the King appointing talented men from the ranks of his followers to important offices in the central administration was already well established by his time.

Figure 83 *Seal Bearer of the King*: Part of a label inscription from the tomb of Hemaka, giving his title as 'King's Seal Bearer' or Chancellor, and indicating the area of his authority – the King's House.

The position of Chancellor was always recognized as a senior government appointment. Wealth was power and a King who could advertise his wealth, in the magnificence of the monuments he built and by his generosity to his loyal followers, proclaimed himself a powerful ruler. The controller of this wealth, the person who knew most about the income and expenditure of the royal treasuries, was almost as powerful as his master. This very power put the Chancellor in a position which could be seen as threatening to the King's authority. The rash of Royal Seal Bearers that erupted in the latter part of the Old Kingdom may represent an attempt to limit the power of any one individual by delegating different areas of responsibility to an ever larger band of lesser-ranking officials (fig. 84). The power of the Chancellor in overall authority was curbed by the accountability of layers of bureaucracy.

Figure 84 *Treasure Under the Bed*: The Vizier relaxes as his wife plays the harp. Beneath them is a collection of sealed jars and boxes labelled 'the best of the sealed things [treasure] – gold, every sort of oil, and linen'.

During the First Intermediate Period, several dynasties ruled from different centres over very limited regions and sometimes simultaneously. The provincial nobility of Thebes founded the Eleventh Dynasty taking control of the whole country at the start of the Middle Kingdom, their success partly dependent on the skills they commanded within the ranks of their followers. Tjetji, the Chancellor who served Intef II and Intef III left an expansive account of his work on his stela which is now in the British Museum:

> ... I was one loved by his lord, praised by him every day. I spent many years in the service of my Lord, the King of Upper and Lower Egypt, Son of Re, Intef, while this land was under his command from Yebu to This, I being his personal servant, his chamberlain in very truth. He made me great, he advanced my rank, he took me into his confidence in his private residence. The treasure was in my hand, under my seal, being the best of everything brought to His Majesty from all Egypt ... as tribute from this entire land, because the whole land was in fear of him ... I accounted for eveything to my Lord without ever having fault found with my administration, so great was my competence. ... I did not overstep the authority he vested in me. ... I took no bribe for the accomplishing of any task. ... every royal duty that my lord entrusted to me I carried out exactly as he desired. ... I am wealthy, I am great. I have provided for myself from my own property that was given to me by my Lord because of his great love for me.

This sounds very impressive, but the area of authority claimed by Intef, from Yebu to This, represented only eight of the traditional forty-two provinces of Egypt. His claim to be King of Upper and Lower Egypt was very ambitious, since he was really no more than a local prince who had acquired a slightly broader sphere of influence than his predecessors or his immediate neighbours, putting Tjetji's grandiose claims rather more into perspective. His authority was based entirely on that of his master. His rank and his success have to be judged accordingly.

The title of Royal Seal Bearer continued to appear in lists of titles well into the New Kingdom, as in inscriptions from the Memphite tomb of Horemheb, now in the British Museum. Horemheb's list is a particularly good example of the wide range of duties claimed, if not actually exercised, by the highest officials in the land. The inclusion of the title which, in earlier times, would have been rendered as Chancellor is a further indication that the significance of such a title is not always easy to determine. Egyptian government was basically autocratic, with the King having absolute power over everyone and everything in his realm, but the Kings of Egypt learned in the very beginning that the support of loyal and efficient officials was essential to their continuing in power.

Officials were not elected, they answered only to their immediate superiors and ultimately to the King himself. It is tempting to call the holders of the principal court offices Ministers of State, with the highest-ranking forming an Inner Cabinet, rather than employing the ubiquitous term 'overseer', as a translation of the title *imy-r*, which applied to almost any senior or middle-ranking official in every level of the administration and in all departments, and so generally that the subtleties of its use are now completely lost. The expression *imy-r* was used throughout the Dynastic era in the titles of both state appointed officials and those in the households of the nobility. The sign used as an abbreviation for this expression was the stylized tongue of an animal, so that the *imy-r*, meaning 'he who is in the mouth', was seen to be one who spoke with the authority of his master or perhaps was thought to act on every word that fell from his master's lips. One application of *imy-r* was in the title 'Overseer of the House of Silver', which may be translated as Treasurer. The Treasurer of all Egypt was known as the 'Overseer of the Double House of Silver', in recognition of the traditional dual nature of the Egyptian state. The Treasurer was effectively the Finance Minister, though his authority in the area of taxation had to be shared with another *imy-r*, the 'Overseer of the Double Granary', just as the Chancellor's control over royal expenditure was also shared with the Royal Steward, a title literally translated as 'Overseer of the King's House'. As early as the First Dynasty there seems to have been a recognized order of precedence for listing official titles, with some honorific or hereditary titles being cited before those relating to royal or administrative appointments. The upper echelons of Egyptian society acknowledged a class structure, but a talented man could work his way up to achieve high rank, though he was always conscious of his origins. Ptah-hotep was very clear on this point: 'If you are poor, serve a worthy man that all your conduct may put you in good stead. . . . Do not recall if he too once was poor, do not be arrogant towards him for knowing his former state; respect him for what he has achieved by his own efforts for wealth does not come by itself . . .'

A code of conduct clearly existed for those in high office or having anything to do with the administration: 'If you work in a government department stand and sit according to the rank you were assigned on your first day. Do not trespass [on another's preserve] for you will only be rebuffed. [The King] will observe any who is announced as he enters and a good seat will be found for one who has been summoned by name. The department has a code by which all behaviour is judged. The King [alone] gives advancement. He who elbows his way to the front will do himself no favours.'

Ptah-hotep also had advice for an official who wanted to advance his career: 'If you are a worthy man who sits in his master's council, concentrate on excellence. Your silence is far better than chatter. Speak only when you know you have something useful to say for the skilled should speak in council. . . . If you are in a position of authority, gain respect through knowledge and gentleness of speech. Do not order people about more than necessary for provocation breeds discontent. Do not be haughty lest you be humbled. . . . When answering one who is angry, keep calm. . . . He who walks with care finds a smooth path . . .'

This very idealistic advice was much more difficult to follow than it was to give but Ptah-hotep stated that the rewards for living according to this code were great: 'If a good example is set by him who leads, he will be recognized as a good man for ever, his wisdom will last for all time. . . . The wise man is known by his wisdom, the great by his actions. Acting with truth [Maat] he is free of falsehood.'

Those officials whose duties put them in closest contact with the King and the royal family claimed to be 'known to the King', a title which is often translated as Royal Acquaintance. This designation was proudly held by both men and women (fig. 85). During the Old Kingdom, Royal Acquaintances formed an inner circle of courtiers with no particular brief, people from whom, perhaps, the

Figure 85 *The King's Acquaintance*: A lady of the court is proud to give her title as 'known to the King', indicating her position in the most exalted company of the King's friends.

King could seek opinions if not advice on a variety of matters. Possibly the most significant role for the Royal Acquaintances was to enable the King to converse in a less formal manner than the precise etiquette of the Court demanded. They were the nearest equivalent to friends that the god-king of Egypt could hope to have. Next below this favoured band was the rank of courtier or Companion which was often augmented with the adjective 'unique' or 'only', to create the expression Sole Companion, showing that this was an honorific title since not every Companion could be the King's only friend. A further rank with no obvious link to any particular government department was defined by the phrase 'he who is over the secrets of the King's house', which could best be translated as Privy Councillor, someone who was given access to all the most intimate matters concerning the administration of the royal residence.

Many of these close associates of the King also held noble titles by right of birth. The provincial ruling families, from whose ranks in most cases the Kings themselves ultimately derived, were necessarily admitted into the government, for to exclude such influential and wealthy nobles from power would have been courting disaster. The terms *rep-a* and *haty-a* were those most commonly used by the nobility and might equate to Duke and Count or Baron. *Rep-a* is usually translated as Hereditary Prince, while the title *haty-a* underwent a gradual demotion in status over the centuries. Originally applied to a provincial governor or nomarch, *haty-a* was frequently held as a subsidiary title by a *rep-a*. Later it was used to designate lesser nobility and senior local officials who were appointed to their posts, rather than having been born to them. By the New Kingdom the term *haty-a* was used by a wide range of officials who might be called 'mayor' or 'headman'. Provincial nobles often held priestly offices associated with their local cults but their most significant posts, those for which they received material rewards, were the appointments to the important departments of the central government.

The text, known as the *Instruction to King Merikare*, is thought to be a statement of intent by a king of that name who ruled during the First Intermediate Period. Written as if by one of his predecessors, it sets out advice as to how a king should govern and the author was very precise about how the monarch should treat his nobles:

Promote your officials so that they continue to enforce your laws. He who has wealth of his own will be impartial. He who lacks nothing is already a rich man [so has no need to take bribes] while the poor man cannot be trusted to speak fairly since he who says 'I wish I had . . .' will incline to whoever will pay him. Great indeed is the great man whose own great men are great. Strong is the king who has good councillors. Wealthy is he who is rich in his nobles (fig. 86).

Merikare was also advised to seek out talent and not to waste it.

Do not prefer the wellborn to the commoner. Choose a man for his skills. . . . Do not kill one who is close to you for he whom you have favoured is thus known to the gods and he is one of the most

Figure 86 *Service Rewarded*: Horemheb is invested with numerous collars of gold beads as rewards for his service to King Tutankhamen.

fortunate dwellers on this earth. . . . Make yourself loved by everyone, a good character will always be remembered.

The key areas of the administration were the Treasury, the Department of Agriculture, the Ministry of Works, the judiciary and the army. In earliest times many of these departments were headed by members of the King's own family. The most prestigious title of all, which emerged in the Second Dynasty, was that of *Tjaty*. This title is conventionally translated as Vizier, a suitably oriental and exotic title for an official whose designated duties covered as many and as great a variety of roles as those claimed by Gilbert and Sullivan's Pooh-Bah. The origin of the word *tjaty* is doubtful. The distinguishing hieroglyph used for this most important title was the duckling or pigeon squab with stubby wings and gaping beak. The sign was used to represent maleness and it is thought that in the title *Tjaty*, the duckling represented the idea of 'The Man' of Egypt in contrast with the King who was 'The God'. This sets the position of *Tjaty* at the very pinnacle of Egyptian society and second only to the King in the authority he wielded.

Little is known about the *Tjatys* and their duties in the Old and Middle Kingdoms, except that they held positions of considerable influence. Almost every *Tjaty* of the Fourth Dynasty, for example, combined the title with that of Overseer of Works for the royal monuments. This was always a very important post, the holder having access to and control over vast resources in terms of both materials and manpower. Perhaps for this reason, the kings of the Fourth Dynasty appointed their own sons to this position, believing that keeping the power within the family was safer than trusting to the questionable loyalty of their followers. During the Fifth and Sixth Dynasties many of the *Tjatys* were related to the King by marriage. Mereruka was married to a daughter of his master King Teti, and his son, Mery-teti became Vizier to Pepi I, taking the honorific title of King's Son even though he was only the grandson of a King. The influence of the *Tjaty* was even more clearly displayed at the accession of Pepi II. The King's mother was one of two sisters, daughters of the provincial governor Khuy of Abydos, both of whom had in turn become the Chief Wife of Pepi I. When Pepi II became King he was still a child so his mother acted as Regent in his minority, with the guidance of her brother the Vizier Djau. This *Tjaty* was brother-in-law to one King and uncle to two more, and for several years his was the power behind the throne. The Kings around this time may have thought it expedient to ensure the loyalty of a particularly powerful family by tying it firmly to the Crown by marriage, or the family may already have become so powerful that the nobles were able to dictate to the King as to his choice of wife and supreme officials.

In the reign of Montuhotep IV at the end of the Eleventh Dynasty, the King sent his Vizier Amenemhet to the quarries of the Wadi Hammamat to fetch the huge block of stone for the royal sarcophagus. Graffiti recording the event state that the Vizier took with him a military escort of 20,000 men, which seems excessive even allowing for the hauling crew required for such a large rock. The expedition was attended by miraculous happenings, such as an antelope giving birth on the very stone chosen for the lid of the sarcophagus. The *Tjaty* Amenemhet interpreted this as a good omen and, taking advantage of the military power at his disposal, staged a *coup d'état*. The Middle Kingdom document known as the *Prophecies of Neferti* implies that at the time, the Eleventh Dynasty had lost all control of the country: 'I show you a land in turmoil. The weak have become strong. One bows to another who once bowed to him. Everything is topsy-turvy . . .'

The author of the *Prophecies* set his story in Old Kingdom times, though the text was more a piece of political propaganda than a work of fiction and was intended to justify the rise to power of the Twelfth Dynasty. The Vizier Amenemhet, a name regularly abbreviated to Ameny, became the first King of that dynasty as 'predicted' by Neferti: 'Then a king will come from the South, Ameny, the justified, by name, . . . a child of Upper Egypt. He will take the White Crown and he will wear the Red Crown. He will [again] unite the Two Ladies. . . . A son of the people will make his name for all eternity.'

Amenemhet I had good reason to fear the power of his ministers. Another document, composed probably during the reign of his successor Senusert I, but written as if by the spirit of the old King himself, warned his son of the dangers posed by disaffected nobles.

> Beware of subjects who are not close to you, who can plot in secret without anyone knowing their schemes. Trust no one, not even a brother or a friend. Make no favourites, form no close attachments. . . . When you lie down, look to your own protection for when the day of woe comes, no man has supporters. . . . I gave success to the poor as to the rich but he who ate my food rebelled [against me]. He in whom I had placed my trust misused it and plotted against me. . . . If one does battle without learning from history, he will have no success.

The text describes how the King was assassinated, treacherously attacked in his bedroom at night with no guard within earshot to come to his aid. His main regret was that he had not anticipated the situation, especially in view of the way in which he himself had come to the throne: 'I had not prepared for it, I had not expected it, I had not foreseen the treachery of my servants.'

Of all the servants to be feared, the *Tjaty* was the most influential. The duties of the Vizier encompassed so many vital aspects of life at court, and in the country as a whole, that he was, as often claimed by such high officials, 'the eyes and ears of the King'. Since the *Tjaty*, unlike the King, was not constrained by religious duties and royal protocol, he had more freedom of movement and action than his master. A loyal and efficient *Tjaty* was a great asset to the King. An ambitious or greedy Vizier was a liability.

Basically, the administration of the country was divided into four major areas of responsibility, the demarcation between them being more or less sharply defined at different periods. The Chancellory or Royal Treasury controlled the Royal Domain, including the income from royal estates, the King's personal possessions and the running of his palaces and his household (fig. 87). The Priesthood controlled the next greatest land-holding, with a considerable income from their estates and authority over large numbers of workers. The Army Department was only really important in times

Figure 87 *Treasury Business*: Ingots and articles made of precious metals, including copper and bronze, were weighed to establish their value.

of war, though, as shown in the case of Amenemhet I, the man who controlled the armed forces was in a potentially powerful position. Virtually everything else came under the auspices of the Vizier.

The way in which the Vizierate was organized during the Middle Kingdom is not known in any detail. The Eleventh Dynasty kings had allowed the provincial nobles who had supported their rise to power a fairly free hand in the governing of their own regions. The hereditary princes took on the responsibilities and also the rewards of government, and the clearest evidence for this decentralization is found in the provincial cemeteries, where the nomarchs chose to build their tombs in preference to having burial places allocated to them in the royal cemetery. The Kings of the later Twelfth Dynasty started to curb the ambitions and reduce the influence of the provincial nobility by giving more and more power to their officials, some of whom were chosen from the ranks of the nobles themselves. In doing so, the Kings created a Vizierate that was far more powerful than perhaps they had ever intended it to become. The ten Kings of the Thirteenth Dynasty maintained a relative stability throughout the country, ruling from the north, but their succession was not as clearly hereditary as that of their Viziers.

Towards the end of the Middle Kingdom, the *Tjaty's* duties were defined for the first time in detail. A document, which is now known as the *Duties of the Vizier*, was drawn up as a formal job description for the office and was inscribed in the tombs of several New Kingdom Viziers, most notably that of Rekhmire, the Vizier in the latter years of Tuthmose III and into the reign of Amenhotep II. The vivid scenes of craftsmen at work, the reception of foreign tribute and the dispensing of justice painted in Rekhmire's tomb give a broad outline of the many and varied responsibilities that went with the title *Tjaty*. Apart from some private estates and many religious foundations which were granted tax exemption, everything in Egypt was liable to assessment for tax purposes. Officials of the central administration, some established in provincial sub-departments, paid regular visits to all taxable properties. Census reports were returned on everything from crops to herds, from orchards to the output of craft workshops. Household census lists from Kahun show that even the people themselves were included in the system. Their labour could be commanded for the royal corvée, even if they produced nothing else in material terms which could be taxed. The grain stores and strongrooms in which the tax payments were kept were under the control of the Overseer of the Granaries and the Overseer of the Treasury, who in turn reported to the *Tjaty*. Gifts from foreign powers and tribute from vassal and conquered territories including war booty was delivered to the Vizier, who saw to its distribution to various storehouses throughout the country and allocated it as directed by the King for use in royal building projects and as donations of all sorts to religious foundations. Under the title of High Priest of Maat, the *Tjaty* was also the supreme judge and so had a major role to play in maintaining law and order (fig. 88). All local magistrates and

Figure 88 *Maat*: The goddess of justice, patron of lawyers and guardian of the scales, wears the feather of truth in her headband and is shown with wings outspread in an attitude of protection.

the *kenbet* courts, the councils of community leaders who met to deal with purely parochial legal matters and minor misdemeanours, were answerable to the Vizier. The *Tjaty* controlled the hiring and firing of administrative personnel at all levels, and in theory any complaint about the conduct of a government official could be taken to the Vizer's court.

The Vizier had access to an extensive messenger network covering the whole country. The overseers of local police forces reported from their guard-posts on the security situation in their regions, including problems caused by people trying to avoid call-up to the national corvée. The *Tjaty* was responsible for the management of the land itself and he issued orders to local government officials, particularly in relation to agricultural tasks and work associated with the irrigation system. The Vizier received daily reports from many agencies and dispatched orders to regional officials.

As a subsidiary title, the *Tjaty* was also known as the Governor of the City, which related to the Royal Residence. This was far more than a single palace or even a personal estate for the King and his family, having more in common with the modern concept of a national capital or centre of government. The Residence City constituted a substantial business concern, as well as an administrative centre with many inter-related departments which mirrored the organization of the country as a whole. At its heart was the House of the King, a formal complex of buildings including the royal storehouses, treasuries and craft workshops – collectively known as the House of Gold – the Reception Hall, which was used as a court of justice as well as a formal audience chamber, the offices of all the principal government ministers, the official residence of the Vizier himself, and the *Per-aa*, the private living quarters of the King. This last expression – literally the Great House – came to be used as a noun representing not just the building but the concept of the authority resident in it. The term was used to refer to that authority in much the same way that the complete organization of the British monarchy is often referred to simply as Buckingham Palace. Eventually the expression *Per-aa* became a euphemism for the King himself, and during the Ptolemaic Period it was enclosed in a cartouche and used as a royal title (fig. 89). The Greeks adapted its pronunciation to Pharaoh, hence the title

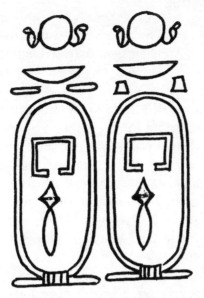

Figure 89 *The Great House*: The term 'great house' became the universally-recognized title Pharaoh under the Ptolemies. Here it is shown in cartouches with the titles 'Lord of the Two Lands' and 'Lord of Thrones'.

most universally used to designate a King of Egypt. In fact, the expression was not commonly used as a royal title until comparatively late in Dynastic history.

In practice, though the King was the ruler of the Royal Domain, the *Tjaty* was its Managing Director and to keep the business running smoothly he had daily conferences with the Royal Treasurer. The Vizier was responsible for the security and the efficient working of the Royal Residence, while the Treasurer and the Royal Steward took charge of its day-to-day management. The Vizier was informed of all comings and goings of both people and goods, ordered the opening and closing of doors and gateways, and his office issued permits for travel on state business and approved the use of the royal messenger service. When the King himself travelled outside the Residence City, the Vizier took charge of all arrangements, gathering together the necessary escort and choosing which of the King's officials should accompany him. The King's House was wherever the King was, and as manager of the King's House the Vizier necessarily travelled with the King. Other important officials may not have been so lucky, since their offices were often duplicated. For example, it was not uncommon for the King to maintain households in at least two cities, with a Chief Steward in charge of each, and Treasurers were appointed to major storehouses such as those attached to the royal mortuary temples. In some circumstances, the *Tjaty* acted as his master's private secretary, keeping the King up to date with all home affairs. The *Tjaty* was the mediator between the King and any petitioner of sufficient rank to be granted access to royal justice. Such cases often related to questions of land tenure and boundary disputes, since all the land of Egypt, in theory, belonged to the King. The Vizier received foreign delegations on his master's behalf, except when a ruling prince visited Egypt in person. On these rare occasions the King himself received the envoys.

Because the duties were so far-reaching and so time-consuming, the institution of the Vizierate in the Eighteenth Dynasty was split, with two officials of equal status ruling from the northern and southern capitals of Memphis and Thebes. This dilution of authority also helped to ensure that no one man should ever again acquire power enough to rival the King. The Vizier was appointed by the King and, unlike the situation in some other professions or offices, the post was not obviously hereditary. Little evidence for the existence of the northern Viziers has survived from Memphis itself, but the information from Thebes, especially the inscriptions in the tombs of several Theban Viziers and their families, provides a reasonable picture of how life was conducted and organized at the top of Egyptian society.

A good Vizier was rarely replaced when a new King came to the throne. The change-over of power had to be as smooth as possible, and sweeping away the old administration was a waste of human resources. When Ramesses II succeeded his father Seti I, he inherited the services of the Theban Vizier Paser, who continued to serve his new master for perhaps as long as twenty-five years, and for the last ten years or so of his life also performed ceremonial duties as the High Priest of Amen. Paser's father had been High Priest at the Karnak Temple, the senior religious office in Egypt during the New Kingdom, and in several cases the Vizierate and the High Priesthood had been held by one and the same man, as was the case with Hapusoneb, the *Tjaty* in Thebes under

Hatshepsut. In the tomb of Rekhmire, the Vizier is shown over-seeing many activities in the workshops of the temple of Amen, including the production of special festival bread for the sacred offerings. In the reign of Ramesses III, the Vizier Tua was sent to gather together the cult statues of Egypt's principal deities and escort them to Memphis for the celebration of the King's jubilee festival.

The southern Vizier was also responsible for the village of the Royal Workmen at Deir el-Medina. The skilled craftsmen and builders who excavated and decorated the royal tombs were paid for their labours by the state. Their regular rations, and extra supplies paid as bonuses or for special occasions, were released from the royal stores at the Vizier's orders. Any misconduct, dispute or crime that could not be dealt with by the village's *kenbet* court was referred to the Vizier for judgment. The Workmen, supported from the royal treasuries, expected the Vizier to ensure that they were paid all that was due to them and on time. The failure of the system in Year 29 of the reign of Ramesses III led to the earliest recorded strike. The Scribe of the Tomb, Amen-nakht, recorded the reason for the dispute on an ostracon: 'This day is the twentieth of the month and still our rations have not arrived.'

Disgusted with this cavalier treatment the Workmen downed tools and marched to the mortuary temple of Horemheb, demanding that their wages be released from the granaries there. Some grain was at last issued, but the problems continued, one underlying reason being that the Vizier was otherwise occupied as Amen-nakht recorded at the time: 'The office of the King promoted the Vizier Tua to be the Vizier of both Upper and Lower Egypt.' Tua, now Vizier of the whole country, was actually away from Thebes on his religious escort duty when trouble erupted and the Workmen again went on strike. When they marched down to the valley once more to claim their overdue pay they made an impassioned plea to the authorities: 'Hunger and thirst have driven us to these lengths. We have no clothing, no fat, no fish, no vegetables. Send word to the King our good Lord about this matter, send word to the Vizier our superior that we may be provided for.' When at last Tua came to hear of their grievances he sent a message via the Chief of Police,

Montmose: 'It was not because I had nothing to offer you that I did not come in person. As for you saying, "Do not give away our due rations", why should I as Vizier give with one hand only to take away with the other? If I had found that there was nothing to give, even in the granaries, I would have given you whatever I could find.'

The situation seems to have arisen as a result of a combination of events, including several poor harvests and a lack of proper administration of the supplies delivered to and released from the royal storehouses. The age-old problem of corruption in high places was exacerbated by the absence of the Vizier from Thebes for longer periods, as his extended duties kept him in the northern capital. Though self-righteous officials would claim, as did the Treasurer Tjetji, that they never took bribes, there was ample opportunity within the Egyptian system for embezzlement. Corrupt officials were responsible for the loss of considerable amounts of state and temple income including an estimated 90 per cent loss in annual corn revenues suffered by one temple alone as a result of maladministration at every level.

Nor was corruption the King's only cause for concern. A cryptic entry in the Great Harris Papyrus, which deals with all the benefactions that Ramesses III made to the temples during his reign, seems to mention an attempted rebellion by an unnamed Vizier, centred on the Temple of Horus in the Delta town of Athribis:

> I arranged the administration of this august house. . . . It was set in decrees carved in stone in the god's name, forever. I set priests and inspectors of his house to administer its workforce . . . I cast out the Vizier who had entered into their midst. I deprived him of all his followers who were with him. I made it one of the great temples of this land, protected and defended forever. I brought back again all its personnel who had been cast out [by the Vizier] with every official appointed to carry on their administration.

When so little is known about the northern Vizierate, it is impossible to put even a name to the *Tjaty* mentioned in this passage, let alone to speculate on the nature of the crime against the state which apparently led him to seek sanctuary with all his followers in the temple itself.

Figure 90 *Commander of the Army*: Horemheb, the Great Commander of the Troops and King's Scribe, amongst a long list of other titles, here claims to be 'the favoured one of the Good God'.

The Vizier played only a minor role in foreign policy which, in ancient Egyptian terms, meant war. During the reign of Tutankhamen, Horemheb held practically every official title available except that of Vizier, which was incompatible with his appointment as Commander in Chief of the Army (fig. 90). In most reigns the King himself took charge of the armed forces, or appointed one of his sons to that position. A serving Vizier is recorded as seeing military action, and that was during the Asiatic campaign of Ramesses II which culminated in the Battle of Kadesh. Surprised by Hittite chariot forces, the King needed to call up reinforcements to prevent a disaster and he sent as his messenger the most senior non-combatant official available, his Vizier, who, though unnamed, could conceivably have been the faithful Paser: 'Then the Vizier was ordered to hurry along the army of His Majesty, which was still advancing south of Shabtuna, in order to bring them as quickly as possible to the place where His Majesty was.'

Though such activities were strictly outside those prescribed in the *Duties of the Vizier*, the description of his office that Paser had had inscribed in his own tomb, the holder of such a prestigious office had to be adaptable. The position that required the abilities to balance the interests of many different people, to keep the peace between the disparate departments under his control, to remain impartial in all matters and to maintain a dignified appearance at all times, was not a job for the faint-hearted. Of all Egyptian officials the *Tjaty* is perhaps the most entitled to call himself 'the King's True Courtier, he who does everything that his Lord desires'.

Hieroglyphs associated with the Men at the Top

cylinder seal attached to bead necklace, symbol of office-holder

tongue of an ox (?), 'overseer'

duckling, 'male'

CHAPTER 10

The King

•

THE KING OCCUPIED the highest position in Egyptian society, like the capstone of a pyramid. The King of Egypt was a god incarnate, a priest and a warrior, who kept aloof from the toiling majority of his people who were prepared to fight and, if necessary, to die for him. Despite his inaccessibility, the King was far more than a figurehead monarch performing purely ceremonial duties. He was at the centre of all things Egyptian, in fact, in a very real sense, he was Egypt.

The Egyptian method of recording history was to make lists of kings. The naming of the leaders of society achieved the same purpose as the modern historical record of events arranged as a continuous narrative. The name encompassed everything that was essentially true about a person. Speculation, commentary and criticism about deeds and motives were irrelevant. The papyrus known as the *Turin Canon*, dating from about 1200 BC, lists over 300 kings, grouping them in families or dynasties, but provides little more historical information than the lengths of their reigns and an occasional terse statement about a significant event. The Palermo Stone appears to hold more information, with its year-by-year account of each reign, but the events considered important by the compiling scribe are not of the dramatic historical significance that might be expected. For example, one of the two remaining year boxes ascribed to a king of the earliest period, contains the entries 'Worship of Horus' and 'Birth of Anubis', both referring to religious festivals. In the nine boxes relating to the next king, all but two references are to religious events, and one of the remaining entries relates to the building of a temple. Conducting the religious affairs of the country was seen as one of the King's

principal functions, if not the most important. From the very beginning of Egyptian Dynastic history the special relationship between
the King and the gods defined the kingship itself.

The Turin Canon names semi-mythical kings of the Predynastic
era and calls them 'Followers of Horus'. Horus was the first divine
patron of the Kings of Egypt and the King was known as Horus.
The hawk standard of the god was used as the hieroglyph for the
personal pronoun when applied to the King. Later tradition gave
divine approval to the exercise of the kingship by Horus, as a
result of his legal action before the gods, the culmination of his
centuries-long battle with his rival Seth. The two gods had been
brothers in the earliest form of the divine family, but in the later
version of the myth cycle Horus was Seth's nephew. The argument
centred around the rights to the throne of Egypt, originally occupied by Osiris. Horus claimed his father's throne as his inheritance,
but Seth challenged that right since Horus had been conceived and
born after the death of Osiris. The supreme sun-god Re presided
over the trial, of which an account is given in one of the Chester
Beatty Papyri in Dublin. After much vacillation, Re eventually gave
judgment to Horus and confirmed him as King of Egypt in his
father's place. Seth was persuaded to relinquish his claim with the
offer of a place in the crew of Re's celestial bark, and with the
promise that his voice would become the sound of thunder. In a
later version of the story, written on the Shabaka Stone, now in
the British Museum, the judge in the case was Geb, the earth-god,
who gave Horus the land of Egypt as his rightful inheritance, and
compensated Seth with lordship over the desert and all foreign
lands. Seth was recognized as the god of storm, chaos, violence
and, to some extent, evil, but whatever dastardly deeds were accredited to Seth, he remained a royal god and patron of the King, who
needed the goodwill of both Horus and Seth to confirm his own
kingship.

The patronage of Horus and Seth was an essential aspect of the
overall duality of Egypt itself. The Pyramid Texts include references to the roles of the Two Lords, as in the hymn for 'awakening'
the dead King: '... Cause the Two Lands to bow to this King
even as they bow to Horus; cause the Two Lands to dread this
King even as they dread Seth.'

Seth continued to be shown as a tutor of the King, especially in the arts of war. The occupying Hyksos princes in the Delta region adopted Seth as their patron because of his similarity with the Canaanite god Baal. At Abu Simbel he is depicted watching his protegé Ramesses II, as the King engages the Hittites at the Battle of Kadesh. Ramesses II was more closely associated with Seth than many other Kings because his family came from that area of the north-eastern Delta which was a major cult centre for the god. Seti I, father of Ramesses II, had inherited his grandfather's name meaning 'Man of Seth' or the Sethian, written with the symbol of the Seth animal, a curious concoction of dog, jackal and donkey, with a hint of anteater, but really none of these. It is sometimes called the Typhonian Beast, after the chaotic monster of Greek mythology which was supposed to be imprisoned beneath Mount Etna. The ambiguity in the nature of Seth had become even more pronounced by the Nineteenth Dynasty, and on monuments like the royal tomb and mortuary temple, which were dedicated to the idea of the dead King becoming one with Osiris himself, Seti's name was written with the figure of Osiris replacing the Seth animal to avoid insulting the King of the Dead. However, Seth was still revered and respected as a royal patron. In the Kadesh inscriptions of Ramesses II, the King was proud to relate that his enemies likened him to the god under the name of Sutekh, which was the pronunciation current at that time: 'He is no man who is in our midst, but Sutekh, himself, great of strength, Baal in person. His actions are not those of a man, but those of a unique being . . . Let us quickly flee before him . . .'

The Horus falcon and the Seth beast were two ancient tribal emblems shown on the standards surrounding the Scorpion Macehead. The oldest centre for the worship of Seth appears to have been Ombos which the Egyptians called *Nubt*, meaning 'Gold Town'. The falcon represented the sky-god Horus of *Nekhen*, near modern Kom el-Ahmar. The Greeks named the city Hierakonpolis which means 'City of the Hawk', indicating the long-established link between the site and the worship of Horus. The Narmer Palette clearly shows the hawk-god as patron of the conquering King who wears the tall White Crown of Upper Egypt. Despite this evidence that Horus was worshipped in the south at the time of the Unification, the hawk-god was traditionally recognized as the divine patron of Lower Egypt and was often shown wearing the Red Crown while Seth, whose cult was practised in the north, was the patron deity of Upper Egypt and wore the White Crown.

The first of the King's Five Great Names was written in the rectangular *serekh* (fig. 91) surmounted by the Horus falcon which was often crowned with the Double Crown of Upper and Lower Egypt. This earliest and most sacred appellation was known as the Horus name, and the word Horus was the most ancient title which in modern terms is rendered as King. In the Bible, the word Pharaoh is used in place of the King's personal name, a custom explained by the Jewish historian Josephus: '. . . All the Kings of Egypt from Menes, who built Memphis . . . were called Pharaohs, and took the name from one Pharaoh who lived after that time . . . Pharaoh, in the Egyptian tongue, signifies a king, but I suppose they made use of other names from their childhood; but when they were made kings, they changed them into that name which, in their own language, denoted their authority.'

Only in the Late Period was the expression *per-aa* used to refer to the King as an individual rather than an institution and the Greek-speaking officials of the Ptolemaic Period were responsible for the corruption of this term into Pharaoh, the title used most often in modern parlance to mean, specifically, a King of ancient Egypt.

The second of the Great Names is composed of the Horus falcon and the symbol for 'gold' which could represent Seth as the god of Gold Town. This title, which is now called the Golden Horus name, seems to acknowledge the dual nature of the kingship, and set the King under the protection of the Two Lords, just as the third name in the royal titulary claimed the patronage of the Two Ladies (fig. 92). The national goddesses Nekhebt and Wadjet were seen as guardians of the crowns and the heads of their sacred animals were placed on the King's brow to demonstrate their protection. In the Deir el-Bahri temple of Hatshepsut, the Two Ladies are shown bearing the Red and White Crowns at the Queen's coronation. These crowns were more than insignia of office. The Pyramid Texts refer to them as deities in their own right, each represented as a serpent:

Figure 91 *The Complete Monarch*: Seneferu is portrayed wearing his jubilee regalia surrounded by his Five Great Names within the rectangular *serekh*. His chosen name was Lord of Maat.

'O King, the dread of you is in ... the White Crown, the serpent-goddess who is in Nekheb ... O King, I provide you with ... the Red Crown, rich in power ... that it may protect you, O King, just as it protects Horus; may it establish your power ... as the two serpent-goddesses who are on your brow.'

The sacred uraeus, the multi-coloured cobra rearing on the forehead of the King, was attached to all crowns, whatever their colour or significance. In fact, the uraeus could be seen not simply as a decorative element of any crown, but as its essential feature. The earliest example so far discovered of the use of the uraeus to identify the King is on the tiny ivory label from the reign of King Den of the First Dynasty, which is in the British Musuem.

The White and the Red Crowns continued to be worn separately long after they had been combined into the *Pa-sekhemty*, the Two Powers or Double Crown of Upper and Lower Egypt. No examples of the crowns themselves have been found, so it is not known of what materials they were made. Possibly the originals were

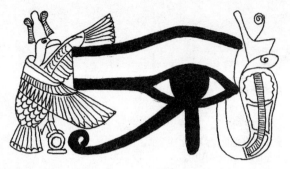

Figure 92 *The Two Ladies*: The serpent Wadjet and the vulture Nekhebt guard the Eye of Horus. The goddesses wear the Red and White Crowns symbolic of their position as patrons of the Two Lands.

woven from plant materials. The White Crown of Upper Egypt is very similar in shape to the crown of Osiris, which was often shown striped, as if made from a bundle of reeds. The Red Crown is sometimes referred to as the Green One, a name also borne by the northern goddess Wadjet, and the curled ornament projecting from it may represent the serpent's tongue. The crowns could have been made of metal, but more probably they were of leather. Since they were sacred, possessing a divinity apart from that of the one who wore them, they were almost certainly kept in shrines or chapels, like those of the Roman legionary standards, attended by their own priests or Keepers of the Diadems, who were amongst the highest court officials. The only truly royal insignia to have been found is that worn by Tutankhamen to his tomb. Made of gold and inlaid with coloured stones and glass, it is a replica of a simple linen headband embroidered with rosettes. At the brow are the heads of a serpent and a vulture, the Two Ladies.

The simplest and probably the most comfortable of all the official head-dresses available to the King was the *nemes*, the blue and yellow striped headcloth, which is so immediately associated with the funerary mask of Tutankhamen. It had shaped lappets hanging at each side of the face on to the shoulders, and the loose cloth at the back was gathered and bound into a sort of pigtail. The cloth, as with all crowns, was attached to a browband of leather or linen, tied behind the head with ribbons or streamers which are often shown emerging from beneath the crown at the nape of the neck. Despite its simplicity, and Hollywood notwithstanding, this striped cloth was never used as a head covering by anyone other than the King. A living King wore, as a mark of maturity and status, a false beard. The priestly purification rituals required of the King prevented him from growing his own beard, but he, or she in the case of Hatshepsut, wore a square-ended beard made of carved and painted wood, or perhaps woven from plant fibres, suspended on strings or wires from tabs on the browband. When the King died, he would be entitled to wear the beard of the gods, the longer, narrower plaited beard with a rounded, up-turned end, and this beard is shown in all funerary portraits, including Tutankhamen's mask and coffins.

The presentation of these and other items of regalia was central to the ritual associated with the King's coronation. The accession of a new monarch was called the 'appearance' of the King. The same word was used for 'dawn', providing a very obvious connection between the King and the sun-god, and as a general word for 'crown' or 'diadem' as opposed to the specific titles given to individual crowns. At the Temple of Hathor at Denderah, one of the Ptolemies recorded the crowns to which he laid claim displayed like sporting trophies in a case. The crowns are shown as objects, as ceremonial hats, rather than as sacred insignia with their own divinity, but at least the Ptolemies recognized the necessity of adopting an Egyptian style in order to lay a firm hold on the kingship, even if they misunderstood the significance of the regalia they adopted.

At the coronation, the two principal officiants were priests representing the gods Horus and Thoth. Purification by means of ritual lustration was essential and the two gods are shown pouring water over the crowned King. As in the scene of Hatshepsut's coronation, carved on the so-called Chapelle Rouge now in the Open Air Museum at Karnak, the streams of water pouring from the libation vases are drawn as chains of the hieroglyph for 'life', as the act confers divine life on the new King. At the coronation, the King was invested with his new titulary, the complete set of names by which he was uniquely identified and which marked his transition from mortality to godhood. The throne name, or prenomen, was the name by which he would be known for all official purposes from that day forward and was introduced by another dualistic title 'He of the Sedge and the Bee'. This title, first used by King Den, is usually translated as 'King of Upper and Lower Egypt', but the significance of the reed and bee symbols is not fully understood. The name written in the oval enclosure, shown as a knotted loop of rope, which is called a cartouche, made reference to the divine nature acquired by the King at his coronation. During the New Kingdom the Sedge and Bee introduction was sometimes replaced by the expression 'Lord of the Two Lands'.

The last of the Great Names was the nomen, the name by which, in most cases, an Egyptian King is now known, the name by which he had been known since birth, though many Kings added epithets such as 'Beloved of Amen' or 'Ruler of Thebes', to distinguish themselves from common folk who used the same personal names. The nomen was also written in cartouche and was introduced by the title 'Son of Re' or, alternatively, from the New Kingdom, by the expression 'the Good God' (fig. 93). This assertion of the King's close association with the sun-god was first made by Seneferu at the beginning of the Fourth Dynasty. The Fifth Dynasty Kings, even more fervent in their worship of Re, had sun-temples built at each of their pyramids, in place of the usual personal mortuary temples. Re, with his cult centred on the Delta city of Heliopolis, continued to be recognized as the supreme royal patron by every King except Akhenaten who revered his own solar deity, the god Aten. During the New Kingdom, when Thebes became the religious and administrative capital of the country, the Theban god was associated with the sun-god under the composite name Amen-Re and, even after the centre of government was removed to one of the Delta cities, Thebes remained the religious heart of Egypt. Kings from the Eleventh Dynasty onwards devoted much time and precious resources to the building, extension and embellishment of the Theban temples in honour of the god who was seen as their especial patron. The royal necropolis was established on the west bank at Thebes and all the New Kingdom Kings, except Akhenaten, were buried in or around the Valley of the Kings. Military campaigns and trading expeditions paid for monuments which advertised the strength and authority of the King, while also rendering homage to his guardian deity. The King always credited his success to the god who stood 'as his father' or 'as his strong

Figure 93 *The Good God*: Tutankhamen enthroned wears the Red Crown of Lower Egypt and his coronation name Nebkheperure is introduced with the title the 'Good God'.

right arm'. Their acceptance of this highly personal relationship between the King and the gods was the chief reason for the people's continued support of the kingship (fig. 94). The King embodied the pact made between the gods and the land itself at the beginning of time. The King's influence with his fellow deities was used to the good of his country and its people who, in return, worked hard and paid their taxes, so that the King might keep the gods in the manner to which they had become accustomed. This system of mutual support ensured the continuity and stability of the kingship and thereby the well-being of the country as a whole.

When a King had reigned for thirty years he would have achieved a good age by Egyptian standards and this was an event worthy of celebration. The thirty-year festival was called the *heb sed*, usually translated as jubilee. The word *sed* means 'tail' and may refer to the animal tail which hung from the King's belt as part of the royal regalia. This is such an ancient element of the King's costume that its origins are obscure. The King was frequently likened to a bull, the ultimate symbol of strength and virility, as on the Narmer Palette, and in several instances a King chose a name making allusion to this idea, as in the Horus name of Tuthmose I, 'Mighty Bull, beloved of Maat'. The jubilee rites seem to have included an event known as the 'Running of the Apis',

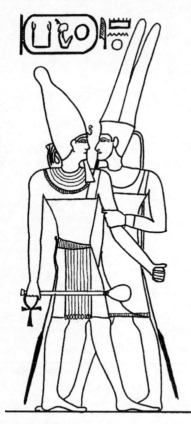

Figure 94 *The King of the Gods*: Amen of Karnak, the King of the Gods, identified by his double-feather crown, embraces the Pharaoh who wears the White Crown of Upper Egypt.

part of the cult of the Apis Bull sacred to Ptah, the first national deity of Egypt (fig. 95). *Sed* also means 'slaughter', and it may be that this ritual was a pale memory of an ancient tradition of king-sacrifice, whereby an aging monarch had to undergo a trial of strength to justify his continued rule. If he failed this test, he would have been sacrificed as a placatory offering to the gods of the land and a younger, stronger King would have taken his place. As with the practice of servant burials, this custom, if it ever existed in Egypt, had been quickly replaced by symbolic rituals.

The physical challenge of the *heb sed* was a run or dance around a court which represented the land of Egypt itself. Crescent-shaped cairns at the northern and southern ends of the court marked the extreme boundaries of the Two Lands and the King had to circle these to re-establish his claim to rule the whole country. Chapels containing the cult statues of the major provincial deities were set along the length of the course and the King would have paid his

Figure 95 *The Running of the Apis*: As part of the royal jubilee ritual the King runs a 'race' with the Apis Bull. The cairns marking the course are shown behind the King.

respects at each and asked for the gods' continued blessing on his reign. Finally, at two larger chapels representing the patron deities of Upper and Lower Egypt, the King was reinstated on the two thrones which are prominent in the hieroglyphic writing of the name of the festival, and was crowned anew, receiving his regalia from priests representing Horus and Seth, Wadjet and Nekhebt. In the earliest dynasties, this celebration was probably quite a private affair, a personal matter between the King and his gods, with only his most trusted followers, family and priests as witnesses. Part of the ritual seems to have involved the burial of a statue of the King, representing his symbolic death, after which he was reborn by means of the coronation. This renewal of the pact between the King and the gods was a suitable occasion for the King to adopt new names, or to add extra epithets to his titulary. On an ebony label from the tomb of Hemaka, King Den is shown performing the jubilee rites (fig. 96), and King Djoser included a full-scale replica of the *heb sed* court in his funerary complex at Saqqara.

Figure 96 *King Den's Jubilee*: The enthroned King is wearing his *heb sed* cloak and the Double Crown, and is also shown running the race between the cairns. At the far right is the palm-rib hieroglyph for 'year'.

By the New Kingdom, the *heb sed* was very much a national celebration lasting for several days and every temple in the land joined in the festivities. Royal employees, like the Workmen at Deir el-Medina, were issued with extra supplies of food and drink to allow them to celebrate in style.

Another important part of the jubilee celebrations was the raising of the *djed* pillar, a fetish of uncertain origin in the form of a tapering column with four horizontal bars or capitals. This aspect of the ritual associated with the *heb sed* of Amenhotep III is shown in the tomb of Kheruef, and at Abydos, Seti I is shown erecting the *djed* pillar under the gaze of the goddess Isis. The *djed* came to represent 'stability', especially the stability of the kingship. The Delta town, whose name meant 'City of the *Djed*', was called Busiris by the Greeks and this is a corruption of the Egyptian name *Per-Wsir*, meaning 'House of Osiris'. The *djed* was, above all, a symbol associated with Osiris whose name, written with the throne hieroglyph, could be translated as 'he who occupies the throne'.

The relationship between the King and Osiris was very subtle. As Horus incarnate, the King occupied the throne of his father Osiris. When he died, even the symbolic death of the *Heb Sed*, he became Osiris. At Abydos, the principal cult centre for Osiris, the tomb of King Djer had been recognized as the burial place of the very first King of Egypt, the god himself. This explains why successive Kings paid attention to the cult of Osiris at Abydos, the most spectacular monuments being the temples built by Seti I and his son Ramesses II. The King embodied every attribute of Osiris. Even in death the King continued to serve Egypt by controlling the harvest and offering all people the opportunity of joining him in everlasting life. The coronation of the King confirmed him on the throne as the incarnation of Horus and successor to Osiris. At death he became united with Osiris and ruled as Foremost of the Westerners, the euphemism for the Blessed Dead who had descended to the realm of Osiris with the setting sun. In the Pyramid Texts, the King was said to become a star and join Osiris in his heavenly form as the constellation Orion, while at the same time the deceased King was said to join Re in his solar bark and travel with the sun-god in his daily journey across the sky. The King enjoyed a very privileged relationship with all those deified ancestors who had gone before him to join with Osiris. The

Figure 97 *The Divine King*: The King wears the diadem and a fanciful *atef* crown, the crown of the gods, composed of horns, feathers, reed bundles and uraeus serpents.

standard prayer for offerings to be made at the tomb started with the phrase 'a boon which the King gives'. This implies that, originally, all funerary offerings, and indeed the right to burial itself, were seen to be provided by the King who, by putting in a good word with Osiris, Anubis, Geb and the other deities commonly named in the formula, nominated those of his followers whom he considered worthy of immortality. The phrase continued to be used long after the King's responsibility had become purely theoretical and all tomb-owners expected to provide for their own eternity.

As usual within families of rank or wealth in any society, a great deal was expected of the members of the King's family. The King himself only became a god when he was crowned (fig. 97). As a prince he was likely to be one of many sons, all of whom had a claim to the throne, some better than others. It was always most likely that the eldest surviving son of the King and his Chief Wife would succeed his father and thus assume godhood. The term now translated as 'prince' was 'Son of the King', and this expression alone does not indicate whether that son was the child of the principal wife, nor even which King was his father. Only the unequivocal expression 'of his body' indicates true paternity, as opposed to an adoptive relationship, and only rarely are both royal parents named.

Some of the largest tombs in the cemeteries of Abydos and Saqqara belonged to royal relatives. The lady Neith-hotep owned a mastaba tomb at Nagada in the same style as those of her husband Narmer and her son Aha. The massive size of the tomb indicates the status of the lady who is thought to have been a representative of an important northern family, taken in marriage by Narmer to confirm his authority over both north and south. Just as there was no Egyptian word for prince or princess, so there was no single word meaning 'queen'. The expressions 'King's Daughter', 'King's Sister' and 'King's Wife' were all used, and in everyday language the word 'sister', was an endearment meaning 'beloved' which was often used in place of 'wife'. The King could afford, and often for diplomatic reasons found it necessary, to take several wives, but as was the general custom in Egypt, only one wife was recognized as his official consort with the title 'Great

Figure 98 *The Queen*:
The Great Wife of the King wears a
coronet of uraeus serpents
supporting the horned crown with
twin feathers which was the prerogative of Pharaoh's principal consort.

Wife of the King' (fig. 98). From the New Kingdom onwards, the
name of the Great Royal Wife was written in cartouche and was
often preceded by the title 'Lady of the Two Lands'.

Often the King's Chief Wife was one of his close relatives, a
cousin or even a half-sister, though marriages between full brother
and sister were not as common as is sometimes believed. The
reasons for this custom of consanguineous marriage were many. It
maintained a 'pure' bloodline and kept the power of the kingship,
both secular and divine, in the one family. It matched the rank of
the King with that of his Queen and avoided rivalry and jealousies
among the nobility which might arise as the result of the King
marrying the daughter of a powerful noble house. This has led to
the popular perception that inheritance was passed through the
female line, an idea followed slavishly by the Ptolemies who, in
their efforts to be accepted as true Kings of Egypt, adopted all the

most extreme and superficial trappings of the kingship. The facts that not all Kings married their sisters and that father-daughter marriages were even more rare, have been overlooked in the glare of publicity surrounding extraordinary cases. For example, if the most recent theories are correct, Tutankhamen married his own half-sister who had already been married to and had a child by her father. When Tutankhamen died, his widow married an elderly courtier who was probably also her grandfather. It may take DNA analysis to unravel the family relationships of the period, and then there will still be room for doubt, since the family connections are already known to be close.

Every Egyptian man was expected to marry, following the divine precedent set by Osiris and Isis. Princes who were not likely to inherit the throne often married outside their immediate family and built careers for themselves in the world at large. The royal harem, a word adopted from the Ottoman court and not precisely applicable to the ancient Egyptian institution, included unmarried or widowed sisters, cousins, aunts and nieces of the King, who was responsible for their upkeep and, where possible for finding suitable marriage partners. The fortunate Princess Tia, sister of Ramesses II, married a gentleman also named Tia who was Controller of the Ramesseum, the King's mortuary temple complex at Thebes. A request from a Babylonian king for an Egyptian bride was rebuffed with a retort to the effect that no Egyptian princess would marry outside her country and with the implication that even an Egyptian husband would have to be of royal blood. There must have been many spinster princesses cluttering up the palace at any time, bringing to mind the entourage of Sir Joseph Porter in HMS *Pinafore*, but there were also many lesser royal wives or concubines, any or all of whom could have children by the King or one of his predecessors, so there were opportunities for royal females to make suitable matches with men who were their own relatives, however distant the relationship.

The children of the King's Chief Wife were the natural heirs to their father, but their chances of surviving childhood were not very much better than those of ordinary Egyptians, and pregnancy and childbirth were just as dangerous for the Queen as for her female subjects. The royal situation was made even more perilous by the consanguinity of marriages and the inevitable consequences of interbreeding. It was not unusual for the son of a secondary wife to succeed to the throne because none of his fully royal brothers had outlived their father. When Amenhotep III succeeded his father Tuthmose IV he was still very young and unmarried. Although several of his brothers and sisters are known by name, it appears that none of them outlived their father and when it was time for Amenhotep to take a wife there were no suitably royal females available. In the second year of his reign he announced his marriage on several large commemorative scarabs:

> The Great Wife of the King [is] Tiye ... The name of her father is Yuya, the name of her mother is Tjuya. She is [now] the wife of a great king whose territory stretches from Karoy [in Nubia] to Naharin.

This defiant inscription, clearly stating the King's break with tradition in marrying a woman of the people, dared any citizen of Egypt to oppose his choice. Queen Tiye produced a large family for Amenhotep and probably ensured the Dynasty continuing for one or two generations more than might otherwise have been expected. In the course of a long reign a King might be fortunate enough to produce a troop of royal sons from whose ranks he could choose his successor. However, the position of the first Great Royal Wife was unassailable and her surviving children outranked all others. The senior prince was given the title 'Eldest Son of the King', which could be translated as Crown Prince, in recognition of his right to inherit. Ramesses II lived so long that he outlived not only his two Chief Wives, Nefertari and Isetnofre, but also their daughters, Merytamen and Bint-anath, who took their mothers' places as Royal Consorts in the latter years of the reign. He was eventually succeeded by Merenptah, his thirteenth son and the fifth to have been nominated Crown Prince.

Despite all protestations to the contrary, the King was still a mortal man and subject to mortal frailty. He could not expect to live forever, so he had to prepare for his death. From the moment he became King, he would have started building his tomb and providing for his mortuary cult. One method of ensuring a smooth transfer of power when the time came was the introduction of co-regency, by which a son was crowned as joint King during his father's lifetime and took on some of the more arduous aspects of the kingship, notably the command of the army. When the senior partner in a co-regency died, there was no hiatus in royal authority, since Egypt was never deprived of a King altogether. Such co-regencies during the Twelfth Dynasty varied in length from one or two years to as many as ten or twelve. The rise to power of the Dynasty may have been as the result of the coup by the *Tjaty* Amenemhet, so the institution of co-regency served to prevent another ambitious nobleman using the excuse of a weak or aging King to stage further rebellion.

The *Story of Sinuhe* indicates that the Twelfth Dynasty Kings were right to worry about such matters. The narrative begins with Sinuhe in a military camp in the company of the junior King Senusert I. When a messenger arrives bringing news of the assassination of King Amenemhet I Senusert rushes back to the capital to establish his right to the throne as Egypt's properly crowned monarch. The plot could have succeeded completely only if both father and son had been killed at the same time. Co-regencies were less common in later dynasties, but the institution was still very useful in some circumstances, as in the changeover of authority between dynasties. Horemheb, last King of the Eighteenth Dynasty, had no child to succeed him, so he appointed his army colleague Pramesse as his co-regent and heir. Since Pramesse was of the same generation as Horemheb himself, he could not expect to rule for long, but his strength lay in his well-established, healthy and energetic family. After less than two years on the throne as Ramesses I, the founder of the Nineteenth Dynasty died, making way for his son Seti I, and Egypt embarked on a long period of remarkable achievements, prosperity and stability.

The most appropriate person to provide guidance for a child king was a member of his immediate family, often his mother, though it was quite possible that she too had already died or was not a senior enough spouse to assume the regency. When Tuthmose II died suddenly, his successor Tuthmose III, the son of a minor concubine, was too young even to be married. He was officially betrothed to his half-sister, the Princess Neferure, but the regency was held by her mother, Hatshepsut, who was more royal by blood than the new King. Ineni, the Minister of Works at the time, recorded the succession in his biographical tomb inscription:

> The King went forth to heaven having mingled with the gods. His son stood in his place as King of the Two Lands, having become ruler upon the throne of the one who begat him. His sister, the Divine Consort Hatshepsut, settled the affairs of the Two Lands by reason of her counsel. Egypt worked for her with respect, she being the excellent seed of the god, which came forth from him ... whose plans are excellent, who satisfies the Two Lands when she speaks.

For the first few years of his reign, Tuthmose III is shown as co-regent with Hatshepsut, and Neferure had her name written in cartouche as befitted the wife-to-be of the King. However, Hatshepsut had acquired a taste for power and assumed the throne as King in her own right. When she died, Tuthmose assumed his rightful place and, having already been crowned as King, he dated his reign from the death of his father (fig. 99).

Figure 99 *Co-regents*: Kings Hatshepsut and Tuthmose III are shown as joint monarchs paying homage to Amen-Re of Karnak. Both wear royal insignia and their names in cartouches show that both had been crowned.

The case of Tuthmose III shows that the successful heir to the throne was not necessarily the son of the Queen, and unless there was a clear candidate from among the children of lesser wives nominated as Crown Prince by his father, any of the King's sons might hope to become King. Instances are recorded of harem intrigue, the most spectacular being the assassination of Ramesses III. This was the result of a plot hatched in the harem by a minor wife called Tiye who wanted to put her son on the throne. The transcripts of the trials of the conspirators imply that Tiye had enlisted the help of some very influential people at court, including Treasury officials and an army general. Since the surviving records are hardly more than abstracts from the trial proceedings, the full story is difficult to make out, but the plot apparently succeeded since the prosecutions were ordered by the new King Ramesses IV. The fate of Tiye and her son is not explicitly stated, but a death sentence is assumed to have been inevitable for the crime of killing a god.

The King was always, in name at least, leader of the armed forces and protector of Egypt's boundaries. The New Kingdom monarchs took this role far more seriously than most of their predecessors and were very proud of their military achievements. As a symbol of this aspect of their kingly authority, the Eighteenth Dynasty Kings adopted a new crown, the *Khepresh* or War Crown, thought to have developed from the leather helmet worn by army officers. The *Khepresh* is always shown with flaring wings and an all-over pattern of roundels, probably embossed in stiffened leather. In some illustrations the *Khepresh* is shown gold or even red, but usually it is blue. The uraeus is always shown on the browband, with the body of the serpent coiled behind the rearing hood or arched over the top of the head-dress identifying it as a true royal crown worn only by the King.

As the focus of military activity moved farther north into the Asiatic territories, it was essential that the Kings of Egypt should be confident of their control over Nubia. To fight major campaigns on two fronts more than 2,000 kilometres apart would have stretched communications, resources and loyalties to the limit. During the Second Intermediate Period, the Hyksos rulers of the Delta had formed an uneasy alliance with the Nubian tribes of

Kush, the region beyond the Second Cataract, while the Medjay of Wawat, the area between the first two Cataracts, remained loyal to the native princes of Thebes. Kamose, the Theban King who started the campaign to expel the Hyksos from Egypt, described the situation on a stela at Karnak:

> ... What use is my strength when one foreign chieftain occupies Avaris [the Hyksos capital] and another is in Kush? While I sit hemmed in by an Asiatic and a Nubian, each in possession of his slice of this land of Egypt, and I am unable to pass even as far as Memphis ... My desire is to deliver Egypt and to smite the Asiatics.

The Medjay troops were a vital element in the strategies of Kamose and his brother Ahmose in driving the Hyksos from Egyptian soil. The restoration of the whole of the Two Lands to Egyptian possession was finally achieved by Amenhotep I, who was the first King to appoint a senior official to control the distant southern territories in his name. The titles given to this official were King's Son of Kush and Governor of the Southlands, but he is commonly referred to as the Viceroy of Nubia. The title King's Son was purely honorific since there is no evidence that any of the Viceroys was a royal prince, but it provided the bearer with a suitable rank from which he could issue decrees and make decisions without reference to any higher authority. In Egypt itself, the Viceroy was of equal rank with the King's own children and may even have outranked the *Tjaty* in certain circumstances. At its greatest extent, the area of his authority stretched from Hierakonpolis in the north to Karoy, the region between the Fourth and Fifth Cataracts, in the south. He was the King's representative, established in his own capital in Nubia, who spoke with the King's voice and acted in the King's name. After keeping the peace, his principal function was to see to the collection of taxes and tithes from the Nubian tribespeople and the safe delivery of that tribute to the King's storehouses in Egypt. The Viceroy had authority over the most important gold-bearing lands under Egypt's control. He had to guarantee the safety of miners and the gold caravans travelling to and from the mines, and if necessary he could call upon the garrisons of the Nubian forts or the southern army based at

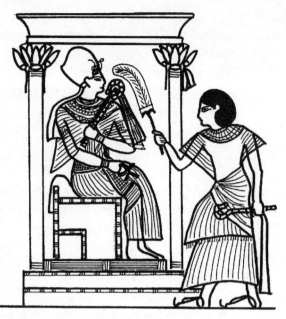

Figure 100 *The Viceroy*: Huy, the newly invested King's Son of Kush, pays his respects to Tutankhamen. He holds the crook sceptre as a symbol of his viceregal authority.

Aswan. As problems occurred, the Viceroy dealt with them immediately. Of course, the King was kept fully informed of everything that happened in the Southlands by means of regular reports made in writing and delivered verbally by eye-witness messengers, but communications between the Viceroy's capital and Thebes could take weeks, if not months, and that was too long to wait for permission to act if a critical situation arose.

The Viceroy of Nubia had to be one of the King's most trusted and loyal courtiers. His job was more diplomatic and economic than military, but the control over the produce of Nubia was vital in maintaining the King's authority both at home and abroad. The investiture of a Viceroy was a grand occasion, as displayed in the tomb of Huy who was installed as King's Son of Kush during the reign of Tutankhamen. As a demonstration of the wealth of his new domain the Viceroy ushered before the King a parade of Nubians in their native costumes, bearing all kinds of produce from their territories including ivory tusks, logs of ebony, ostrich eggs and feathers, animal skins and even live animals such as cheetahs, baboons and a young giraffe. The Vizier accepted these gifts on the King's behalf then led the Viceroy before the King to receive his seal of office (fig. 100):

> 'Handing over the office to the King's Son of Kush, Huy, [giving him authority] from Nekhen to Karoy ... appointed in the royal Presence of the Good God to be the Viceroy and Governor of the Southlands, Huy. Nubia is assigned to him and Upper Egypt is enclosed under his supervision in order that he might govern it for the Lord of the Two Lands.

Egypt had bad Kings as well as good, but the institution of kingship was so deeply rooted in the hearts and souls of the people, as well as in the soil itself, that a true King would emerge, even after a period of turmoil and uncertainty, with a determination to restore the country to greatness and to uphold the rule of Maat. Until other nations started to impose their forms of kingship on Egypt, the system had served the country well for nearly 3,000 years. No other ancient civilization could claim such continuity and stability. No other nation was as lucky as the people of the Pharaohs.

Hieroglyphs associated with the King

the Horus Falcon

the Seth animal

the uraeus
serpent worn at
the King's brow

'appearance',
'crown', 'diadem'

the White Crown
of Upper Egypt

the Red Crown
of Lower Egypt

animal tail symbol,
emblem of the
Sed festival

canopied double
throne used in the
King's jubilee
celebrations

Acknowledgments

•

The quotations used throughout this book are free translations based on English versions of ancient Egyptian original documents and some Classical works. The principal sources used for these texts are as follows:

BREASTED James Henry, *Ancient Records of Egypt*, (5 vols), New York, 1906
CUMMING Barbara, *Egyptian Historical Records of the Later Eighteenth Dynasty*, (1–3), Warminster, 1982–4
DAVIES Benedict G, *Egyptian Historical Records of the Later Eighteenth Dynasty*, (4–6), Warminster, 1992–5
ERMAN Adolf, *The Ancient Egyptians; a sourcebook of their writings*, New York, 1966
FAULKNER R O, *The Ancient Egyptian Pyramid Texts*, Oxford 1969
FAULKNER R O, *The Ancient Egyptian Coffin Texts*, (3 vols), Oxford, 1973–8
FAULKNER R O, *The Ancient Egyptian Book of the Dead*, London, 1985
GARDINER Sir Alan H, *Egypt of the Pharaohs*, Oxford, 1961
HERODOTUS, *The Histories* (Penguin Classics edition), London, 1954
JOSEPHUS, *The Complete Works* (Hendrickson edition), Massachusetts, 1987
LICHTHEIM Miriam, *Ancient Egyptian Literature*, (3 vols), Berkeley, 1976
PARKINSON Richard B, *Voices from Ancient Egypt*, London, 1991

Biblical quotations are taken from the *New English Bible* translation.

Individual hieroglyphs used throughout the text have been reproduced using the *Inscribe for Windows* software from Saqqara Technology.

Every effort has been made to trace the copyright holders of the photographs in the plate section. The publishers would like to thank the following for their permission to reproduce photographs:

Oriental Museum, University of Durham pp. 4, 6b, 13b; The Metropolitan Museum of Art pp. 8, 14; Peter Funnell pp. 10a, 10b, 11, 12, 13a, 15, 16b; The Hutchison Library p. 6a; Liverpool Museum p. 7.

Bibliography

•

INTRODUCTION: RESOURCES

BAINES J & MALEK J, *Atlas of Ancient Egypt*, Oxford, 1980
HEPPER F Nigel, *Pharaoh's Flowers*, London, 1990
LEWINGTON Anna, *Plants for People*, Kew, 1990
LUCAS A, *Ancient Egyptian Materials and Industries*, London, 1948
MANNICHE Lise, *An Ancient Egyptian Herbal*, London, 1989
MASPERO Gaston, *The Dawn of Civilization; Egypt and Chaldea*, London, 1901
SHAW Ian & NICHOLSON Paul, *British Museum Dictionary of Ancient Egypt*, London, 1995

CHAPTER 1: THE FARMER

HART George, *A Dictionary of Egyptian Gods and Goddesses*, London, 1986
JAMES T G H, *An Introduction to Ancient Egypt*, London, 1979
JAMES T G H, *Pharaoh's People; Scenes from Life in Imperial Egypt*, London, 1984
JANSSEN Rosalind & Jack, *Egyptian Household Animals*, Aylesbury, 1989
KEMP Barry J, *Ancient Egypt; Anatomy of a Civilization*, London, 1989
MURNANE William J, *United with Eternity*, Cairo, 1980
SCOTT Nora, *The Daily Life of the Ancient Egyptians*, New York, (undated)
STROUHAL Eugen, *Life in Ancient Egypt*, Cambridge, 1992
TOOLEY Angela M J, *Egyptian Models and Scenes*, Aylesbury, 1995
WILSON Hilary, *Egyptian Food and Drink*, Aylesbury 1988

CHAPTER 2: THE BUILDER

ALDRED Cyril, *Egypt to the end of the Old Kingdom*, London, 1965
BARNES, BRIGHTWELL, von HAGEN, LEHNER & PAGE, *Secrets of Lost Empires*, London, 1996
DODSON Aidan, *Egyptian Rock-cut Tombs*, Aylesbury, 1991
EDWARDS I E S, *The Pyramids of Egypt*, London, 1972
EMERY Walter B, *Archaic Egypt*, London, 1961
HOFFMAN Michael A, *Egypt Before the Pharaohs*, London, 1980

LAUER Jean-Philippe, *Saqqara*, London, 1976
see also LUCAS A (1948)
TRIGGER, KEMP, O'CONNOR & LLOYD, *Ancient Egypt; a Social History*, Cambridge, 1983
UPHILL Eric P, *Egyptian Towns and Cities*, Aylesbury, 1988

CHAPTER 3: WOMEN AND CHILDREN

DESROCHES NOBLECOURT Christiane, *La Femme au Temps des Pharaons*, Paris, 1986
FILER Joyce, *Disease*, London, 1995
JANSSEN Rosalind & Jack, *Growing up in Ancient Egypt*, London, 1990
MALEK Jaromir, *The Cat in Ancient Egypt*, London, 1993
MANNICHE Lise, *Sexual Life in Ancient Egypt*, London, 1987
ROBERTS Alison, *Hathor Rising; the Serpent Power of Ancient Egypt*, Totnes, 1995
ROMER John, *Ancient Lives*, London, 1984
TYLDESLEY Joyce, *Daughters of Isis*, London, 1994
WATTERSON Barbara, *Women in Ancient Egypt*, Stroud, 1991
WHALE Sheila, *The Family in the Eighteenth Dynasty of Egypt*, Sydney, 1989

CHAPTER 4: THE SCRIBE

FAULKNER R O, *The Egyptian Book of the Dead of Ani*, San Francisco, 1994
GILLINGS Richard J, *Mathematics in the Time of the Pharaohs*, New York, 1972
GRIFFITH F Ll & PETRIE W M F, *Two Hieroglyphic Papyri from Tanis*, London, 1889
NUNN John F, *Ancient Egyptian Medicine*, London, 1996
PARKINSON Richard & QUIRKE Stephen, *Papyrus*, London, 1995
see also PARKINSON (1991)
REEVES Carole, *Egyptian Medicine*, Aylesbury, 1992
ROBINS Gay & SHUTE Charles, *The Rhind Mathematical Papyrus*, London, 1987
WATTERSON Barbara, *Introducing Egyptian Hieroglyphs*, Edinburgh, 1981
WILSON Hilary, *Understanding Hieroglyphs*, London, 1993

CHAPTER 5: THE PRIEST

DAVID Rosalie, *Cult of the Sun*, London, 1980
DAVID Rosalie, *The Ancient Egyptians; Religious Beliefs and Practices*, London, 1982
FORMAN Werner & QUIRKE Stephen, *Hieroglyphs and the Afterlife*, London, 1996
HART George, *Egyptian Myths*, London, 1990
see also HART (1986)

LURKER Manfred, *The Gods and Symbols of Ancient Egypt*, London, 1980
NIMS Charles F, *Thebes of the Pharaohs*, London, 1965
SHAFER Byron E (ed), *Religion in Ancient Egypt*, Cornell, 1991
SPENCER A J, *Death in Ancient Egypt*, London, 1982
WATTERSON Barbara, *The Gods of Ancient Egypt*, London, 1984

CHAPTER 6: CRAFTSMEN

ALDRED Cyril, *Jewels of the Pharaohs*, London, 1971
ANDREWS Carol, *Ancient Egyptian Jewellery*, London, 1990
BROVARSKI Edward (ed), *Egypt's Golden Age; the Art of Living in the New Kingdom*, Boston, 1982
HALL Rosalind, *Egyptian Textiles*, Aylesbury, 1986
HOPE Colin, *Egyptian Pottery*, Aylesbury, 1987
KACZMARCZYK A & HEDGES R E M, *Ancient Egyptian Faience*, Warminster 1983
KILLEN Geoffrey, *Egyptian Woodworking and Furniture*, Aylesbury, 1994
NICHOLSON Paul T, *Egyptian Faience and Glass*, Aylesbury, 1993
REEVES Nicholas, *The Complete Tutankhamun*, London, 1990
SCHEEL Bernd, *Egyptian Metalworking and Tools*, Aylesbury, 1989

CHAPTER 7: THE ARTIST

ALDRED Cyril, *Akhenaten and Nefertiti*, London, 1973
ALDRED Cyril, *Egyptian Art*, London, 1980
BOURRIAU Janine (ed), *Pharaohs and Mortals*, Cambridge, 1988
JAMES T G H, *Egyptian Painting*, London, 1985
MEKHTARIAN Arpag, *Egyptian Painting*, Geneva, 1978
PECK William H & ROSS John G, *Drawings from Ancient Egypt*, London, 1978
ROBINS Gay, *Egyptian Painting and Relief*, Aylesbury, 1986
RUSSMANN Edna R, *Egyptian Sculpture; Cairo and Luxor*, London, 1989
WILKINSON Charles K & HILL Marsha, *Egyptian Wall Paintings*, New York, 1983
WILKINSON Richard H, *Reading Egyptian Art*, London, 1992

CHAPTER 8: THE SOLDIER

GARDINER Alan H, *The Kadesh Inscriptions of Ramesses II*, Oxford, 1960
HANSEN Kathy, 'The Chariot in Egypt's Age of Chivalry', (in *KMT* vol. 5:1), San Francisco, 1994
HARDY Robert, *Longbow; a Social and Military History*, (third edition), Yeovil, 1992
HEALY Mark, *Qadesh 1300 BC; Clash of the Warrior Kings*, London, 1993
KITCHEN Kenneth A, *Pharaoh Triumphant; the Life and Times of Ramesses II*, Warminster, 1982

LEAHY Anthony (ed), *Libya and Egypt* c. 1300–750 BC, London, 1990
NEWBY P H, *Warrior Pharaohs*, London, 1980
SHAW Ian, *Egyptian Warfare and Weapons*, Aylesbury, 1991
WISE Terrence, *Ancient Armies of the Middle East*, London, 1981
WOOD Michael, *In Search of the Trojan War*, London, 1985

CHAPTER 9: MEN AT THE TOP

Van den BOORN G P F, *The Duties of the Vizier*, London, 1988
DAVID Rosalie & Antony E, *A Biographical Dictionary of Ancient Egypt*, London, 1992
see also KEMP (1989)
see also KITCHEN (1982)
LESKO Leonard H (ed), *Pharaoh's Workers*, Cornell, 1994
MARTIN Geoffrey T, *The Hidden Tombs of Memphis*, London, 1991
NEWBERRY Percy E, *Ancient Egyptian Scarabs*, London, 1905
QUIRKE Stephen, *The Administration of Egypt in the Late Middle Kingdom*, New Malden, 1990
SPENCER A J, *Early Egypt; the Rise of Civilization in the Nile Valley*, London, 1993
STRUDWICK Nigel, *The Administration of the Old Kingdom*, London, 1985

CHAPTER 10: THE KING

CLAYTON Peter A, *Chronicle of the Pharaohs*, London, 1994
CONWAY Liz (ed), *Ramesses II; the Great Pharaoh and his Time*, Denver, 1987
DESROCHES NOBLECOURT Christiane, *Tutankhamen; Life and Death of a Pharaoh*, London, 1963
DODSON Aidan, *Monarchs of the Nile*, London, 1995
GRIMAL Nicolas, *A History of Ancient Egypt*, Oxford, 1992
HART George, *Pharaohs and Pyramids; a Guide through Old Kingdom Egypt*, London, 1991
see also NEWBY (1980)
PARTRIDGE Robert B, *Faces of the Pharaohs*, London, 1994
QUIRKE Stephen, *Who Were the Pharaohs?*, London, 1990
ROSE John, *The Sons of Re; Cartouches of the Kings of Egypt*, Warrington, 1985

Origins of Line Drawings

•

Tombs prefixed TT are in the Theban necropolis.

Those prefixed KV or QV are in the Valley of Kings or the Valley of Queens respectively.

1: Seated statue of Ramesses II, Luxor
2: Tomb of Ipuy (TT 217)
3: Tomb of Horemheb (KV 57)
4: Tomb of Mereruka, Saqqara
5: Tomb of Sennedjem (TT 1)
6: Temple of Ramesses III, Medinet Habu
7: Tomb of Menna (TT 69)
8: Tomb of Paheri, el-Kab (after Griffith)
9: Tomb of Haty (TT 151)
10: Tomb of Ipuy (TT 217)
11: Tomb of Rekhmire (TT 100)
12: Tomb of Nebamun (TT 90)
13: Tomb of Sennedjem (TT 1)
14: Stela of Penbuy, British Museum
15: Ostracon, Louvre
16: Ostracon, Fitzwilliam Museum, Cambridge
17: Book of the Dead of Hunefer, British Museum
18: Tomb of Anherkau (TT 359)
19: Tomb of Sennefer (TT 96)
20: Book of the Dead of Ani, British Museum
21: Tomb of Sennedjem (TT 1)
22: Tomb of Amenemhet (TT 82) (after Davies)
23: Relief from tomb of Seti I (KV 17), now in the Louvre
24: Sarcophagus of Kawit from Deir el-Bahri, now in Cairo
25: Tomb of Ipuy (TT 217)
26: Tomb of Ti, Saqqara
27: Tomb of Paheri, el-Kab (after Griffith)
28: Tomb of Nebamun (TT 181)

29: Tomb of Sennefer (TT 96)
30: Book of the Dead of Ani, British Museum
31: Book of the Dead of Hunefer, British Museum
32: Tomb of Ramose (TT 55)
33: Tanis Sign Papyrus (after Gardiner)
34: Tomb of Ti, Saqqara
35: Tomb of Idut, Saqqara
36: Ostracon, Cairo
37: Ostracon, British Museum
38: Tomb of Hesyre, Saqqara, now in Cairo
39: Tomb of Tutankhamen (KV 62)
40: Gerzean vase, Cairo
41: Tomb of Ra-wer, Giza, now in Cairo
42: Tomb of Khaemwase (QV 44)
43: Tomb of Menna (TT 69)
44: Book of the Dead of Hunefer, British Museum
45: Tomb of Nakht (TT 161) (after Manniche)
46: Tomb of Ipuy (TT C6)
47: Tomb of Horemheb, Memphis (after Martin)
48: Shabti, University College, London
49: Tomb of Ramose (TT 55)
50: Tomb of Rekhmire (TT 100)
51: Tomb of Rekhmire (TT 100)
52: Tomb of Rekhmire (TT 100)
53: Tomb of Ipuy (TT 217)
54: Tomb of Rekhmire (TT 100)
55: Tomb of Rekhmire (TT 100)
56: Tomb of Amenemhet (TT 82)
57: Tomb of Sobekhotep (TT 63) now in the British Museum
58: Stela of Neferhotep (?) from Deir el-Medina, now in Chicago
59: Tomb of Ptah-hotep, Saqqara
60: Tomb of Itet, Meidum, now in Cairo
61: Fragment of relief from Hermopolis, now in Brooklyn
62: composite
63: Temple of Luxor (after Habachi)
64: Tomb of Ramose (TT 55)
65: Tomb of Nebamun, now in the British Museum
66: Tomb of Mereruka, Saqqara
67: Tomb of Rekhmire (TT 100)
68: Statue from the Serapeum, now in the Louvre
69: Stela from Tel el-Amarna, now in Cairo
70: Ostracon, Brooklyn
71: Battlefield Palette, British Museum and Ashmolean Museum
72: Temple of Hatshepsut, Deir el-Bahri

73: Tomb of Khety (TT 311)
74: Bowcase from the tomb of Tutankhamen, now in Cairo
75: Wooden label from Abydos (after Hoffman)
76: Tomb of Nefertari (QV 66)
77: Tomb of Hapu (TT 66) (after Davies)
78: Relief from Luxor, now at the Luxor Museum
79: Towns Palette, Cairo
80: composite
81: composite derived from Newberry
82: after Newberry
83: Label from Abydos, now in the British Museum
84: Tomb of Mereruka, Saqqara
85: Stela of Nefert from Giza, now in Berkeley
86: Tomb of Horemheb, Memphis
87: Tomb of Rekhmire (TT 100)
88: Tomb of Nefertari (QV 66)
89: Temple of Hathor, Denderah
90: Tomb of Horemheb, Memphis
91: Relief from the Bent Pyramid at Dashur, now in Cairo
92: Jewel from the tomb of Tutankhamen, now in Cairo
93: Gilded shrine of Tutankhamen, now in Cairo
94: Obelisk of Hatshepsut, Karnak
95: *Chapelle Rouge* of Hatshepsut, Open Air Museum, Karnak
96: Ebony label from Abydos, now in the British Museum
97: Gilded throne of Tutankhamen, now in Cairo
98: Gilded throne of Tutankhamen, now in Cairo
99: Stela from Western Thebes, now in the Vatican Museum
100: Tomb of Amenhotep known as Huy (TT 40) (after Erman)

Index

•